MW01278396

To MELISSA,

May the joys of growth
always be the awareness
of your time.

VcToria

THEN
NOW
AND
FOREVER

a Memoir by
VcToria Gray

Then Now and Forever

Copyright © 2018 by VcToria Gray

No part of this publication may be reproduced, distributed,
or transmitted in any form or by any means, including
photocopying, recording, or other electronic or mechanical
methods, without the prior written permission of the author,
except in the case of brief quotations embodied in critical
reviews and certain other non-commercial uses permitted by
copyright law.

Tellwell Talent
www.tellwell.ca

ISBN
978-1-77370-927-7 (Hardcover)
978-1-77370-926-0 (Paperback)
978-1-77370-928-4 (eBook)

ACKNOWLEDGEMENTS

I wish to thank Linda, John, Blake, Laurie, Sandra, Kirsten, Angel, Louise and anyone else who helped place dates and times for this memoir. I also would like to thank myself for having the insight to save love letters and photographs that are forty years old and allowed me to write this book.

Based upon memories of these people above, I was advised to look at a book called The Montreal Irish Mafia by D'Arcy O'Connor. I found it a helpful and informative read. I also used the internet to clarify some information that the above people could not fully recall.

I particularly would like to thank Savita for the time and energy she put into helping me turn the characters into a story.

Also to those who have now gone before me: My parents, my brother Jeremy, Debbie, Moira, Roman, Denise, Sharon, Shorty, Gil, Ronny, Jimmy and Patsy. You all now know the mystery of life before I do.

My beloved cats who truly showed me the way to love deeply. Chocolate, Kali, Sammy, Lucas, George, Princess and Solomon. May I see you again on the other side.

Disclaimer: Some of the dates may not be entirely accurate. I have come as close as I could to tracking down the day, month and year using photo's, letters, court records and other people's memories. Every incident in this book is true and I have proof to back up any questions.

The two main characters Victoria and Donald were known as Vikki and Brother during the relationship. I have chosen to use our birth names.

Media or talk shows may contact me via e-mail: vau@alternativeuniverse.ca

Website: www.alternativeuniverse.ca

1975

MONTREAL, QUEBEC, CANADA

CHAPTER 1

As I turned, my green eyes met his piercing blues, and I knew I had just given my heart away.

"Hi, Donald." My best friend Debbie introduced us. "This is Victoria. Victoria, this is Donald."

I blinked and quickly returned to my body. "Do you have a gun?" I asked.

"No," he answered simply.

"Well, then, get the hell out of my car."

Donald and his two friends piled out of my Buick 225 back onto Closse Street, getting lost in the sea of light and people gathered in front of The Mustache Club. Debbie looked at me, waiting for me to drive.

"Who was that guy?" I asked.

"That was Donald," she replied.

"I have to have him."

Debbie's barely-there eyebrows arched and she smiled. "You two would suit each other. We can go to his mother's tomorrow."

I didn't say anything, turning the Buick back towards home. The reason I needed the gun seemed so much less important when I pictured his dark hair and smirk. Today I can't even remember the reason why I wanted it.

CHAPTER 2

As late as noon can be for some people, it was early for me. I dragged myself out of bed and over next door to Debbie's. It was already shaping up to be a good day. I had missed my roommates and their godforsaken monkey. I'm not sure if it was even legal to own a live monkey but this family did.

"Debbie!" I pounded on her door. Eventually, she opened it. I had no patience for coffee—my bones pricked with excitement and anticipation, in agony with the unfulfilled promise of seeing him again.

Debbie had found me a room to live in with a family who lived next door. She had met my ex-husband after I left him and had moved in with him. Leaving my husband, I also left behind two children who, we both agreed, would be better off with him as he had family in Montreal and I did not. I left on good terms and could see the kids at any time. Debbie was currently six months pregnant with what would be my ex-husband's third child. She was sixteen years old, about to turn seventeen on January 15, 1975. I was twenty-one.

We left for Pointe-Saint-Charles where his mother lived, about a thirty-minute drive from our apartment complex. The January cold made everything seem crisper. The sky was extra blue, rising above the snowdrifts. Two-storey brick duplexes dotted the sides of the roads with churches and shops in between.

"This is it." Debbie pointed to a nondescript unit. Kids and dogs loitered around the white-columned front porch, and hockey sticks, balls and sleds littered the front yard.

"Debbie!" A few of the kids ran over to greet us.

"Hello, munchkins." Debbie pulled one kid's hat sideways.

"Don't call me a munchkin!"

Debbie rolled her eyes at the little girl. "Is your mom home?"

"Yes," the kids said in unison.

"Great. Now scram." Debbie moved past them.

We walked up to the white door. Debbie didn't knock. "Patsy?" She strode through into the warm kitchen.

"Debbie!" A small red-haired woman stood up from the kitchen table. Everything about her was soft: her skin, her voice, her eyes.

"Hey, kid." Debbie nodded towards Cathy, Donald's sister.

"Hey," Cathy shot back.

"This is my friend, Victoria. She's looking for Donald."

Patsy laughed. "Me, too. He hasn't been home in three days." She smiled. "But don't worry, he always turns up."

I guess it was fate, or whatever you want to call it, because as if on cue he walked through the door, stomping the snow from his boots. "Mom!" he called, coming from the living room. I could see him over Debbie's shoulder. She pushed me in front of her. "You?" He breathed. "I still don't have a gun."

I licked my lips and smiled. "That's okay. There's something else I wanted to talk to you about."

"Oh?" He clearly wanted me to elaborate but I was making it up as I went.

"In private."

"Sure, Victoria." Donald smirked as he motioned for me to follow him into his bedroom. He closed the door behind us and said, "So, what's so important?"

I stood there thinking. It wasn't easy. His body stood parallel to mine radiating heat. A beat passed and his smirk grew. His face descended towards mine, and he took me into his arms, locking me to him. Everything around us fell away. We went back and forth, each of us daring to take the embrace deeper. I broke the kiss to take off his shirt, kissing his neck. I felt the bed beneath me and then he was on top of me. Nothing else mattered in that moment; nothing else existed but us…

I pulled a cigarette from my abandoned coat. "Want one?" I offered.

"No thanks, I don't smoke." He lay stretched out on the bed. I put the cigarette away unlit and crawled back in beside him, laying my head on his chest. Everything just felt right. Until Donald shifted to get up. Panic crawled up my spine; I wasn't ready for this to end. I sat up and drew the blanket around me.

Donald looked me up and down. "You have your car here, right?"

"Yes." I nodded.

"Good, I need you to give me a ride."

"All right."

CHAPTER 3

I won't go into the details of our outing because they aren't important. While our trip did revolve around me driving him to pick up mescaline, and while that was illegal, it was also mundane. In our world it was no different than any other business transaction. Like going to pick up stock for your store to sell later. Things became interesting when we returned to his house, business concluded. On one of the streets nearby, a group of boys waved us over. I rolled down my window.

"What's up?" Donald asked.

"The cops are at your house. They're looking for you," one of them said to Donald.

For a moment I considered the implication, but Donald didn't miss a beat. "Thanks, kid." He handed the kids some change and turned back in his seat. "Take me to Saint Jacques Street—I'm going to get a motel." We drove off, leaving his family to handle things with the police.

In the '70s if you drove down Saint Jacques Street, you would see different variations of the same motel repeated. It didn't matter which one we pulled into; they were all the same.

"Wait here," Donald said. He went inside the office and returned, holding keys. "Come on." He motioned for me to get out of the car. I fell in behind him, as we made our way to the room. He took the keys from his pocket and unlocked the door. He hesitated for a second in the doorway, then turned to look at me over his shoulder and stared deep into my eyes. "I'm a criminal. Don't try to change me."

"I won't," I said, and I meant it.

"Good," he mumbled as he ushered me into the room, holding the door. Once inside, he latched the security chain. "Sit down," he said, gesturing to the faded brown couch. I did as he said and Donald joined me. I looked at his arms, noticing his two tattoos for the first time. I looked down at his black jeans, then at the carpet.

It was covered in stains and cigarette burns. The bed quilt was faded, and the pillows looked lumpy, but it still felt a million times more like home than my current room.

"Hey." Donald's voice brought me back to attention. "You're staying, right?" His demeanour was cool, but his eyes betrayed him. I saw in them a look of urgency.

I nodded my head slowly. "All right." He patted my knee. "Go get your things. I want you to be wearing different clothes the next time I take them off you. We may be here for a few days."

Donald walked me to my car and then headed off to use a payphone.

I drove aimlessly for a few minutes, considering the last six hours. *I love him.* The words erupted from me. Last night I had been dreaming of him and tonight I would sleep beside him.

I don't remember what I threw in my laundry basket to take with me. Clothes obviously, shoes for sure, my important documents, maybe? I didn't have any mementos or keepsakes. Separating from my husband two years ago had reduced my life to fit into the single room I rented.

On my way to the motel I let my mind drift back to earlier. Something was different with Donald. My instant attraction to him wasn't new. I had experienced that before. It was something else I felt but couldn't express. Looking back, I know now what I felt was the familiarity left over from our previous lifetimes together. I felt totally and wholly accepted for the first time.

CHAPTER 4

Later, when Donald looked back he admitted to feeling something as well. He also felt the pull of destiny.

I found him stretched out on the motel bed. "Good, you're here," he greeted me, taking my laundry basket. He never said much, but he always seemed to know what I was thinking. Everything in me melted when he touched me. His hands found the small of my back and caressed me; our bodies fit together. Our nakedness felt as normal as when we were clothed.

Donald laid me down on the bed, kissing my chest on his way to unzipping my pants. His dark hair brushed my face as he kissed my neck. I didn't think; I didn't think about what he was thinking, I just felt. It was intoxicating.

After, he took me out for dinner before returning to the motel to rest and watch TV.

Our days and nights fell into a routine. I wasn't working and Debbie came by every day to visit. Donald had arrived in my life at the perfect time. I decided to join him in his life of crime. It wasn't that I wanted to, but I felt compelled. I had to prove to myself that I could keep up with him.

Breaking and entering was the most common felony for people our age. Debbie and I decided that we would try our hand at this.

Most days, Debbie and I would just drive and drive. Rarely did we find a house that we thought was worth breaking into. One that we did try was a former foster home of Debbie's. She gave directions for how to get there.

"Follow me," Debbie said as she got out of the car. "I know where they keep the spare key."

"Sure," I said and followed Debbie inside. We went straight upstairs to look for jewellery and other valuables. After a few minutes, we heard someone come home. The door opened and we heard a woman taking off her shoes. I froze.

"Be cool," Debbie said calmly. She started heading down the stairs. The woman, Debbie's ex-foster mom, startled when she saw us come down the stairs.

"Hi." Debbie smiled at her.

"Hi," the woman replied.

"We've been trying to get in touch with Holly. I thought she might be upstairs sleeping." Debbie started moving towards the door. "You know how she likes to sleep in." Debbie laughed.

"Holly hasn't lived here for a while. I would try Kevin—he's still her boyfriend." The foster mom kept staring at Debbie.

"Really." Debbie sounded surprised. "Okay, I guess we'll head over there now. Thanks!" Debbie opened the door. I followed behind her, smiling at the foster mom and walking calmly to the car. Once we were inside, I started driving, and Debbie broke out laughing.

"That was so close," I said.

A few days later we tried our luck again. Debbie and I drove to a duplex in Westmount and picked a door at random. Debbie was working hard to get the lock to break backwards with the crowbar. I heard a rustle inside, and suddenly the door flung open. I flattened myself against the wall. Debbie gasped and ran. A large, hairy man burst out of the apartment and chased after her. I waited until he was a ways away, then I ran behind them. I ran as fast as I could across the road.

"Shit! There are two of you!" I heard the man yell. He was catching up to Debbie. He grabbed her by her arm.

As soon as he touched Debbie, she screamed, "Rape! Rape! Help! I'm being raped!"

"You little bitch." He pushed her away from him.

Debbie and I caught the first bus from Sherbrooke Street to Atwater Plaza. We headed straight to the Red Lion Bar. My brother-in-law Jimmy was always there.

"Jimmy." I walked in and went right up to him, taking the seat beside him at the bar.

"What's up?" he asked, looking from me to Debbie and back to me. "You look flushed."

"It's kind of a long story. Could you please grab my car for me?" I asked.

"Sure, but why do you need me to get your car?"

"I'll tell you when you get back." I handed him my car keys. Jimmy got up without asking any more questions and returned in half an hour.

"What the hell did you two do?" he asked us as he walked back into the bar.

"What do you mean?" I asked.

"That place is infested with cops. I could see the lights and sirens five blocks away." Jimmy sat down, and the bartender put a beer in front of him.

"We may have tried a B & E." I tried to look calm.

"And the owners were still in the house?" Jimmy looked at me.

"Yeah. He wasn't impressed. He chased Debbie down the street and caught her."

"How did you get away?" He looked at Debbie.

"I cried rape, he called me a bitch and let me go," Debbie said.

"Nice." Jimmy chuckled and grinned.

"I would have never thought to do that," I added.

Debbie just smiled.

I looked at the clock; it was getting to be late. I was ready to go home to Donald. I had been at the motel for six days now. Tomorrow would be a week. He had only paid for the motel for one week. We already felt like we had lived together forever. I couldn't imagine ever living apart.

I thought about it all night tossing and turning, so when I awoke I asked him point blank, "Are we staying together or not?"

"Sure." He smirked, kissed me and went off to pay for another week.

For three Sundays after that I asked him, "Are we staying together or not?" He said yes every time, until the fourth week. That day at the beginning of February, Donald handed me sixty dollars and told me to go and rent a place for the two of us.

"This isn't enough for a hell hole," I told him.

"Of course it is," he responded.

"Where?"

He shook his head. "Go find my sister, Cathy. She'll show you." Donald grabbed his coat and I followed him out and watched him get into Gil's waiting car.

"I guess we're moving in together," I said to no one in particular.

CHAPTER 5

I was certain I wouldn't find anything for sixty dollars unless it was a super dump. Even in the '70s, rent in Montreal was higher than his measly sixty dollars.

At Donald's mom's house, I didn't bother to knock. I let myself in just like everyone else.

"Victoria, what a pleasant surprise." Patsy smiled at me.

"Hi, Patsy. Is Cathy here?" I said.

"Cathy!" Patsy yelled.

Cathy looked a lot older than she was. Her eyes took everything in at once; she was always on alert. She remembered everything that was said and done in the Pointe.

"Donald said you would help me find a place for us," I told her.

"Sure."

Cathy made a few phone calls and no more than twenty minutes later, she turned to me and said, "I found one."

"Excellent!"

We hopped in my car. She directed me to Evelyn Street in Verdun. A row of triplexes occupied both sides of the street for as far as the eye could see. Cathy knocked on a neighbour's door, retrieved a key and we walked up the outdoor staircase to the second floor, my floor.

The inside of the house was bare but clean. A double living room (meaning you could combine the bedroom with the front room by putting up a curtain), kitchen, bathroom—everything we would need until we could get more. I had been living alone for the past year. Now that Donald and I would be living together I would enjoy being his "little woman"; the idea of domesticity suited me just fine.

I picked him up from the motel and drove him to our new home. I always drove. It's one of the things I'm known for. I can do amazing things with a car.

I looked over at him in the passenger seat. Four weeks ago, when I first met him, felt like a lifetime ago, a previous life.

"What?" Donald asked me.

"Nothing." I smiled, looking back at the road. From the corner of my eye, I saw him smirk.

"When we get there, we'll have to christen the new place." Donald put his hand on my thigh and kept it there. The warmth of his palm seeped into me and spread.

When we arrived, the evening sounds of Evelyn Street were setting in. Dinners cooking, cars passing on the street. Few people were out because of the cold, so the air around us felt like our own bubble.

We walked up the wooden stairs, leaving foot prints in the fresh snow. My hand was tucked into the crook of his arm, as he guided me up to the landing. Donald stopped with his hand on the doorknob, turned, and kissed me on the lips before opening the door.

CHAPTER 6

The days slipped by, filled with small moments of domestic bliss that added up to a fulfilling life. Like any other couple we began and ended the day together. But unlike other couples we were free to choose if we wanted to spend our daytime together or apart. Often we met up for an early afternoon nap.

It took us some time to furnish the apartment. Our couch, kitchen chairs, table and hutch came from a lovely house north of us, our colour TV from a different house. We had found all this furniture on the side of the road one day; I guess the furniture fell off a truck, right before we drove by.

When you walked in the door to our new home, you would see on your right, a double front room. The big windows were nice because they let in so much light. However, the house didn't come with curtains. Even though we could see all of our neighbours, and they could see us walking around naked, Donald refused to spend the money. I made do with flimsy sheets that I tacked up. I don't know what it is, but I've always had a thing for curtains. When I go into a house, one of the first things I notice are the window dressings. In the home I own now, I installed remote-control blinds. I never get sick of using them.

"God, these make-believe curtains are so ugly!" I said one day out of frustration. When Donald didn't reply, I pushed on. "Well, don't you think so?"

"It's going to take some time before any fall off the back of a truck," he said and kissed my temple. "Get your coat on—you're coming."

I grabbed my jacket and followed him to his brown Chevy Malibu. It was a car no one would bother to remember.

In Montreal at that time we didn't have license renewals staggered monthly; they all expired in March.

"You have got to be kidding!" Donald swore. A line snaked back and forth across the room, culminating in a row of four tellers. Neither of us liked lines. Donald looked down at me. He played with one of my belt loops and half-heartedly caressed my butt. I felt his hand still. I looked up at him and he was looking around the room, taking it all in properly. I could tell by the look in his eyes he was coming up with a plan. He looked at the walls, the tellers, the people in line around us, the rooms behind the tellers. Our long wait was no longer a bad thing; it had given him time to case the place. He looked at me then, a big grin breaking out across his face. Leaning in, he gave me a kiss, pulling me to him.

"Oh my God, Victoria. Did you see?" he asked me back in his car. "All those people there, all paying cash. The amount of money that is in there."

"That's great, Donald."

I walked up the stairs to our apartment. "Effin' curtains," I cursed as I made my way inside. I started to ready the ribs for our dinner and could hear Donald walk into the bedroom. Then came the *whirl, whirl, whirl* of the telephone dial.

He must be calling someone to come over and plan the job, I thought to myself.

I heard little snippets of the conversation, "Hey, Victoria! Can you make enough for another person, if it's not too much trouble?" he yelled away from the phone.

"Donald, you know I love to cook and that I always make too much food. Of course, another person is no problem. Who's coming?"

"Billy F," Donald replied.

Billy F was in for a treat! I had planned to make oven-baked ribs with lima beans, gravy from the rib drippings and my secret-recipe mashed potatoes. The secret was adding lots and lots of butter and then using whipping cream. I mashed the potatoes with an electric beater.

Billy F arrived within twenty minutes of getting Donald's phone call. The ribs had another hour to go before we could eat. I made myself busy while Donald and Billy F talked. They didn't care that I came and went and heard almost everything. Anything I didn't hear Donald would tell me later tonight.

"This smells so good!" Billy F took the pot of ribs and put some on his plate right away.

"Thank you, Billy." I smiled at him.

"Victoria is an excellent cook." Donald took some ribs for himself.

"Do you mean you get to eat like this every night?" Billy F stopped shovelling food in his mouth and stared at me.

"Almost every night." Donald winked.

"You're a lucky, lucky man, Donald." Billy F went back to eating.

"I am a lucky man," Donald said quietly looking at me.

I blushed just a little at that.

I cleared away the dishes and then joined them back at the table. It was decided I was going to drive the getaway car.

After Billy F left, I settled down to read in our bed. Donald got up and went to the fridge. "Victoria!" he yelled from the kitchen. "We're out of Coca-Cola."

"I'll buy some tomorrow," I yelled back.

"But I want some now." Donald pulled on his coat. "I'll want some for tomorrow, too."

"Okay." I looked up at him for the kiss I knew was coming. "Hurry home."

I didn't hear Donald come in. He flopped down on the bed beside me and rolled onto his stomach and took the book from me. "I'm so happy," he said as he put the book down. "If this keeps up, I'm going to marry you."

I smiled wildly at him. "Nothing would make me happier."

Donald pulled me a little closer so he could look into my eyes. He didn't wait for permission. His lips touched mine, pushing them apart, and his hands moved from my elbows down to my hips.

We became a single entity when we came together. His energy flowed into me and I felt as if I knew everything inside of him and he knew everything inside of me.

He undid my jeans and pushed me onto the bed, tugging my pants off. Then Donald removed his clothes and descended on top of me, taking off my shirt and my bra. He went painfully slow, curling my toes with small twitches of pleasure. I moaned and bucked my hips.

"Just wait." His arm slid across my stomach, pinning me to the bed. I could feel his mouth kiss lower and lower… His tongue knew every curve and crevice of my body. He never faltered; sex with him was natural. He took control; he decided how much pleasure I would have before he took his own. Secretly, I thought of him as the Cunnilingus King.

CHAPTER 7

"You really are the best driver I know, Vic." Donald smiled at me from the passenger seat.

"Tell me something I don't know!"

The sun felt warm shining in through the Buick's windows. With the heater going full-blast you could enjoy the morning rays. February wasn't usually this cold. But we had been hit with a cold snap. Everything froze: ponds, sidewalks, pipes, even your eyelashes. You could feel the cold prickle in your lungs every time you breathed in.

I wasn't nervous about the job we were on our way to do. Donald had always been the perfect criminal. He was the one in control, not just of me but of everything. Saying no, or thinking this might not work, didn't occur to me.

"Turn here." He pointed towards Billy F's house.

"I know where I'm going."

When I parked, Donald didn't get out of the car, so I waited, too. Billy F jumped in, cursing and rubbing his hands.

"Hello, Victoria," he greeted me.

"Head towards the east end," Donald directed.

Everyone was quiet in the car, focused. We were each going over our part in our minds.

"Pull over here." Donald pointed to a residential road. He got out, bent down, and tried to remove the license plate of the car in front of us. "Damn, it's frozen!" He gave up after a few minutes, sliding back into the car. "Keep driving, we'll try another on the way."

I gave him a quizzical look.

"Don't worry. We'll find one."

On our way to the bureau we tried a few different cars. We stopped on different side streets and in several parking lots, with no luck.

"You'll have to park farther away." Donald climbed back into the car for the last time.

"Okay," I said.

I stopped two blocks away from the bureau and waited. Donald gave me a quick kiss then followed Billy F.

I wasn't nervous; it's not in my personality. I was alert. The street was quiet. I watched a taxi drop his fare off farther down the road. A few people walked along the sidewalks, but their heads were down as they focused on not slipping.

I saw Donald and Billy F approach. Everything in me stilled. I could feel myself coil. It was my job to take off the second the last person was in the car. And it was the last person's job to make sure the door was shut as I drove away.

The guys jumped in and I snapped into action. I drove quickly, trying not to draw attention. I could hear sirens in the distance, but they faded the farther we drove. We hadn't planned a route in advance because I knew to drive away from the job, but also away from home. I checked the rear-view mirror to see if anyone was following us, but there was no one. I did see Billy F in the back seat breathing deeply and evenly.

"Easy job, everyone behaved," Donald declared after we had been driving for about ten minutes. Relief spread through me. "You can head towards home, Victoria. Wait till you see what I got."

CHAPTER 8

The next day after the job was much like the one before, only now I had more money to spend. I was paid $200 out of the $5000 that was stolen.

The following Friday, Debbie and I drove up Mountain Street, my trunk full of groceries. It felt like any other day, busy and warm. The cold spell had finally lifted.

A car cut me off and blared its siren. I slammed on the brakes in time to avoid hitting the cop who jumped out, gun drawn.

Debbie and I looked at each other; it was the only communication we needed.

"Get out of the car!"

Debbie slowly opened her door and got out, hands up, pregnant belly out. I mirrored her on the other side of the car minus the belly.

A police officer roughly cuffed me and threw me into the back of a squad car next to Debbie.

Both the cops had been armed and ready. Their faces stone cold, their stance firm and ready to shoot. It was a little comical considering I'm five foot six and at the time weighed all of 128 pounds. Debbie was five eight, and due to deliver her baby in less than two months. I didn't laugh, though. I kept my face frozen in a look of cool disdain, ready to express my indignation at any moment. After all, we were innocent; we hadn't done anything wrong. That was the front Debbie and I put up.

We were taken to the main police headquarters in Montreal.

"I want to use a phone." Debbie looked at the cop. Her attitude was starting to show itself.

"I don't give a fuck. You're going upstairs till I figure out what to do with you."

"I'm seventeen. You have to let me use the phone."

"I don't have to do anything," the cop shot back. He grabbed her elbow as she pulled away from him. Another cop came up from behind and took her other elbow. They pushed her up the stairs kicking and screaming, "You pigs! You can't do this to me… I'm a minor! I have rights! I'm a minor and I'm pregnant. You can't do this to me. I'm going to sue you!"

"Your turn." A plainclothesman jerked me downstairs into an interrogation room. The hallway was musty; it smelled like sweat from a hundred different people mixing together and oozing from the walls.

"Those are huge! Do you think they're real?" the cop at my elbow asked his partner as he ogled my breasts.

I ignored them. They sat me at a table and asked my name and age. I told them. Then they asked me what I had been doing the day the license bureau was robbed. "I was at home."

The cop rolled his eyes. "And your Buick was where?"

"It's not my Buick. Everyone in the house has access to the keys."

The cop was not impressed. He looked to his partner. "We know you're involved, Victoria. We don't want you. We want the guys you drove for."

"I told you I was at home."

"Fine!" The cop who had been standing, silently glaring at me, grabbed me and forced me to my knees. "You think for a while." The bad cop stormed out, followed by the good cop. A uniformed cop stayed in the doorway.

I took a break and tried to remember that day, to picture who might have seen me. I came up blank. Later, I would learn it was a taxi driver who had reported us, going above and beyond his civic duty.

Both cops returned about forty-five minutes later. My legs were just starting to go numb.

"Enjoying yourself?" Bad Cop sneered.

I stared right back. I wasn't scared. I had dealt with cops before. I knew what to expect.

"You think you're so tough, but really, I think you're just a scared little girl." The bad cop leaned forward, entering my personal space.

I didn't flinch; I didn't move. I just kept staring back. I could see how that frustrated him.

"This is funny to you isn't it, Victoria? You think this is all a game. Well, you can laugh yourself all the way to prison. We don't want to charge you, but these charges carry some serious time."

This time I cocked my head to the side and raised my eyebrows, unamused.

The bad cop slammed his fist down on the table.

"Let's try this differently," Good Cop intervened. "You're only twenty-one, Victoria. Where are your parents?"

"They live in BC now."

"Really." Good Cop smiled at his partner. "BC is lovely this time of year, much better than Montreal. If you help us, we'll help you. Give us the names and we'll put you on a plane to your parents tomorrow."

"I don't want to live in BC."

Bad Cop scoffed so hard spit flew out of his mouth and over my right shoulder. It was hard not to roll my eyes. "Leave her here a while longer. If that doesn't work, we'll try something harder." Bad Cop let the threat hang in the air.

In Montreal in the '70s, the cops had two tactics they relied on. One was making a person kneel. Which I was already doing so that left only the phone books. A phone book was thick enough and large enough to distribute the force of a punch, but not really lessen the force. The cops could hit away without leaving any marks.

I didn't think they would hit me much. But I was beginning to worry about Donald. He would be going out of his mind by now. On the other hand, maybe Debbie had gotten to a phone and they were just waiting for me to be bailed. God help them if they hadn't yet let Debbie use a phone…

When Bad Cop returned, Nice Cop wasn't with him. He was flanked by two uniformed officers instead. "Sit for a bit." Bad Cop helped me into a chair. He stared at me for a while. I stared back nonchalantly. "We need a name, Victoria. If they were in here, they wouldn't hold out for you."

I didn't flinch.

"You look like a nice girl from a nice family. You have a family of your own?"

I turned my gaze to one of the uniformed officers, then back to the bad cop. His face was starting to turn a little red. They couldn't get me to give them the information they wanted if they didn't first get me talking.

"Damn it! Get down!" Bad Cop pushed me back on my knees.

The blood in my legs had just started circulating again. I felt every angry muscle, tendon, and nerve scream at me. I didn't make a sound.

"One last time, Victoria. Give us the names of the guys and we'll put you on a plane to BC."

Maintaining my silence, I just stared down at the floor.

One uniformed cop held my shoulder, and the other held the phonebook to my ear. Bad Cop punched me a few times. I don't know why they chose my ear. I could feel my brain rattle around a little after the first punch. It wasn't that bad.

After the second, third and fourth punch, I realized it was really bad; they would have to stop soon or I was going to pass out.

Bad Cop fed me a few more shots then threw the phonebook on the ground in disgust. "Bitch!" He stormed out.

I blinked my eyes a few times. I had a headache.

Good Cop and Bad Cop left me alone for a few hours this time. They probably stopped to get a meal and relax. *Pigs...*

When they finally came back, I decided I'd had enough. The comment about my breasts earlier flashed through my mind. *They think I'm a damsel in distress, nothing but a woman.* Damsels faint; if I fainted, they'd leave me alone for a while. I closed my eyes and breathed deeply, trying to make my swoon look as real as possible. The cold floor kissed my cheek. I lay there, listening. I could hear them whispering, the police sounds getting more and more agitated. I blinked furiously: my performance of coming to.

Good Cop and Bad Cop looked at me. "Take her upstairs." The uniformed officers helped me to my feet and led me up to a cell block. If I had thought to look at a clock, I would have realized seven hours had gone by.

I felt something wet and sticky between my legs. I looked down to see a red spot expanding from the crotch of my orange dress pants. Dumbfounded, I kept staring. Then I just burst out laughing. I laughed uncontrollably for a long while. I had gotten my period and it had saved me. The bastards must have thought they made me miscarry. After all, they had commented on my breasts. It would have made sense to them. I don't know what would have happened if I hadn't gotten my period at that second.

I blinked and wiped away the tears from laughing. Never in my life, before or since, have I ever been so thankful to get my period.

CHAPTER 9

I had been taken in on a Friday night and was bailed out the following Monday, after I was charged with the robbery. The cops kept my Buick 225. They claimed it was evidence; where the groceries ended up, I'll never know.

Shorty, one of Donald's best friends, was waiting for me, keys in his hands. He gave me a big hug, "Let's go. He's waiting for you." Shorty looked me up and down. "Long weekend?" he asked.

"You could say that."

Shorty nodded and closed the passenger door.

Donald was waiting for me in the doorway. He pulled me into his arms instantly. "I was so worried about you! We spent the whole night looking for you in ditches."

I pulled back and looked at him. I could see relief written all over his face. He kissed the top of my head. "They finally let Debbie out at 3:00 a.m., Saturday morning. I guess she clogged the toilet in her cell and flooded the whole cell block."

I laughed. "Good for Debbie."

"Are you okay?" Donald's voice was serious.

I nodded my head. "They made me kneel a bunch. It was no worse than church."

Donald smiled. "You stayed here all weekend?" I asked.

"Of course, I stayed here. This is our home. Where else would I go?"

"I don't know. I just thought…"

He kissed me softly. "I knew you wouldn't rat."

I leaned my head against his shoulder, enjoying the smell of him. My eyes glanced down at the floor; it was spotless. I looked up to see luxurious green velvet curtains hung in our front window. "The truck came around?" I questioned.

"No, Santa brought them," he shot back with a grin. "Of course it was me. I measured and picked them out myself. I had my sisters clean the floor. Do you like the curtains?"

"Of course I do!" I took a step forward, fingering the soft material.

"Enough of that." Donald scooped me up and carried me into our bedroom. He set me down gently on the bed and began tracing the corner of my ear with his thumb. He instinctively seemed to know. His expression was neutral, but I could feel his emotions welling up and spilling out of him. He pushed me down on the bed and kissed me deeply. Then he pulled back to look into my eyes. "From now on, Victoria, you don't work!"

CHAPTER 10

I looked up at the clock: a quarter past six. I tried to turn my attention back to the sink and the dishes I was washing. Donald had been good to his word. I kept the house and he worked. The minute hand seemed stuck, moving glacially slow. I put the cups and plates back in their places just so. It was now March and still winter, but not the brutal cold of a few weeks ago. *That bastard, who does he think he is being this late? This is crap. I'm going to kill him.* Just then I heard the door open. Donald walked through the door, a big grin on his face. He kicked off his boots and walked toward me. "Where the hell have you been?" I said.

"Vic, I'm not that late, and it was an easy job." He smiled at me.

I gave him an icy stare.

"Enough of this." Donald pinned me to the sink and kissed me long and deep.

It pissed me off that he was happy. He had a big smirk on his face. He always came home from a job like that, wanting to celebrate his hard work. I didn't feel like celebrating; I wanted to claw his eyes out.

I felt him pull me a little closer and his hand moved to the back of my neck. His face angled downward and his lips pressed against mine, his tongue exploring my mouth deeper and deeper. Then he just stopped, looking down at me, my face flushed.

I wiggled my hips against him. Donald knew how to make me feel better. Stoke the fire that burned in my veins.

"Not now." He gave me a final quick kiss. "Let's go purchase a car for you. A reward for all your hard work." Donald winked at me. After my arrest, I had not gotten my Buick back. The cops claimed it was evidence, but really it was just one more thing they tried to leverage against me.

Donald was silent as we drove to the first lot. He sighed often, and I could see he was turning something over and over in his mind. I knew it was our job. He never said sorry; his mind didn't work like that. But he did feel responsible. The *if onlys* haunted him. If only he had thought to get the plates earlier in the day. If only he had thought to use hot water to thaw the license plate. If only he hadn't screwed up and I didn't get arrested.

We strolled through various car lots, hand in hand, chattering with the salesmen. At the third lot, I stopped in front of a green Buick Skylark convertible! The soft top was white; it matched the interior and tires. It was clearly labelled $1600, a significant sum of money.

"Nice choice. It's got a 440 under the hood. It's lightning fast," the salesman said.

I liked to go fast.

"Easy to burn rubber in that car."

I liked to burn rubber. "Yes, it's definitely a contender," I told the salesman, and began to move away from the car.

"Wait, Victoria. Do you really like this car?" Donald saw my desire written all over my face. "We'll take it," he said to the salesman.

I knew that with this purchase, Donald was trying to make up for the arrest that I didn't hold against him on a conscious level. But I no longer trusted him to be the perfect criminal. I worried when he went out. Deep inside, I felt betrayed that he hadn't been more careful with the license plates, that he hadn't been more careful with me.

At that moment, though, my mind was totally focused on my nice new car. I peeled out of the parking lot on my way home, enjoying the freedom of being behind the wheel again. Donald had a hard time keeping up with me in his Chevy Malibu. Eventually, he gave up and I beat him home.

As we went up the stairs, Donald turned to me and said, "I have another surprise for you, but it can wait till later."

Later came, and he pulled out a joint of hash. "What?" I exclaimed.

"Come on, let's smoke a joint together. We've never done this." We lay back on the bed, lit the joint and passed it back and forth between us, inhaling deeply. Time stood still; I couldn't tell what was happening. It was not a feeling I liked. It brought me back to my hippie days—once I found out I was pregnant, I had stopped taking all drugs. After I had my two children, I tried to get high on hash again but it caused me to get paranoid, and I didn't like being unaware of my surroundings.

The phone rang around midnight. I looked at Donald and said in a voice that seemed to echo, 'No, please don't let it be Debbie in labour." But it was. I stared at Donald in horror and let him take charge. We jumped into his car, and drove quickly over to Debbie's. She climbed into the back seat and Donald took off like a madman.

I hadn't said a word and finally Debbie leaned forward and looked at us. "Are you two high?" she asked with a loud laugh. No one had ever seen us high.

"No," I tried to proclaim.

"Yes, you are!" She laughed until she had a contraction. That shut her up. Arriving at the Montreal General Hospital, we pulled into Emergency. Donald asked if she wanted us to stay but Danny wasn't far behind. He had stayed behind with the kids until his mother arrived to look after them and then hopped into a taxi. As it turned out, it was false labour, and it wasn't until two weeks later that Christine was born on March 25, 1975.

CHAPTER 11

Our days had an order to them. We woke up around 8:00, had breakfast. Then, being a news person, I went across the street and bought the daily newspaper. As soon as I had filled myself with the news, sometimes sooner, we made love. By 1:00 p.m. we were both spent and napped in each other's arms. When we awoke, we might go to his mother's house for dinner, go for a drive or take his siblings to the movies. Life felt like it was painted with pastel colours, made warm and bright by our love.

When the snow melted, we added fishing to our calendar. Lying in the small motor boat we would rent I would lie back and read *True Confessions* magazines as Donald steered us out to the middle of the water. I always shared the most outrageous stories. I liked watching Donald shake his head, dumbfounded by other people's drama. Lancaster, Ontario, a mere forty-five-minute drive away, was beautiful in the warm days leading up to summer. The banks of the St. Lawrence River bloomed with spring flowers, and the water was a dark blue that brightened on the horizon as it mixed with the sky.

I remember the sky because I would glimpse it as Donald enjoyed his favourite activity, the reason I called him The King.

"Put down the magazine, Victoria." I put it back in the picnic basket. Donald put his hand on my shoulder, lowering me flat on my back. I looked up at the sky while he flipped up the skirt of my summer dress. His hands were warm as they massaged my thighs, a counterpoint to the cool breeze. I wiggled my hips impatiently. "Hold on, I'm admiring the view." He spread my legs a little farther apart. His breath and then his lips caressed mine. Slow upward licks sent pleasure shooting up my hips. When his lips pressed fully into me, I gasped. His cue to stroke me with his finger, tracing light circles, then press harder, until his finger was inside me. Slowly, in and out, in time with his mouth. Every muscle in my body tightened, completely at his mercy. When he curled his finger up, my hips bucked on their own, faster and faster.

"Donald!"

When my breath began to slow down, he lifted his face and smiled a big wicked grin. "Again, Victoria?"

An hour passed, and we were both satisfied. I sat up, moving my clothing back into place, smoothing my hair. The banks of the river looked unfamiliar. We had definitely drifted way off course. "Where are we?" I asked.

Donald shrugged his shoulders. He steered us towards shore. Farther up, a family played on the beach. "Excuse me, Sir," Donald said to the father. "Where are we? I seem to have drifted off course."

"In the USA," the man replied.

"How far down did we drift?" Donald turned and looked at me.

"Well, enough distance to put us in another country!" I laughed. Donald just grinned.

"Thank you," he said to the father, and pushed us back out into the river. "Still worth it." Donald winked at me.

I rolled my eyes ever so slightly.

"I saw that. Keep it up and I'll throw you in," he said, laughing.

CHAPTER 12

As much time as we spent together, I still needed to be alone a few times a week. It's always been that way, in all my relationships before and since. "Can you go to your mum's for a bit, I want to clean the house." I informed him, coming out of the kitchen.

"Okay." Donald got up from his rocking chair. He never questioned me; he seemed to already understand. "I'll be at Mum's. Call me when you want me to come back." He kissed my cheek. "Thank you."

Donald smiled. "Of course."

The first thing I did once his car pulled away was pull out the ironing. In those days, I found ironing very calming. So, I ironed everything, even our sheets. When we got together, I forbade Donald from wearing jeans. I hated them. That meant a lot of dress pants to iron.

After that, I did the dishes, dusted, and scrubbed the floor. Then I sat down to enjoy my handiwork. Our home felt fresh and clean again.

"Okay, Patsy. Tell him to come home."

"He says he's putting on his shoes and heading out the door."

I hung up the phone and lay on the couch. Daydreams played out in my mind. But my sense of time caught up with me. I could feel the change in my body. My bones felt cold and prickly. I tried not to look at the clock. When I did, the clock showed it had been forty-five minutes since I called Patsy. I began doing the math in my head. If he stopped to say goodbye to everyone, that would add ten minutes. Worst case, at this time, traffic could add ten minutes. That still left fifteen minutes unaccounted for. I looked out the window, pacing a little.

It's not easy to love a criminal. Before my arrest, I blissfully thought Donald was the perfect criminal. It never occurred to me he could mess up. My arrest had changed everything. I didn't worry about getting arrested again. I worried about him. My mind tortured me.

In the '70s we didn't have an integrated view of the mind, body and soul. Everything was separate. People didn't talk about their feelings. The word "stress" did not exist. So, I didn't have words to explain my emotions. I didn't understand that I was worried sick about him. I felt frustrated with him. Like a dog with a bone. I asked myself repeatedly: *Why isn't he home? Why isn't that little bastard home yet?*

When Donald finally got home he could tell I was upset. He knew I didn't like him being late. "Don't worry about me, don't worry about me. I'll always come home to you, Victoria." He thought I was worried he would leave me for another woman. He still thought he was invincible.

"Gordy showed up as I was leaving. He got a new M1. I had to help him figure out where to saw." Donald loved guns. "I'm going to Ottawa to look at a gun store. Want to come along for the ride?" he asked, even though he already knew my answer would be yes.

CHAPTER 13

Autoroute 40, also known as the Trans-Canada Highway, is a pleasant drive on a May long weekend. Our second trip to Ottawa was warm and peaceful. The forests we passed were still, lit only by the moon and our headlights. We had the road mostly to ourselves. Though we didn't work a regular schedule, the long weekend mood seeped into our consciousness.

This drive felt different than the one a few weeks ago, when we had first scoped out the gun store. Tonight, Donald had brought a chainsaw, crow bar, and garbage bags. He had checked the motor and oiled the chainsaw the day before.

"Come on, Gaetan, help me pry the door," Donald said, once we arrived at our destination. He grabbed the crowbar and walked to the vacuum cleaner store adjacent to the gun shop. The gun store had a fancy alarm system connected to their doors. The vacuum store, however, had only a steel door. What both stores shared was an interior wall.

Donald and Gaetan went at the back door with the crowbar.

"There. You two stay here," Donald said as he went inside. I could see him work through the open door. He laid out his tools, chainsaw, crowbar, and hammer, all ready to go. He picked his spot on the wall and plugged in the chainsaw. It roared to life.

I saw a flash followed by a bang. The chainsaw sputtered and died. "The bloody fuse blew!" Donald swore.

We joined him inside and fanned out, helping Donald look for the fuse box. Sure enough, it had blown.

Gaetan and I looked at each other. It was after midnight. We didn't really know anyone in Ottawa, and hardware stores were the only place you could buy fuses. Donald swore some more, packed up his gear and we headed back to Montreal.

When we returned three hours later, Donald once again instructed, "You guys stay on lookout," then he pried open the vacuum store door. He brought in the fuses, installing them in the fuse box. He plugged in the chainsaw, flipped the switch, and this time it roared to life. I watched Donald lift the chainsaw, chuckling at his own cleverness. Once he disappeared farther into the store, I could only hear the chainsaw work. Then it stopped. A few seconds later, I heard a chorus of glass breaking. Donald smashed into the glass cases that displayed the guns. He was like a kid in a candy store, a bull in a china shop. In his excitement, he still took the time to pick out a tiny pearl-handled gun. A lady revolver. When he was finished, Donald had loaded around sixty guns into garbage bags then into the car. He had a big smile on his face the whole way home.

The sun was starting to rise when we pulled into Verdun. My eyes felt gritty and I kept yawning. "I'm going to bed," I told the boys, leaving them to unload the guns.

The next day I heard Donald up and about early. I ignored him for as long as I could. But the continuous opening of our front door, the voices of people coming, buying a gun and leaving, was unescapable.

"Did you sleep?" I asked Donald from the kitchen, pouring myself a coffee.

"Not really," Donald responded. He was totally engrossed in the handgun he was cleaning.

There was a knock on the door. "Could you answer that, Victoria?"

"Sure."

A man I vaguely recognized entered my house. He went to Donald, they talked for a moment, and money was exchanged. The man walked out with a bag that I presumed held a gun.

I had settled in at the kitchen table to read my morning paper. A few moments later there was another knock. I didn't get up; I didn't look up. *It was going to be a long day.*

Later in the evening, Donald told me, "I think I'm going to look into renting a garage tomorrow." He kissed the top of my head.

I looked up at him. "Yeah, I think that would be very wise."

The next morning the cycle of customers arriving at our home and leaving with guns began again, and it continued all day long until the afternoon.

CHAPTER 14

"Debbie called. Her hot water has been turned off. She wanted to know if she could come over for a bath," I told Donald.

He nodded. "Sure, Victoria. I'll see you when you get back. I'm almost done for the day."

We kissed, and I left.

"Thanks, Victoria," Debbie said, when I picked her up some twenty minutes later.

"No problem." I shifted the gears and took off. We exchanged the latest gossip. Our gossip consisted of subjects like who was sleeping with who, who was pregnant now, who was being cheated on, and what all of them were wearing at the time. We stopped at the red light before the last turn into my neighbourhood. Construction on the intersection had been going on all month. The light turned green and I gunned the engine, sailing through the intersection. My car went up on two wheels, avoiding a load of construction materials. The car behind me, the one I had just cut off, exploded with red-and-blue lights.

"Shit! That's an undercover cop car!" I pulled to the side of the road. We readied our IDs.

The police officer was burly, red-faced, and sweating. "What did you do that for?"

I didn't respond, and he wasn't done yelling. "Give me your license."

I handed him my ID. He stared at it for a moment. The red left his face.

"Don't do that again!" He threw my license back at me.

I pulled away from the curb. "That was really weird, Vic." Debbie said what we were both thinking.

"Divine, simply divine," Debbie said as she emerged from the bathroom, towel-drying her hair.

I nodded. We stood in the kitchen. A moment passed.

"Victoria, there's no food in the house..."

"Okay." I cut Debbie off. "But you'll have to distract Donald. You know how he feels about Danny. I'll set some things out on the porch for you to take home."

"Piece of cake," Debbie smiled. "I'll just ask him about his new guns. Hey, Donald! What kind of gun is that?" she asked, as she moved into the kitchen.

I took a ham I had cooked for dinner and put it in a clean garbage bag. I took a few tins of peas and put them in as well. Then I walked past Debbie, bent over the kitchen table, doing a good job of pretending to be interested as Donald gleefully showed her the different features of the gun. I opened the door and set the bag outside. Undetected, I walked back to the kitchen and finished cleaning up.

Debbie stayed maybe fifteen minutes after that, then was on her way. Normally, one of us would have driven Debbie home. To this day, I still wonder why we did not drive her home that night as we always had.

CHAPTER 15

The house was finally quiet and tidy. I reclined on the couch, enjoying the glorious stillness.

It didn't last. Donald came in from the kitchen. He sat down to clean the gun he had been showing Debbie. Donald still seemed restless and, after a few minutes, got up and started pacing.

Seriously! "Oh, are we missing Debbie?" I joked.

Donald turned to me, looking sheepish, "Oh yes, very much."

"Well, I guess you better make sure she didn't fall down the stairs." I settled back on the couch.

Playing along, he pulled back one of the green velvet curtains. He paled and yelled at me "Cops!"

I jumped up and raced to the kitchen. I pushed open the back door, Donald right behind me. We heard the glass on the front door being smashed and the heavy footsteps of cops racing up the interior back stairs. Donald and I both hopped the small fence dividing our balcony from our neighbour's.

"Get down!" I pushed Donald down so he wouldn't be seen. "Help! Help! Someone is trying to break in!" I banged on the neighbour's door.

A small woman opened the door. I rushed inside, dragging Donald behind me. Her adult daughter stood in the space between the kitchen and the living room. She watched us and she watched her mother close the back door.

"Please. I'm really sorry about this, but we just need a moment," I said trying to catch my breath.

Both nodded.

"Pay them, Donald."

"I can't. I don't have any money. I didn't grab any."

"Shit," I muttered, thinking of my purse laying on the couch.

Neither of the women were saying anything. They weren't freaking out, either. "Come on." I grabbed Donald's wrist. "Don't let go of my hand, don't say anything, don't look left or right. Stare straight ahead like the whole thing is normal."

"Sure, Victoria…"

Slowly I turned the doorknob. The second the door opened, I could see cops still rushing into our place, guns drawn. With our heads held high, we walked down the stairs with less than two feet between us and the cops. Then we turned and began walking down our long block.

With each step I took, I tried not to cringe.

Don't think about the cops.

Don't think about being seen.

Don't think about being shot.

My heart beat loudly in my chest. I could feel the blood rushing through me. My hands were icy cold and sweat ran down my back.

I repeated my mantra.

Don't think about the cops.

Don't think about being seen.

Don't think about being shot.

I didn't dare look at Donald. His tension flooded into me through his grip.

Eons went by. I hadn't noticed before how long the blocks were in Montreal. Turning the corner, we ran as fast as we could. Donald pulled at my hand, helping me keep pace.

We stopped at the main road. Donald looked around for a taxi. A whistle came out of me before I knew I was whistling. A taxi halted immediately.

"My God, Vic! Were you the one whistling?" Donald asked me inside the cab. "Yeah."

"You're just full of surprises today." He grinned as he gave the driver an address. Gil let us in and paid for the cab.

CHAPTER 16

Debbie had been in the back of my mind, as soon as Donald yelled "Cops!" Now that our escape was complete, a sick feeling began overtaking my exhaustion. I walked to the phone, leaving Donald to regale Gil with the details of our escape.

"Hello?"

"Debbie, thank God you're home. Are you okay?"

Debbie laughed. "I'm fine. I gave those pigs the surprise of their life."

A sigh escaped out of me and my knees slowly caved. "What do you mean?"

"The same undercover cops that pulled us over followed me to the metro. They had to follow me all the way to Atwater Metro Station for my bus transfer. You should have seen, Vic. They ambushed me while I was standing in line waiting for the bus. The pigs ripped the garbage bag out of my hands. They thought they'd hit the jackpot."

I groaned.

"Oh my God, Victoria! The look on their faces when the ham rolled into the gutter and the tins of peas followed. Their faces went red. I think they stopped breathing for a second! Neither of them said anything to me, or to each other. One cop threw the garbage bag at me and they both walked back to their car."

My groaning turned into a chuckle, which exploded into laughter. The image of their faces seeing the ham instead of the guns they had been picturing the whole drive over made me roar even harder.

Donald came over. "What's so funny?"

"Debbie…" I handed the phone to Donald. His eyes grew wide. "Christ, can you imagine? They heard on the radio about all the guns found in our house. Then they had to go back and tell them they took a ham off a little girl." Donald laughed. "Serves them right."

I nodded, then motioned for the phone back. "But you're okay, Debbie?"

"Yeah, Vic." Debbie's voice grew serious. "I thought of you then, and thank goodness you didn't drive me home that night. It would have been all over for you and Donald."

"Yeah," I replied. "It's weird that we didn't." I then finished the story about how we got out before the raid. "Deb, I'll call you later. I'm going to call Carol and see what's going on at home. Thank goodness we know our neighbours across the street".

"Sure, Vic, and take care, okay?"

I disconnected the phone and dialed my neighbour.

"Hello?"

"Hey, Carol. It's Victoria."

Carol laughed. "You're missing all the entertainment."

Oh, God. "What are they doing?"

"Well, right now they're on the roof, screaming through a megaphone that they see you and they want you to come out with your hands up. Obviously, they can't actually see you, can they?"

"Nope," I responded.

"Figures. Cops can't find their shoelaces with both hands on a good day."

"Carol, you have no idea. Are our cars still there?"

She paused. "They already towed Donald's car, and it looks like they're getting yours ready."

My poor new car... "Damn. Thanks, Carol. I'll check back in with you later."

"I'll be here," Carol said.

I handed the phone to Donald to hang up. He sat down beside me on the floor. He had heard our whole conversation.

Donald kissed my cheek and then stood up. "A megaphone, eh?" He pulled me to my feet.

"Apparently." I moved towards our temporary bedroom. There was nothing left for me to do, and it finally hit me. Alone together, I crumpled into Donald's arms, sobbing. He rocked me back and forth, then put me to bed when I was quiet.

CHAPTER 17

The next few days were horrible. I felt anchorless, drifting around Gil's house. The house wasn't mine. I felt uncomfortable doing most basic daily things. Our cars were gone, so I couldn't leave. I was trapped. The shock I felt that first day only lifted a little. A thought was becoming more and more prominent. If I got arrested, would they repeat the previous beating? I became more and more jumpy. I didn't admit that being arrested bothered me. But it was frequently in the back of my mind. That thought led me to a question. I knew if I turned myself in, then our cars and our home would be released. Could I then pass before a judge and get bail, all without getting beaten?

Donald sent someone to break into our home and get the $150 he had hidden behind a picture in the hallway. He used the money to pay Joel Guberman. Joel was one of the best lawyers in Montreal.

"Mr. Guberman will see you now," His perky secretary said when I arrived at his office for the first time.

I got up from my chair in his waiting room. Joel's office looked like any other lawyer's office. It had a big desk and shelves filled with books. Joel didn't look like the average lawyer, though. He had clear brown eyes, tan skin, and strong features.

"Victoria, have a seat. I understand you want to surrender yourself?"

"Yes, that's right." I sat down again.

"Based on what you have already told me, you have a very good chance of getting bail."

I nodded my head.

Joel got up and moved to the door. "Shall we?"

I followed him out of the office and out of the building. It was June. The sun was shining, birds were singing, and you could smell the fresh cut grass.

"So, this is your first offence?" Joel asked me as we walked in the direction of the Montreal police headquarters.

"Correct," I responded.

"And you have no other matters before the court?"

"No, I don't," I lied. I knew I was out on bail already for the license bureau robbery. I'll chalk it up to my shock and naïveté. I honestly thought if I didn't tell them about the other charges, they wouldn't find out.

"My client Victoria is here to surrender herself." Joel pointed to me as he spoke to the desk sergeant. A stream of cop talk and lawyer speak passed between them. I didn't understand it, so I didn't hear them. I looked around the station house. Every muscle in my body was clenched. I didn't let my mind focus on my last arrest, but my body remembered.

Once Joel finished his conversation with the sergeant, the sergeant began the booking process. I was put in a holding cell to await my bail hearing the next day.

The following morning, I was brought with the other prisoners to the docket. Joel approached, and he did not look happy. "Why didn't you tell me you're already out on bail? You're not going to get bail this time."

"Really?" The thought of not getting bail had never entered my mind.

"No, I can't get you bail." He still tried, though. The Crown prosecutor made a big deal out of my previous arrest, my refusal to cooperate and how dangerous the guns I "possessed" were.

Joel pointed out that I had turned myself in, and that that should count for something.

The judge had not looked up once during the proceedings. It appeared as if he was looking at a photograph or something. He squinted then, and looked at me for the first time.

I heard the gavel bang before I registered what the judge had said.

"Bail denied!"

Later, Joel told me the judge had been looking at the photograph of me that is on the cover of this book. Apparently, that made his decision.

CHAPTER 18

All the cell doors opened at once with a loud bang. I didn't stir.

A voice yelled into my cell, "Time to get up!" Sandy, one of the younger screws, banged on my cell door, waiting for me to obey.

I had ignored the 7:00 a.m. morning bell. My sleep had not been restful. Without Donald beside me, I had no motivation to get up. I dragged myself to our common room. I learned yesterday, when I arrived, that we ate in our cell block. Women being held for trial were not allowed to mingle with prisoners. At some point in the day, a screw would put your mail on your bed, if you had any.

Time passed slower in Tanguay. All we could do was watch TV. I enjoyed my few hours in the yard each day. Smoking was allowed, so I was always engulfed in a cloud of cigarette smoke.

To clear a person for a visit took two weeks and a bunch of paperwork. The only time we were allowed to use the phone was with special permission from our social worker.

I was trapped in a world of women now. When I arrived yesterday from the courthouse, a male screw had driven me in a van. We moved through the high gate, past the roundabout into the non-descript main house. He left me to wait on a bench. Then, the first of many stern-faced matrons brought me to the strip-search room. I saw gyno stirrups, but I wasn't forced to lie down and put my legs up. I guess they didn't want to check if I tried to smuggle anything in my vagina.

After, they let me put my own clothes on. At this prison, we all wore our own clothes, for better or for worse. The screws wore uniforms that turned them into variations of the same person.

I was given some neatly folded sheets, blankets, a towel, a facecloth, and a bar of soap to carry with me to my cell on the pre-sentencing block. That first walk was eye-opening. There was a surreal tension walking past what today would be called the psych ward. I heard squeals, laughter, stilted conversation. Sounds heard nowhere else in the prison. Many of the women in that ward today would not be jailed.

The English and French women had separate blocks. Like the rest of Quebec, we didn't mix.

The pre-sentencing block began with a large common room that had an adjoining bathroom, a TV and some tables. Following the matron, I was left in the third cell, down the hall on the right. I would live in this eight-by-ten-foot space for the next few months. My cell did have a window, so I got some sunlight. But it didn't open, so it didn't let in fresh air or a cool breeze. I had a bed, a desk, a chair, and that was it.

I unpacked my few items, made my bed, and lay down. My mind didn't want to process the mistake I had made.

It still didn't.

CHAPTER 19

"It's good to see you, Vic. How are you holding up?" Donald slumped in a chair on the other side of the Plexiglass, a black phone propped against his ear.

"I'm all right." I moved forward, closer. I put my hand on the glass and he covered it on the other side with his. I could feel tears prick at my eyes.

"Don't cry, Victoria. I have a plan."

I looked into his brilliant blue eyes. They seemed earnest, adamant that I not feel bad.

"I put some money in your canteen. Two hundred dollars. That should be enough for you to live it up for a little while until Joel gets you out."

"You said you had a plan?" I asked.

"Yeah, I'm staying in a trailer in Ontario. Joel strongly advises me to stay out of the province. He's up to something, working some angle with The Crown." Donald laughed a little.

"Okay, so how long do you think this will take?"

"I'm not sure, Vic. A few weeks maybe. I'm paying him in installments. So, he's plenty motivated to get the job done."

I said quietly, "Did he ask you for the full amount?"

"Yeah, but you know how lawyers are, Vic. If I pay him in full he'll take his time 'cause there's no more money to be had. It's always about money with lawyers."

My hand slipped from the glass. "Maybe you should just pay him." I wanted to add, *just in case.*

"It'll be okay, Vic. You'll see."

I nodded. "How is Debbie doing?

"I've been lying low, so I haven't been in touch with her."

Our conversation transitioned to the world outside and, before long, a matron made her presence known behind me. My time was up.

"Looks like it's time for you to go." Donald smiled weakly.

"Yeah," I agreed.

"I'll come and see you next week. We'll actually be able to sit in the same room."

I smiled. "I'm looking forward to it."

The matron ushered me out of the room. We walked in silence through the beige hall. The walls, the tiles and the ceiling were all painted a shade of beige I despised.

The matron left me in the common room after my visit. I chose to go to my cell. After two weeks I felt more uncomfortable, not less. It had been nice to see Donald. He looked good. I really liked the thought of him safe in Ontario. My mind often tormented me with thoughts about all the stupid things he might get up to and their consequences.

Prison life is stifling but it was the loneliness I found excruciating. I would roll over in the middle of the night and wake up realizing Donald was not touching me. During the day things would happen and I would think, "I can't wait to tell him," but I couldn't.

"Big plans for today?" Sandy asked.

"Oh, yeah, tons," I responded.

"Well, don't forget your meeting with Madame Lafayette."

"Right." I nodded. "Madame Lafayette, my social worker."

"That's the one," Sandy said and left.

I had forgotten about my meeting. I had thought it was Monday when it was Friday already. I had been certain yesterday had been Sunday. The days blended together in Tanguay. I could see the daily passing of time watching the sun rise and set from my window. But there was little variation to our days. Each day began at 7:00 a.m. with breakfast, then lunch at noon.

Dinner was at 5:00 p.m. and then we had more free time. Lights were out at 11:00 p.m. Free time is a cruel way to describe the unstructured time we had at Tanguay. On the outside, I lived a life filled only with free time. I woke up when I wanted, ate when I wanted. I shopped, visited, cleaned, whenever and wherever I wanted. I was truly free to indulge my every whim. The endless possibilities of those days were what I missed the most.

Here, I was in a box. They didn't always tell us what to do, but they always told us where to be at every second of the day. We were counted, checked constantly, watched by the matrons in their cushy glass bubbles. I was always accounted for. I despised it. The matrons controlled everything we did, because they controlled the list of things we could pick from: clean, crochet, knit, watch TV, read, play cards, write letters, bathe, gossip. More often than not I chose to sleep. I became like a cat, taking my naps whenever I could. I didn't feel free when I slept. I didn't dream pleasant things. I didn't do or feel anything; everything was black.

CHAPTER 20

Jeannie, Sharon and Claudia were the women I became closest with. We were all waiting for our court dates. So, we talked a lot about what our lives were like on the outside. Our main topics were our children and boyfriends. But mostly our boyfriends.

"The Cunnilingus King, I like that." Claudia smirked.

Jeannie, Sharon and Claudia were all good people. That was true about most of the women here. If you left them alone, then they would leave you alone.

"So, Donald's coming for a visit tomorrow?" Sharon asked.

"That's the plan." I knew he was coming for sure.

"Okay." Claudia smiled, mostly to herself. Like she knew something I didn't.

But I didn't correct her. It was important to fit in, get along and most important, not stand out. That included boyfriends. Donald was different, better. However, it didn't pay to be smarter than anyone else, or to brag. I knew, and that was enough. "We get to visit in the room this time."

"In person is better," Jeannie agreed.

"Fish!" Claudia said loudly as she ended the card game with a big grin.

The next morning when the bell rang I was already awake. I couldn't stop smiling. I was dressed, waiting for Sandy. "Good morning, Sandy."

"Good morning, Victoria."

The morning seemed to drag on forever. Visiting hours were after lunch until 4:00 p.m. Donald liked to be on time. I expected him to come early.

"Morning, Victoria." Claudia smiled at me. "Ready for your big date? I like your dress."

I chuckled.

"I hope you have a good time."

Lunch did not get eaten. My body was too full of energy. I couldn't sit still long enough to swallow. I didn't have any visits with my parole officer, social worker or the priest. So, I sat with the others, picking at my knitting. A green blanket for my mother. I had mastered knitting easily, but I didn't see the appeal.

"What are you doing? The blanket is almost done!" Sharon grabbed my knitting.

"I messed up. It wasn't right."

Sharon handed my knitting back, shaking her head.

Somell, the matron who worked in administration, entered our block. Her green eyes passed over me. "Frieda, Lacey, Joan, come with me."

The clock said 1:00. I still had lots of time.

The women returned an hour later; more were taken.

"I'm sure he's just had car trouble," Claudia offered.

I felt like a moron even agreeing.

Everyone nodded.

What if something happened? I asked myself. *What would that something be?* I got up and went to my cell.

By 4:00 p.m. I couldn't ignore my questions any longer. In my heart, I knew something had happened. If it was possible, then Donald would have come. That left a few horrifying reasons why he didn't. Had he been arrested? In an accident? Shot? Killed? He couldn't be dead. Someone would have called. I would have gotten the news right away. Unless it happened on his way here…

I didn't go out for dinner. I couldn't face their smug sympathy. Claudia came into my room. I looked at her, but she didn't say anything. She set two Valiums on my desk and walked out.

Bitch! I looked out the window. It was completely dark, so sometime after 9:00 p.m. I took both Valiums, not bothering to get water. Really, I was grateful. Something terrible had happened and I needed to keep my mind off the worst possibilities.

CHAPTER 21

"**Debbie! Oh my God! What** happened to Donald?" I flung myself into a chair, grasping for the phone.

Debbie smiled. "It's okay, Vic. He was in an accident. The day before he was supposed to come see you. He's going to be fine."

"An accident" I squeaked,

"Yeah, he drove a motorcycle into a wall. He broke his back, but otherwise he's fine."

"What motorcycle? Whoever was stupid enough to lend him that motorbike, I'm going to kill them! Who was it?"

Debbie was starting to laugh. "Cucut, I think. I'll make sure to let him know you're coming for him."

"Debbie, he's never driven a motorcycle in his life. Why would he pick now to learn to drive a motorcycle? Why couldn't he have just stayed hidden, like our plan?"

"I don't know, Vic. I'm sorry..."

Donald was alive and safe in a hospital. He wasn't arrested trying to pull some new job, or shacked up with some other woman. He was safe. *"Motherfucker..."* A stream of curse words flew out of my mouth along with a sigh of relief. "What kind of stupid stunt did he try to pull that made him drive into a fucking wall? And why is he not in Ontario like he told me? Is he looking to get arrested?"

Debbie laughed. "I don't know, Victoria. He should be out in three weeks. He told me to tell you he's coming to visit you as soon as he can."

"Well, tell him I'm pissed, scaring me like that. Not showing up, that bloody bastard!"

"I'll be sure to tell him."

"Exactly like I said, Debbie."

"Of course, Victoria!" She sighed and sat back. "How else are you doing, Vic? Are you doing okay?"

I nodded. "Yeah, I'm okay. How are my kids and Christine?"

"Good. All of them get along and your boys love their new sister."

Everyone back at the cell block was so relieved when I told them Donald had been hospitalized. But, until he showed up, I knew they wouldn't fully believe me.

CHAPTER 22

"It's good to see you, Victoria." Donald looked almost back to normal, except for the back brace.

"Finally!" I smiled at him,

"I know." He looked a little sheepish. "Debbie said you were really pissed."

I gave him a look.

"And rightly so." He took my hand. "I have some big news."

"Oh?"

"Yeah. Joel worked out a deal with The Crown. If I turn myself in, you'll get released. We both know I'm not going to get bail." Donald winked at me. "I have no intention of turning myself in."

I cocked an eyebrow at him. "What are you getting at, Donald?"

"You've been in here long enough. It's time for us to get away. I have a car lined up. As soon as you're out, we're going west."

"That sounds amazing."

"Doesn't it? We can start over. We'll tell everyone we're married. I'd marry you for real, if you weren't still married."

I broke out laughing softly. "That would be perfect, Donald."

"Good." He took my face in his hands and kissed me deeply.

I rested my head on his shoulder; we didn't talk much more until the matron came.

"I have to go now, but I'll see you next Sunday before court on Monday," Donald assured me, looking deep into my eyes.

I nodded. "Be safe."

"Of course. I'm heading back to Ontario. You don't need to worry about me."

I don't remember the days that followed. Except Saturday night. I almost crawled out of my skin. I knew he was coming; I just had leftover jitters from the last time.

He didn't come.

CHAPTER 23

Monday morning Joel moved towards me. I sat at the docket, scanning the courtroom.

"He's been arrested. He was taken into custody late Saturday night." Joel didn't bother with a greeting. "There isn't going to be any deal."

"But, Donald said he was at the trailer in Ontario."

"I don't know what to tell you. They picked him up in a vehicle outside of the Pointe, near Saint Catherine Street."

"No." I shook my head.

"Yes, and I've only been paid $500. I'm going to need more money if you want to keep fighting the charge."

I didn't have any money; Donald had it. He had only paid the lawyer in installments. *Little bastard!* "What happens if I plead guilty?" I asked Joel.

"I'll go find out." He went off to negotiate with The Crown.

Arrested. I wasn't getting out; he wasn't getting out. We were not going out west.

"Two years less a day," Joel informed me, snapping me back to reality. "It's the best I can do. You'll have provincial time and only a provincial criminal record. With good behaviour, you can be out in no time."

"Okay," I nodded. *Even one more day in Tanguay felt unbearable.* I did the math in my head. By "no time," I figured out Joel actually meant eight more months.

He signalled to The Crown and court clerk.

"How does the defendant plead?" the judge asked me.

"Guilty, Your Honour."

CHAPTER 24

I went back to the prison in the same van, driven by a different man. My stuff was moved to an identical cell in an identical cell block, farther down the hall in the English section.

I'm not staying in this monotonous, dreary, watch-what-you-say place a minute longer than I have to. I sat on the bed of my new cell.

My determination dimmed the next morning when I heard the morning bell and a new matron got me up to go get breakfast. I ate breakfast in the cafeteria now. Grunt food is what I called it. My appetite just was not there. I picked at my toast and the yellow guck that was supposed to cover it, tasteless eggs, and watered-down coffee. How I missed my perked morning coffee. Then to add insult to injury, we were searched each time we left the cafeteria, making sure no one smuggled out cutlery that could or might be used as a weapon.

I don't remember much from June to January. I honestly can't recall that Christmas. What I do remember was Tanguay's awful pinkish-beige walls and complete isolation.

In provincial jail, there is a constant cycle of new prisoners. Women came and went. Prostitution would get you a few months, drug smuggling a little longer, assaults a little longer still. We did have a few federal prisoners who chose to spend their time in Quebec. There was no federal prison in Quebec, so most female prisoners went to Kingston in Ontario. However, the choice was yours.

Our hairdresser, Donna, was a federal prisoner. She was also someone who would not have been imprisoned today. After suffering years of abuse, she killed her bastard husband. It didn't matter to the court what he had done to her. She had killed him, and that was what mattered. They gave her a full life sentence.

Really, The Crown had done me a favour, sentencing me to two years less a day. You could get on with your life a lot easier with only a provincial record.

I never had problems with people in Tanguay. I understood them and their rules. Trying to be the toughest women there didn't work. There would always be someone tougher. The secret was not to provoke people, be friendly, and not overly curious.

My friend-to-be, Donna S, wore her karate kimono complete with her yellow belt when she first arrived. I guess she thought it would intimidate people. Two French girls dumped her unceremoniously in a garbage can at the end of her first day. They didn't hurt her. We all laughed. But it was a clear message.

The other women were what made life in Tanguay bearable. On the English side, I made friends. My first friend was Janette. She stood out, but there was nothing she could do about it. Janette had a brown wig, brown eyes, and a thick Scottish accent. She was a hooker by trade, but was in for fraud. I liked her dry humour and the fact that we never got tired of talking about our boyfriends. She had her Daniel and I had my Donald. Talking about him to her always made life on the outside seem more real.

One day, a few months in on the English side, Janette, Sharon, Carla and I were in the gym. I heard someone speaking French. I looked over and saw a tall, leggy woman. She had green eyes and long, luscious brown hair all the way down her back. "Holy crap, she's beautiful," I exclaimed.

"That's her, Victoria," Sharon whispered.

"Her who?" I asked.

"The new girl, Linda," Janette informed us.

"What's she in for?" Carla asked.

Janette replied, "Hash smuggling, I think. She has the best hash, apparently."

Janette was right. Linda did in fact have the best hash. She and her Beaconsfield Boulevard husband had competed with each other to see who could smuggle the most hash in from India. Apparently, it had been a short trip for her to Tanguay after that. As for him, he was off to Bordeaux—a provincial jail for men that sat across from our compound on Gouin Boulevard. We could see their yard from our windows.

Linda told me the story of how she first heard about her husband-to-be, Ronny. One day she had been driving down Beaconsfield Boulevard in Beaconsfield. Jane, Linda's best friend, was driving her Porsche. The top was down, and the wind was blowing in their hair. "Hey, look over there." Jane had pointed at a massive mansion. "The richest boy on the lakeshore lives there," she'd said.

"Well, then, I will marry him," Linda had replied. And she did.

That's why I liked Linda; she knew what she wanted and what she was worth.

The last member of our circle was Denise. I knew Denise from the outside. She was a sweet girl with soft brown eyes, and dark brown hair. She had been a heroin junkie. A deal she did with her boyfriend went wrong, and Denise shot a man. Thankfully, she only wounded him. Being eighteen, the judge went easy on her and gave her eighteen months. She was clean now, and I could appreciate how much her personality had resurfaced. She was still quiet, but now she could join in quickly with a comeback.

CHAPTER 25

On one of my visits from Debbie, she brought me acid to smuggle in. I loved acid. It made me go to places in my brain that opened up amazing awareness and feelings. I was tapping into the unknown parts of life, seeing things that appeared as I visualized them. People called them hallucinations, but I saw them and that made them real.

Acid is the kind of thing you want to do when you have time to yourself. A screw or your social worker could really ruin your trip.

So finally, a few days after I got the acid, the stars lined up and Carla, Janette and I had a "free day." Sharon had been released, so our tight-knit group had been reduced to three. No one had any social worker visits, meetings with the parole board, lawyer conferences, health checks, or spiritual advisements. It would be a day with minimal interruptions from the screws.

We sat around a table in the common area. I divided up the tabs, then handed them out, a giddy smile plastered on my face.

Thirty minutes later, I was noticing things at the periphery of my vision. The acid was kicking in! I looked at Carla and Janette. Carla smiled, and Janette gave me the thumbs up. I leaned back, letting my eyes find the stars, and spirals above my head.

"Janette!" We all jumped.

George stood in front of us. Her name was actually Georgina, but people only called her that to her face. She was a larger woman and had a square face covered with freckles. Her eyes were always squinting.

"What bloody now?" Janette asked.

"Madame Lafayette wants to see you," George replied.

"What does that bag want?" Janette muttered under her breath.

Carla and I grabbed each other's hands, trying to contain our giggles. We laughed for what seemed like forever after they left.

"Oh my God, poor Janette!"

"What does the social worker want?" I asked.

Carla rolled her eyes. "Who knows?"

We were both tripping.

"Should we go check on her?" I looked down the hall.

"Probably," Carla responded.

So we crept down the hall towards the social worker's office. We were giggling, staggering, supporting one another. Each of us egged the other forward. Looking back, it's difficult to say if the matrons in the tower were distracted, or chose to save themselves the hassle and paperwork. I assume it was the latter. Because even though Carla and I were trying our hardest to act normal, we looked like a couple of giggling kindergarteners.

Madame Lafayette's office door was closed. But it had a window. The social worker sat at her desk, facing Janette. Janette sat in front of her with wide eyes, a mildly horrified look plastered on her face.

"I hate to think what she's seeing right now," Carla whispered.

"Me, too. Lafayette goes on and on about nothing"

"She's such a bitch," Carla said.

Janette's eyes met ours and Carla and I took off, squealing. We didn't stop until we were back in the safety of the common room.

There is no consistency to the passing of time on acid. We waited for Janette, maybe an hour, maybe only a few minutes.

"Bitches! Bloody bitches, the both of you!" Janette muttered.

"What did she want?" Carla asked.

"I don't fucking know. She went on and on, talking about nothing. I thought my brain was going to start dripping out my ears."

We nodded in solidarity.

It took a few minutes, but Janette began enjoying her trip again.

We giggled at the things we saw, and the things we gossiped about.

Keys jangled behind us, getting closer.

"This had better be for one of you two," Janette said without opening her eyes.

"Janette."

"What!"

The matron backed up a little in surprise. "It's time for your visit."

"What visit? I don't have any visitors today." Janette finally opened her eyes and looked up at the matron.

The matron ushered her to her feet. "Well, Daniel wants to see you."

"What? Daniel is here? Daniel is truly here?" Janette straightened her wig and checked her face. She jumped up and down before following the matron out.

Carla and I looked at each other. Daniel was serving time at the prison in Cowansville. Janette had put in for a special request—though one which was rarely granted—a pass to visit a spouse in another prison.

"Well, good for her, I can't believe he's here." I said to Carla.

She shrugged her shoulders and we both went back to enjoying our trip.

When Janette came back she described her ordeal. The matron had brought her to the chapel. It turned out our new priest was also named Daniel.

"When is Daniel coming?" she had asked the priest.

"I'm Father Daniel, my child," the priest responded.

"Oh, this is too fucking much! I can't take this!" She stormed out of the chapel. We heard her long before we saw her. "Never again! Never fucking again!" I heard the metal of her door rattle as she entered her cell. We didn't see her for the rest of the night.

CHAPTER 26

I was granted a weekend pass out of the jail in January. My parents had flown down from Vancouver to visit. They picked me up from the prison. We drove far from Saint Jacques Street and its motels, downtown to Stanley Street and an upscale boutique hotel.

The lobby had dark carpets and bright lights. People spread out, coming and going from the elevators. It was everything you would expect in a nice hotel. I sat on my bed, in the room I had all to myself. It was disorientating in some ways. Not the change in setting, but the lack of change in my mindset. I had the illusion of being free, but the screws cast out unseen threads, hemming me in. Knowing where I would be and waiting for me to get back.

There was a knock on my door, and I opened it to see Donald's best friend Roman. He kissed me on the cheek. "Are you ready for dinner?"

"Sure," I responded. I followed him into the dining room. My parents were already seated on one side of the booth. Roman and I shared the other. I sat on the outside.

I kept blinking, my uneasiness growing.

"Are you all right, Victoria?"

"Yes." I looked the menu up and down without reading it. I tried to slow down, but my eyes couldn't process the written words into information my brain could use.

"The steak sounds nice," my father said.

"I think I'll have that, as well" my mother added. "Victoria?"

I looked down at the menu again. No words swam to the surface. "I'll have that, too, please," I told the waitress.

The night wore on and I thought more and more about Donald. My mother was taking me to see him tomorrow. Roman was there to give me a message to pass along for their work.

Roman was a good-looking guy, tall and slender with brown eyes. He was sexy in his own right. He was personable and made my parents laugh the whole night.

"He's a nice lad," my father remarked while Roman had gone to the bathroom.

"Really, Victoria, what's wrong?" My mother waved her hand in front of my face. My thoughts shattered. "My mind is not a part of me," I blurted out.

Now Roman and my father were staring at me.

"I mean, I'm just not myself tonight." I swallowed and tried to moisten my lips.

"Of course, you're not yourself. You've been in prison. It takes time to readjust, I'm sure," my mother said.

My father waved my mother off. "Nonsense. The girl just needs some rest."

I tried again to understand my swirling emotions. I had been inside alone for so long. I had let myself go. It was the only way to bear my loneliness in prison. To make myself into the kind of person who could survive inside. Now, surrounded by family, in a bright warm restaurant, I had to put myself back on. My old self felt like a cold wet bathing suit, struggling to put it on as it stuck and crawled up my body. Mercifully, the longer you wear a swimsuit, the more it warms up. Allowing you to forget you were ever uncomfortable.

"I think I'm going to go to bed now." I smiled at my parents.

"Of course, dear." My father stood as I left the table.

"I should go as well." Roman shook my father's hand and followed me up to my room.

"You look exhausted." Roman poured me a nightcap.

"I am." I took a sip.

"You can't let this break you." Roman took my hand.

"I know, Roman."

"No, I mean it, Victoria. You're becoming used to living in a cage. The outside world is unfamiliar to you now. Don't let yourself become too comfortable in there. Survive, but never get comfortable."

I nodded. "What did you want me to tell Donald?"

"Just tell him we're working on it."

"Okay, I can do that." I looked at Roman.

"Get some sleep." Roman gave me a hug and I closed the door behind him.

CHAPTER 27

I woke up with the late January sunrise. Frost ringed my windows. I dressed, picking out a nice long skirt and matching top. An outfit I knew Donald would appreciate.

My mother was waiting for me in the dining room. My father had gone off to meet his publishers already. He was in town to see me but he was also working on his second book. His first book, 'The Miracle of New Avatar Power,' had sold well and he was in the middle of a follow-up to this one.

"Are you sure you won't be too cold in that?" my mother asked.

"Thanks, Mom, but no." I refused to let her get on my nerves today. I ate quickly, not tasting my food. My mother fussed and took her time eating. It took every ounce of strength not to fling her plate across the room. Or better yet, take some money, grab a taxi and go by myself.

Finally, she called a taxi and we headed to Laval.

Snow drifted across the road. I had missed so much: summer, fall, Christmas. I had seen the weather during my yard time. But when I pictured the outside, all I saw was the summer I left behind.

"We're here." My mother did not look impressed. She was dressed in orange pants and a blue top. Prison was something far below the life she had invented for herself when she came to Canada. She walked swiftly from the car. She was afraid, I realized; she'd never set foot in a prison before.

"Name?" the desk sergeant said.

"Victoria... I'm here to see Donald. My social worker, Madame Lafayette, arranged our visit."

"Yes." He handed me a few forms. "Sign these. We'll call you in a bit."

"Thank you."

The prison waiting room was packed with families from all walks of life. But my mother still stood out. She chose to sit in the farthest corner, folding herself up as small as possible. Looking back now, I wish she had had a smart phone to occupy her. My mother would have loved Instagram and Facebook. In many ways, she was ahead of her time. My mother was primed to compete in our digital version of keeping up with the Joneses, and bask in the synthetic celebrity of social media.

"Victoria!"

"That's me."

"Right this way please." A screw ushered me inside.

My mother caught my arm. "Please don't take too long."

"Yeah, Mom."

Donald's face lit up when his blue eyes met mine. "Victoria…" He pulled me into his arms, pressing my cheek to his neck. I could feel myself start to tremble. "It's okay, Vic. Let's sit down." He guided me to a chair and took one for himself. Donald settled across from me, holding my hands in his. "I like your outfit. That colour suits you."

"Thank you. That colour suits you, too." I made a show of looking up and down at his prison uniform. Donald laughed wholeheartedly.

"Oh, I've missed you, Donald."

"I've missed you, too, Victoria. Have you seen Debbie lately?"

"She's been up to see me a few times. Seems her and Danny are having major issues and are about to split. She keeps talking about this guy, Hal. I'll keep you updated." I grinned. "I've also made a few friends inside. So far, Janette is my favourite."

I decided not to tell him about our acid trip. Instead, I asked him some questions about his own time inside. As he talked, I began to understand the cold fire filling me. I had longed to see him; so much so, it was unreal. Now I felt as if I couldn't get enough of him. And I knew too soon I would get up and walk out the door. Not knowing when I would see him again. I squeezed his hand and kissed him. He kissed me back slowly.

"Wow. That kiss will keep me warm for a lot of nights." Donald rubbed the pad of his thumb across my cheek.

"Were you able to meet up with Roman?" he asked me casually.

"Yes, he joined my parents and me for dinner last night. We talked after my parents went to bed. He wanted me to tell you he's working on it."

"Excellent!" Donald's face lit up again. "Things are starting to line up."

I nodded.

"Okay, enough about business," Donald concluded.

He seemed reassured about our prospects on the outside.

"Are you okay in Tanguay?" He put both my hands in his and looked me straight in the eye.

I forced a smile. "I've adjusted, and my time is almost done." I chuckled. "I've learned to knit and crochet. I made my mother a shawl."

"Really? Maybe you could make me some socks."

"Sure, I'll get on that right away," I said as I rolled my eyes.

"No one is bothering you there, right, Vic?" Donald's voice changed, hardened.

"I keep a low profile. People don't bother me."

"What about the screws?"

What could I say? "They're a hell of a lot better than the Montreal PD."

Donald's face crumpled into a grin, dissolving into full blown laughter. I wanted to bottle it up and take it with me.

"Okay, I just want to make sure. In some of your letters it seemed like life was really hard for you."

"Don't worry about me. I'm working on getting out, not staying in. I hope you're doing the same?" Out of the corner of my eyes I could see a screw open the door. I kissed Donald hard one more time, my mind searching for a reason to extend our time. "Come meet my mother, Donald." We made our way to the window looking at where my mother sat.

"Mom!" I waved to her. She looked up. "This is Donald." I pointed at him. My mother nodded, a bewildered look on her face.

"That's it. Say goodbye," the screw said.

Donald took his time kissing me. "I love you. You really are my whole world, Victoria. I promise I'll write you tonight."

I nodded, squeezed his hand, and then broke contact.

Donald kept looking back as he was pushed towards the strip-search room.

"Do you know it's been three hours?" my mother said in greeting.

I shrugged my shoulders and began walking to the car. I didn't feel the January wind. I didn't feel the weak sun. I didn't feel anything; I was numb. For three hours, my life had been almost normal. Now I had to prepare myself to leave Donald and go back inside.

CHAPTER 28

Everything was exactly where I left it in my prison cell. Nothing had changed for my friends; they had stayed inside. I felt like a completely different person, though. Time on the outside had allowed me space to evolve, expand. You couldn't do that in Tanguay. It was like being chained to a treadmill: you walked and walked but you never moved forward.

Carla did her best to cheer me up. She asked about the hotel in detail, trying to imagine herself there. Then about my parents and Donald. "God, if I could see any man now." She paused, thinking. "Oh, the things I would do to him!"

Janette and I laughed. Knowing Carla was in for prostitution made me laugh even harder. I thought she had been enjoying her break from work.

When I returned and was first being strip-searched, I began to understand how right Roman was. I had to be uncomfortable now, so I could survive on the outside. From that day on, when I lay down in my bed, I thought about the first thing I was going to do when I got out. I weighed the pros and cons of how important that activity was, and who I wanted to do it with.

During the day, I made a point of noticing things that would have bothered me when I first arrived. I looked outside myself and thought about what my loved ones would say if they saw what I was seeing.

When you want to survive in prison, you change how you think about the outside world. You make it a far-away promised land that you will go to someday. It's important that you are vague and superficial about the things you want to do outside. Then doing without them isn't so hard. To steel yourself to the reality of prison, you have to gloss over and not notice all the humiliation and frustration. Those things have to become normal. Once they become normal, you don't notice them, so they don't bother you.

CHAPTER 29

A few weeks later I was sitting in the common room when something began to prick at me. Something felt off. I glanced around the room. It was empty. "Where did everyone go?"

"I don't know," Linda replied.

"Do you think we should go find out?"

"Probably." She got up and I followed her. We walked first to the hallway of cells and then into the bathroom. There wasn't anywhere else to look.

Everyone was huddled around Janette, jostling and whispering.

Janette seemed oblivious, fussing with her lighter and spoon, a needle resting in her lap.

"Hey, Victoria, do you want some?" Carla offered.

"What the hell is it?" I asked.

"Speed. Janette is cooking it up."

"I can see that, Carla." I moved back. "I'll pass," I said. I had never been one to do hard drugs. Needles were out of the question. I had watched too many friends die because of overdoses.

"Me, too," Linda seconded.

"Are you guys sure you don't want some? This is good shit." Janette finally looked up.

"No, I'm sure. Listen, when Denise G comes in, tell her you've run out." I put an emphasis on the "run out" part.

Janette nodded. "Sure, Victoria. I'll tell her we ran out." She went back to her work.

I returned to the common room, enjoying the silence of having the place to myself.

"What the hell, Vic?" Denise flew out of the bathroom a little while later. "If I want to do something, I'm going to do it."

I stood up; clearly Janette had not told her they were out of speed. Denise was flushed, breathing hard, twitching, and in full junkie mode. She picked up a chair and hurled it at me.

I raised my hands instinctively, catching the chair in mid-air. "I've known you a long time, Denise. Don't you remember everything drugs took from you? You're clean now. That's not worth giving up? I did this because I care."

"Well, I don't want your fucking mothering!" Denise screamed.

"Fine. You want to kill yourself, then go right ahead!" I slammed the chair onto the floor for effect and stormed back to the bathroom. "Thanks, friend," I hissed at Janette. "Just go ahead and give her some. She's not worth saving."

There's no point in being here. Why do I even bother trying to help these people? I thought to myself as I went back to my cell.

CHAPTER 30

Clang.

My eyes blinked open. I could hear a matron's keys jingling at her hips. Women were up, talking amongst themselves. I heard another buzzer. *It's the middle of the night. What is going on?*

I heard someone else ask, "I really need to go. Can you take me, too?"

"No!" the matron spat back her.

The speed.

Morons, I thought, as I lay back and closed my eyes. *Clang*, and then two more buzzers. *I'm not going to get any sleep tonight.*

Our cells didn't open the next morning.

Women began to complain.

"Don't even try. You're all on a lockdown!" The head matron's face was frozen in a mask of anger. I had never seen her like this. Her cool, unaffected disposition totally evaporated. "Anderson!" The first girl was hauled out. The screws didn't wait; they tore into her room. Everything was thrown on the floor, her books were handled roughly, her picture frames tossed on the mattress, and her clothes spread everywhere.

A few hours went by while the matrons worked their way down the hall. When it was my turn, I calmly got up and walked with them to the interrogation room. I sat myself down on the chair, legs crossed, hands folded.

"What do you know about the drugs?" the head matron demanded.

"I don't know anything about drugs," I replied.

"I don't believe you. Search her." A screw on each side grabbed my arms, checking for track marks. Another grabbed my feet, bending my toes this way and that.

"She's clean."

The head matron narrowed her eyes. I raised my eyebrows ever so slightly, meeting her gaze directly. "Get her out of here," she said quietly.

I was escorted back to my cell and locked in.

The women around me were starting to come down. They were crying, paranoid, pacing. *Morons.* I didn't feel any sympathy for them. I turned on my little black-and-white TV as loud as it would go and began putting my cell back together.

CHAPTER 31

On March 18, 1976, the letter arrived. [unedited]

Dear Victoria,

Sorry I cannot come and visit you for quite a while. But me and Beaver and Hal had a car accident. Hal got a few pieces of glass in his face. Beaver broke his leg in two places and has eight stitches behind his ear and a black eye. I have twenty-nine stitches around the top of my head. I was scalped. You know like the Indians do. Half my hair is shaved off. My left hip was dislocated. Something cut me near my ass and went right up me which cut me about six inches down there and now I am full of stitches down there. My left leg and my left ankle is broken. I am in a cast and up on strings. I can't move fuck. I'll be in the hospital for four more weeks = 1 month. My phone number is 761-3551. Maybe you can get a pass to come see me. I hope so. Well, there isn't much to say, so take care of yourself and be good.

Lots of love and pity,

Debbie

PS. Do you know that the doctor said? That I should be dead and I am lucky.

"WOW" I thought, as tears welled up in my eyes just thinking of her there in the hospital. I went and made a request for an emergency phone call.

On March 29, 1976, Debbie wrote again. In this letter she told me how she had dumped Hal, as apparently he was the cause of the accident that wrapped them around a pole in their stolen vehicle. She talked about being so depressed and now she still had another five weeks to go. She could not even get out of bed to go to the bathroom. This meant two months of hell for her. Lying on her back. Not being able to move. Since the accident, she said she had a bad memory. I imagine that she must have had a concussion, but back then these things weren't as well known. She ended the letter by telling me that the following week she would be going for plastic surgery on her leg. A bone had pierced through her shin. I know that from this surgery she had a metal plate put in the leg. She also had a permanent limp.

I felt relieved that she was on the mend and quickly wrote back with jokes and things we had done in the past, hoping to cheer her up.

CHAPTER 32

My eyes opened and my excitement grew. Summer was almost here and today I was heading out on another pass. I had packed the night before and grabbed my bag when I was called.

Lorna, my sister-in-law, Jimmy's wife, was waiting outside for me.

I hopped into her Monte Carlo.

She looked me up and down. "You don't seem all that excited to be out this time."

I shook my head. "It's been a long couple of months."

"Well, tell me about it on the way home."

We reached Lorna's house around 10:00 a.m. It was close to the duplex Donald and I had shared. I settled into the room they had prepared for me.

"Christ, you look like shit." Debbie gave me a big hug. She had been staying with Lorna since getting out of the hospital, while she recovered from her accident.

"Because you look so much better, hop-along." I hugged her back, hard.

"Come on, Victoria. Let's go to the kitchen. I'm starving." Debbie knew not to ambush me with a lot of questions. Lorna brought me a drink and I settled into the warmth of their easy conversation. Carol and Lawrence showed up about half an hour after I got there. They joined in the conversation. I smiled and nodded a lot. It was nice to be out in the world. Carol and Lawrence stayed with us for dinner. Lorna was the block mom; she always had enough for company, and everyone was welcome at her house.

After dinner, friends came and went. Coli and Bret stopped by for an hour; other people stayed for a shorter amount of time. It was one of the best evenings I'd had in years. I went to bed happy, not thinking about anything.

In a big city like Montreal, it's never quiet. Someone is always doing something, some kind of machine is always running, cars drive by, dogs bark, people pass in the street. My room was filled with familiar and sustaining sounds, soothing me.

I closed my eyes for just a moment and unknowingly drifted off till I felt a hand on my shoulder shaking me.

"Hey, phone is for you," Lorna said.

"What? Is it morning?"

"Yes, it is, and the phone is for you," she repeated. "I think it's the jail."

I got up and walked to the kitchen wall phone. "Hello?"

"Is this Victoria?"

"Yes, it is." *God, what now? Why would the prison be calling me?*

"It's Madame Lafayette," the person on the other end said. "I'm calling to inform you that you have been granted early parole. You don't need to come back to Tanguay."

That phone call took a few moments to process. Debbie was overjoyed to not have to drive me back to Tanguay, and Lorna welcomed me into her home with open arms. She had testified before the parole board a few weeks earlier when my passes were being reviewed.

"What did you say to the parole board, Lorna?" I asked her.

"I told them that you're easily led. That's the truth, Victoria. I told them you are a good person but you go along with things."

"Well, whatever you said worked." I hugged her excitedly.

CHAPTER 33

"This is a pleasant surprise." Donald's eyes shone when he walked into the visiting room and saw me. "It's good to see you out and free. How did you swing early parole?"

"Simple. I hate needles. So there was no way I was letting Janette shoot me up with speed. Even if I was into speed, it wouldn't be worth risking my early parole." I looked at Donald. "Don't you agree?"

Donald burst out laughing. He ignored my question about good behaviour. "That simple, eh? You can come visit me all the time now."

"I know," Donald squeezed my hand and smiled. I thought about saying more to him but I wasn't ready to spoil our first of many visits.

"Are you and Debbie getting along? How's life at Lorna's?"

"Hop-along is doing well. She's on crutches now and gets around as fast as you and me. Uses her crutches like a weapon to make sure we cater to her." I laughed. "The rest of us are all getting along fine. You know Lorna's house—it's busy. I'll be happy to get my own place. A place for us. I have to meet with my parole officer, Lewis, on Wednesday. My father's found a job for me with one of his publishing friends. I start next Monday. I'm sure it'll be a gas." I rolled my eyes.

"Don't worry, Vic. I'll be out soon. Then you'll never have to work again."

"Seven more months," I replied.

"See, I'll be out in no time. We'll get our life back on track. The things I'm going to do to you, Victoria. I'm going to lick you all over until you beg me to stop."

"That will never happen, Donald. I always want more."

CHAPTER 34

Parole isn't true freedom. Sure, I was free to find whatever horrible straight job I could. I was free to schedule my weekly visits with my parole officer when I wanted. I was also free to pick the time I had to check in with the Montreal PD. Any time left over I could spend how I wanted, as long as I didn't move without reporting it to my parole officer, own or be near any firearms, or leave the city.

I always suspected a nine-to-five job would feel like a trap, a different kind of confinement. I was right. Since leaving home at sixteen, I had slept when I wanted, got up when I wanted, spent my days and nights how I wanted.

I didn't last a month at my first job. I was a kind of receptionist for a publishing company. Since I was working for the publishing company my father used to publish his books, the owner called in a favour with one of his friends and found me a new job. Again, with a publishing company. But this time I worked in a warehouse. It turned out to be not so horrible at first. After a few weeks, Debbie was off her crutches and I was able to get her a job there with me. Each day, we drove from Lorna's in our own separate cars, parked beside one another and walked together inside. We both loved to drive. It was that simple.

The warehouse was owned by a husband and wife. Chris, their nineteen-year-old son, also worked there when he wasn't training. He was an Olympic marathon runner: tall, blond, and sweet. Debbie and I enjoyed teasing him as he ran laps. Debbie and I once went to watch him compete and dropped pennies over him at the starting position until he looked up to see us.

I was fired from this job after a few months but it wasn't my fault. Chris had found out that I had recently been released from Tanguay. He didn't care. In fact, he was proud of his parents for hiring someone on parole. The problem was, his parents didn't know I was on parole. Chris mentioned it in passing when his parents asked him something about me.

I was fired on the spot, along with Debbie to boot.

"You're still looking tanned and lovely, even though it's fall." Donald almost always began our visit with a compliment.

"Thanks, I got fired from my job. They found out I had been in Tanguay. They fired me and Debbie on the spot."

"Bastards," Donald spat. "You hated that job anyway, Victoria."

"Yeah, you're right. It wasn't bad at first but holy heck it got tedious quickly. Now Lewis says I have to find a job next week. I've found a few in the help wanted ads already."

"Four more months Vic, we're almost there."

"I know, Donald. I've been saving. As soon as I get this next job I'm going to get my own place. There's one in LaSalle I want."

"Our own place. I'm going to make you scream in every room in the house"

"It's always about sex with you, Donald!"

Donald laughed. "That's not true. Sometimes I think about cuddling."

"Yeah," I joked back, "after sex"

CHAPTER 35

The third job I found stuck. It was bookkeeping for a bakery. I love numbers. Numbers are my thing; they have always made sense to me. I've always been able to do math in my head. Numbers are one of the few things I love as much as driving. Almost as much as I love Donald.

At the end of October, I moved into that apartment in LaSalle. Once in that house I completely changed. I had gotten it into my head that I wanted us to have a straight life. No more "jobs," no more cops, no more chance of arrest. No more talking through a telephone, staring at him behind glass like a zoo animal. The closer it came to him getting out, the harder it was for me to see him.

The more time that went by, I realized I didn't like my friends when I was sober. Chaos and drama seemed to follow them around. I didn't want any of that anymore. I didn't make friends at my new job. I didn't really fit into that world, either. Donald was the only one who knew what I was going through. He became the centre of my existence.

But Donald couldn't seem to get his head on straight. His priorities were all wrong. He tried to fix things in the moment instead of planning and waiting, tolerating the current problems. I needed money for furniture for the new apartment. Donald wanted to help. He began working a connection on the outside to smuggle in hash. He sold the hash and gave me some of the money.

One visit, they found the money he was giving me in a strip search on his way out. Someone ratted for sure. They found $325. They didn't let me see Donald and assuming I had drugs to exchange for the cash, I was taken to the police station to be searched. Donald would never use me as a drug mule. When the cop didn't find any drugs on me they let me go. I went back to the prison and demanded to see Donald. I knew they would cut our visits after this stunt and I needed to see him. Typically, I got what I wanted when it came to Donald. The guard I was dealing

73

with was stuck having to work a long-weekend holiday. He was the highest-ranking person there. He couldn't call any of his superiors, because it just wasn't worth the hassle. Saying no and getting rid of me was also not worth the hassle.

"This is above my pay grade," the guard finally muttered. He picked up the phone and called downstairs for a guard to bring Donald up. Donald was readied, and I had one last contact visit before the visits were cut entirely.

"Hey, Victoria." Donald leaned the phone against his shoulder. His eyes were still bright blue, his hair long and thick. The bloody glass prevented me from touching his face and stroking his hair.

When they cut all of Donald's visits, they had the nerve to say they weren't trying to punish his family, just him. After a few weeks, they were reinstated but only through glass.

"Hi, Donald."

"Man, it's good to see you. I've been thinking about you a lot. Did you get my letters?"

"I did, Donald. They get me through the week."

"Good." He put his hand to the glass. It was cold and sticky. "You don't look happy, Victoria."

I'm not. Seeing you through the glass makes me miss you even more. So close, yet unable to touch you, your voice garbled by the phone. "No, I'm just tired," I said.

"How are things at the bakery? Are you still liking it?"

"I am. I'm doing well, adding to our savings account every week."

"That's good. I'll be out soon to take care of you. I can't wait to have you in my arms again." Donald's eyes darkened.

A shiver went through me.

"I am going to wear you out, Victoria!"

"I think I'll give as good as I get," I shot back.

Donald leaned forward. "Tell me about the bedroom again in the new place. I want to imagine us making love there."

"All right. You walk into the bedroom from the hall. The room is open and airy, lots of light colours. It has hardwood floors, off-white walls and light blue curtains. I bought us a new bedroom set."

"Tell me about the bed," he prompted.

"It's a queen-sized bed. New mattress. I've put soft sheets on it. The dresser is at the foot of the bed. There is a mirror on it and I can see myself in it when I'm lying down…"

"Oh!" Donald's free hand clenched. "The things I'm going to be able to watch me do to you. I'm going to make you scream."

My whole body felt on fire. We had been separated since September, and three months had passed now. The visits before today had been contact visits. We could kiss and touch. Now I could only see him through the glass.

Just like that, I came back to earth.

Our hands had warmed the glass between us but it was still sticky. "The screws are going to come soon, Donald. Is there anything else you want to tell me?"

"Yes. Victoria, I miss you so much. You are my whole world, my wife-to-be."

I smiled at him. "My husband," I whispered quietly, almost to myself.

CHAPTER 36

Christmas came more quickly than I expected. It was a simple Christmas. Donald and I had made plans to celebrate in late January when he was out. After Christmas, time stalled. The week between Christmas and New Year's seemed as long as the ten weeks previous. January 1st was a marker. It meant we were in the month of his release. Days, not weeks or months left.

"How the hell did this happen? You had days left. They could have charged you with this any time this last year." I almost put my fist through the visitation glass in frustration.

"I don't know, Victoria." He sighed. "Either the system is out to get me or maybe there is something to all this past life stuff you keep talking about." Donald would have to wait for his new court date. It was set for May. He was going to be moved to Parthenais, where pre-sentencing prisoners are kept. "May, Donald. May! That's five months more of this bloody phone and bloody glass. I can't take this." A tear slid down my cheek.

"I know the judge will throw it out. They are just trying to do everything to keep me inside. It's a 'stayed' charge. No more evidence will come to light. I don't know what they think they have on me."

I sank my head into my hands, the phone balanced hazardously on my shoulder. "I had everything planned. Our home is all ready. Now it's ruined."

"Vic, look at me. We'll get through this, too."

On November 7, 1974, two months before we met, Donald had his assault charges stayed. He and his friends Bob, Richard and Anita had a regular job they did. It was nothing original. In fact, Charlie Manson's mother and uncle were arrested for pulling the same kind of job.

Anita played the part of a hooker. She would get a john and walk him down the lane. Richard, Donald, and Bob would be waiting a little farther down in the dark. In a very straightforward manner, Donald, Bob and Richard would rob the john and send him on his way. Most of the time no one got hurt.

One fateful night on September 7, 1974, Anita, Richard and Bob went to work without Donald. A john arrived at the lane with no money. He had planned to stiff Anita. Richard and Bob were shocked and offended on Anita's behalf. So they beat the man bloody. A very clear statement had to be made for the other johns. Worried they'd been seen, one ran to a pay phone and quickly called Donald. Jumping into his vehicle, Donald raced downtown and the three of them jumped into his vehicle. The cops pulled them over and all four were charged.

This case was based on the testimony of one witness, and it was flimsy. That was why the charge had been stayed in the first place on Donald's charges. He still however was denied bail and not released until November 7, 1974. Richard got twenty-two years and Anita five. I cannot recall what happened to Bob. All this took place before I met Donald and he really didn't talk about it. As far as he was concerned he had nothing to do with that night and thought that the beating was a very stupid thing to do.

Donald's court date got closer and closer. We wrote each other almost daily. The biggest news I had to tell him was that my ex-husband, from whom I was now finally divorced, was moving out west with the three children. Lorna and Jimmy and their two kids had moved a few months previously and Danny was following his brother. I was fine with this, as was Debbie. That is what airplanes are for, and before they left we arranged for the kids to come stay with us in the summer and some Christmases.

I worked hard putting as much money as I could in our savings account. Donald was using Joel Guberman as a lawyer again.

I decided to pay the lawyer fee in full. I still felt uncomfortable that my guilty plea had been forced due to a lack of money.

It's not often that I say this, but Donald was right. Lawyers don't work as hard when they have already been paid. Joel had missed appointments with Donald two weekends in a row. There is no winning with lawyers; just existing with lawyers. They are a necessary evil for criminals. I didn't want that life. I didn't ever want to see a criminal lawyer ever again.

CHAPTER 37

May 3, 1977

I wore a blue form-fitting dress that went just past my knees and up to my collar. It was one of my favourites and quick to take off. Donald looked handsome in his new court suit. His long hair would have normally seemed out of place, but on him it was perfect. Donald turned to me as the judge entered. I could see his eyes move over my body. He grinned wolfishly as he turned back to face the judge.

"So, it's my understanding"—the judge looked at the paper in front of him—"that Mr. Donald is being charged with assault causing bodily harm from a stayed charge from September 1974."

"Yes, Your Honour." The Crown stood up.

"I see here only the testimony of one witness, a Mr. Chandra, and he is not here?" The judge looked at Joel.

He gestured to the judge. "No Your Honour he is not. As you can see, The Crown's case is flimsy at best."

"I see that."

The Crown presented their case. No witness showed.. Then it was done. A whole five months of time Donald and I would never have together.

The judge looked over his notes once more. "I'm ready to rule. Please stand, Donald. I find you not guilty. You are free to go."

CHAPTER 38

"Janette, he's getting out!" I called my old friend from the courthouse.

"That's wonderful news, lassie." Her Scottish accent sounded even thicker on the phone.

"Can you come pick us up?" I asked her.

"Of course, I'm at your service." She hung up the phone and drove to meet me right away.

I waited outside on the steps of the Montreal Court house. It was a lovely May day. The sun was shining warmly, I could hear birds singing and people were happily milling about. Everything was right in the world. It had taken a few extra months but Donald was finally out. I could feel my heart singing; I smiled at everyone I saw.

Janette pulled up and I climbed in. I could barely sit still in her car. We talked about how Donald was finally out and what that would mean. Daniel was still in Cowansville, getting regular visits from Janette. Janette told me all of the things she planned to do when Daniel was out. It made me even more excited.

I saw Donald walk out of Parthenais holding a suitcase. I burst out of the car and threw myself at him. Donald dropped his suitcase and pulled me into his arms. He leaned down and kissed me. It went on and on.

Honk!

"Let's get a move on love birds. I'll take you home and you can properly get to business," Janette yelled through the open car window.

Donald laughed. "Hi, Janette. I'm glad to meet you. I've heard so much about you."

"Welcome home, Donald." Janette started the car.

I climbed into the back seat next to Donald. We were like two teenagers in the back of the car. His hands wandered under my dress and over my breasts. Janette smirked when she noticed. It would be no different when she finally got to bring her Daniel home.

"Thanks again, Janette." I waved to her as we got out of the car.

"No problem. Call me in a few days when you get out of bed." She winked at me.

"It might be a week," Donald warned her.

We all laughed.

Donald and I headed up the stairs to our new home. After opening the front door, Donald went straight to our new bedroom. He sat on the bed. "This mattress is softer than I imagined."

"Well, you've been sleeping on a sack on top of metal for the last two years." I walked up to him so his face was level with my chest and his hands went around my waist.

"The dress." He looked up at me. "Take it off."

I undid the back zipper and let it fall to the floor. The dress pooled around my feet. Donald pulled me onto his lap. He had my bra off in seconds. Then I could feel his kisses all the way down my neck to my breasts.

After a few minutes, Donald pushed me up and pulled my panties down. From there he stood up and laid me down on the bed. He removed all of his clothing and climbed on top of me. We were kissing, getting ready for the moment of full-body contact.

Ding, ding, ding!

I thought I heard the door. I listened, and I heard it again.

Ding, ding, ding!

"Someone's at the door, Donald."

"So?" he replied, kissing my neck.

Obviously, the annoying person was not going to go away. I grabbed a sheet, wrapped it around myself and peeked over the balcony.

"Open up, you horny rabbits! Donald left his suitcase in my car."

"That didn't take long, love." Janette winked at me. "Here, take his stuff and get back to it." She handed me Donald's suitcase and got in her car.

I walked back up the stairs, and closed the front door, making sure I locked it. I threw the suitcase on the couch and went back to the bedroom.

Donald ripped the sheet off me as soon as he could reach. "Now, where were we?" he murmured as he pulled me close.

CHAPTER 39

Donald fit into my LaSalle apartment instantly. Our rhythm returned and set the pace for our new life. I had planned to keep working when Donald got out. But the second I was in his arms, I knew I would never go back. I quit the day after he was released.

Right away, Donald began making up for lost time. While in prison he had cooked up a master plan. Plain old bank robberies were falling out of fashion. The hot new thing was extortion. Donald planned to kidnap a bank teller and ransom them back to the bank. Extortion jobs require money to set up. So, that meant a bank robbery first.

The first bank job failed because the bank had been robbed a few hours before. Now it was locked up tight and swarming with cops.

The next one fizzled because Donald miscalculated the day of the robbery. There was a holiday the day before, so the payroll had not yet arrived.

The third job, Donald interrupted a bank robbery already in session. The rule among criminals is 'first come first serve'. When Donald walked in, he saw everyone was already on the floor. There were already guys with guns stationed around the room.

"Can I help you?" One of the robbers asked him.

"Sorry." Donald chuckled. "I didn't know you would be here." Donald shrugged his shoulders at the other bank robbers. "Good luck," he said and motioned his guys to leave.

Donald's fourth job was an old standby. He waited outside a shoe store. From casing the place earlier, he knew the clerks, a man and woman, would take the nightly deposit to the bank. As Donald told the story, he waited until the last moment, and just as the man began inserting the bag into the slot…

"Stop or I'll shoot!" Donald grabbed the female clerk. The male clerk turned around. He looked Donald straight in the eye and dropped the bag into the safe.

Donald swore and pushed the girl away grabbing the bag she was carrying and took off.

"Hey, you're home," I greeted Donald.

Donald stalked into the kitchen. "Here." He dropped the shoebox on the table.

"Thank you, dear. You've never bought me shoes before."

Donald mumbled something before heading towards the bedroom.

I opened the box to try on the shoes, which is what I always did when he brought home something new for me. "Why are these shoes so big? They're not even close to my size. Donald?"

"I don't want to bloody talk about it." He slammed our bathroom door.

As these failed jobs piled up, I began thinking about a straight life again. Donald even said, on his way out the door for his fifth robbery attempt, "If this goes wrong, Victoria, I'll get a straight job."

CHAPTER 40

At that time, we didn't have a lot of money or a car. But still I prayed the job would go wrong. A straight life would mean rules, schedules, and monotony. But it was worth all of that and more to know that the cops could never take Donald away from me again.

Waiting is the hard part of being a criminal's girlfriend. Staying behind, all you could do was pace and count the minutes. I'm the type of person who likes to get things done. I couldn't get us money right away, but I could do something about our lack of a car. I used my last $200 to buy a bright orange Volkswagen Beetle. It burned oil like something else, but it ran well.

"Victoria, I'm home."

"How did it go?"

"Perfect." Donald picked me up, spinning us around. "It was an easy job. We got $10,000 and that will set up the extortion." As he moved forward, so did the three fellows behind him. Shorty, Peter and Red all looked happy. I grinned at them and said, "So, you must all be relieved that the fifth job went well? Were you thinking you all had a curse on you?" I laughed.

Shorty replied, "Yeah, what a relief. At least now we can get on with the main job, which is why we've all been working together"

I smiled back at them. "I bought a new car."

"What?" Donald asked.

"It's a Volkswagen Beetle. I got a really good deal."

"The orange one out front?" Shorty asked.

"Yes. What is it, Donald? Why do you look so pissed?"

He looked at me for a moment. "The guys and I decided on the way home to pitch in $1500 for you to buy a new car."

"Well, I'll still take the money," I quipped.

"They won't give it to you now." All three nodded. I glared back at them.

Damn... I screwed myself twice: no straight life and no flashy car!

CHAPTER 41

The next day some guys Donald met on the inside came over to our house. I had never seen any of these people before, but I made dinner anyway. Donald and his guys sat at the table talking and laughing.. Comparing stories from the joint.

"Victoria, I'm going out for a while." Donald grabbed his coat.

I looked at him. "But you—"

Donald kissed me and cut me off. "I'll be home soon."

I finished the thought in my head: *You already have the money for the extortion. Why are you going out again?*

"Okay…" I looked from Donald to Guy #1, then to Guy #2. "If anything happens to him, you'll have to deal with me." They laughed.

But I was serious.

Twelve forty-five a.m. Donald should be home any minute. TV held no interest for me. My fingers tapped as the minutes when by. Worst-case scenarios alternated in my mind. Each of my thoughts came along unbidden—a conveyor belt dumping thought after thought, adding to my already roiling emotions.

The phone rang; it was him. "Listen, Vic. The job went sideways. I was in the car and we were pulled over for a broken tail light. The cops lined us up against the wall while they searched the car. I heard one cop say they found a gun. I thought of you in that moment and I just ran." Donald sounded like he was still out of breath.

"Fine, I'm glad you're okay. Go to Carol's. I'll call you in the morning. I'll have more energy to be pissed at you, you little bastard."

First thing the next morning, I called Carol. She put Donald on the phone.

"Good morning, love of my life."

He was trying to butter me up. "When are you coming home?" I asked him point-blank.

"Not right now. I want to lay low a while longer in case any cops show up."

"Did the other two guys run as well?" I asked.

"No," he replied.

"Will they give up your name?" I asked, even though I was already pretty sure of the answer.

"No, but you never know. I've been surprised before."

Yeah, someone will probably rat, just like they always do…

CHAPTER 42

Ding, ding, ding!

I answered the door. It was later that afternoon. I had spent the day cleaning and seething.

"Can we come in?" one of two plain-clothed officers asked.

I nodded.

The cops moved from room to room, poking and prodding. "Is this where Donald lives?" one cop asked after not finding anything in the duplex.

"Yes, but he's not here right now." I moved a little closer to the front door.

"Do you know where he is?" the other cop asked.

"No, I haven't heard from him, I don't know where he is, and I don't know when he will be back." Now I was standing right next to the front door.

"Are you sure?"

"Yes, officers, I'm sure." I opened the door and one of the cops gave me his business card on the way out.

"Give us a call when he comes home, or when you hear from him."

"Of course, officer." I shut the door.

From my balcony, I watched the cops walk to their car, get in, and wait.

A few minutes went by and they were still there. *I guess they don't trust me to call.* I went back to my housework.

Maybe an hour passed, and then the phone rang, freezing my breath.

"Hello?"

"Hey, it's me Victoria."

"Are you okay?" My voice was shaking.

"I'm fine. I'm still at Carol's," Donald assured me.

"Well, don't come home 'cause you got ratted out once again," I said. "The cops came by looking for you. They gave me a business card and parked themselves in front of our duplex." I looked out the balcony door. "They're still here."

"Shit. Okay, well, tell them I'm not coming home and that I'll be in touch. I love you."

"I love you too, Donald."

I went down the stairs and walked up to the cop car. The cop in the passenger seat rolled down his window the second he saw me. "Donald just called. He told me to tell you he's not coming home. He doesn't want to waste your time, so he'll be in touch soon."

One partner looked at the other. Their unmarked car smelled of fast food. Each cop had sweat stains forming in their armpits. "Okay, we'll expect to hear from him soon," the cop on the passenger side said, narrowing his eyes at me a little.

The other cop started the engine and they drove away.

Donald came home that night undeterred. He had the money he needed, and he began to make serious plans. The date of the extortion was set for July 7, 1977.

CHAPTER 43

The world doesn't stop turning no matter what is going on in your life. Children get older and the seasons still change. Now it was summer. In Quebec, summer houses are common. Almost every year I've rented one. This year wasn't going to be any different; however, I now had to find one quicker than I had anticipated due to Donald's stupidity. I found a charming house beside Lac Malo in L'Annonciation. The house was off a little-used road. Our driveway began there, passing over a bridge, before finally snaking up to our front porch. The lake formed a natural moat. Inside the house were a cosy kitchen, three bedrooms, and a screened-in porch.

The lease on our apartment was up at the end of July and it was now mid-June. We paid the rent until the end of the lease and moved north.

Donald and I stayed at the lake house unless he was needed in the city to help plan the upcoming extortion. I allowed only those I trusted to know our location and even though Donald said Peter was trustworthy, I put my foot down when it came to him coming to visit. Something was wrong with that boy. In my heart of hearts, I didn't believe he was solid. Why? Just a hunch, an intuition I felt. I had this feeling a lot in life and if I ever went against it, I ended up paying for it. Donald just grinned and said, "Okay, we'll meet in town."

One house guest, though, became more regular than the others. Red was one of the guys who had helped Donald with the bank job and would be doing the extortion, as well. He was a redhead, fairly short, chunky, and awkward. Red had recently run away from prison while out on a pass. He was serving a life sentence that he had been given in 1970. Donald had known him for some time and took pity on him. I didn't like him much. Red had beady eyes that were always looking where they weren't supposed to. He was creepy.

Red would tell anyone that would listen he was never going back to prison. He kept a .45 calibre gun by his side always. In his mind, the best way to avoid getting arrested was committing suicide by cop. I assumed that any person being helped out when they were on the lam was solid, particularly one doing life.

Donald assured me he was good people. I trusted him on this.

We didn't see Shorty, Donald's third partner, as much only because he was married and had his own home. He had known Donald forever and was solid as a brick. He and Donald trusted each other completely because they kept the same code. I trusted him, as well. I have always been able to read people and their motives well.

CHAPTER 44

"Here I come!" Donald cannonballed into the pond. He swam over. "Oh, it's so cold. Will you keep me warm?" He pulled me into his arms.

"You'll get used to it." I splashed water in his face.

"Why you…" Donald began tickling me and pulling at the strings of my bikini. I splashed and squirmed, trying to get away. We were both laughing and shouting.

"There." Donald pinned my arms with one of his. He wrapped his other hand around the back of my neck. The kiss was firm, punishing. My whole body lit up, and I felt Donald's arousal.

He glanced over my shoulder. "Let's go find a place in the woods."

I looked back. Red was sitting on the bank, staring at us. He didn't bother to avoid eye contact and look away.

Thankfully, towards the end of June, Red started coming around less and less.

"I wonder what's up with Red," Donald said one day.

"He's probably got a girlfriend," I replied.

"No… he's too ugly." Donald made a sour face.

I didn't disagree with him on that. "Just wait. You'll see, Donald."

As always, I was right. Red had found a girlfriend, and they had moved in together.

"Listen, Victoria, are you sure you don't want to drive? Your cut would be $5000."

Donald and I sat together on the porch, watching the sun go down.

"Not if you use Peter."

"Why?"

"Donald, I can't explain it, but I don't trust him. Something's off about that guy. It's a bad idea to use him for the job."

Donald shook his head. "He's already done a job with us. He's proved himself."

"If you say so, Donald." I rested my head against his shoulder, enjoying the last rays of sunshine before it disappeared below the horizon.

CHAPTER 45

Suddenly, it was July 7th, the day of the extortion. We woke up in a motel on the edge of town that Donald had picked for me to wait for him.

"Donald, think again about not using Peter." I caught his elbow on his way out the door.

"We've been over this, Vic. He's proved himself. He's proved himself, and he's done a job with us already." Donald drew me into his arms. "I'll be home in no time with all that money."

I kissed him quickly and stepped back. "Just come home, with or without the money. You know you're all I care about."

"I've got this." Donald smirked at me as he left.

I knew the gist of their plan because Donald had told me. But no meetings were had at the country house, so I wasn't privy to any of the details.

To my understanding, Shorty and Red's job was to grab two bank tellers and take them to a Saint Jacques Street motel.

Donald was then to contact the bank manager and negotiate the ransom and a pickup spot.

Once Donald had the money, it was Peter's job to pick it up and lose any tails.

The plan worked; they got $100, 000. The only hiccup was Red's chivalry. He gallantly opened the car door, then pulled the front seat forward for the teller he had kidnapped. The second his hand left that woman's arm, she took off like a shot.

The remaining bank teller was frightened out of her mind. At the motel, she went to the bathroom with the door open. Both Red and Shorty told her to close the door. They promised not to hurt her. She hadn't seen their faces. They were going to let her go as soon as Donald had the money. Shorty explained this as they ordered pizza and hung out watching TV. In their minds, this was just another day at the office and a pleasant one at that. They didn't notice, but I doubt the pizza and soft drinks made a difference to that poor girl.

Peter grabbed the money from the pickup spot, and ran down into a nearby metro station. He jumped a few tracks, got on a train, and disappeared.

Donald, Shorty, Red and Peter met up somewhere later; I don't actually know where. The money was split, and Donald came back to the motel.

CHAPTER 46

"Hey, Vic, ready to go?" Donald walked into the motel room we had rented the day before.

I jumped up. "You're back!" I gave him a big kiss.

"Was there ever any doubt?" he asked.

"No, I'm just really, really happy to see you." I tugged at his hand and pointed to our small amount of luggage. He tugged back at my hand and pointed to the bed.

He won. I could barely keep my hands off Donald. The nervous tension I endured waiting for him at the motel room bloomed into ecstatic joy. *He came back to me. No problems, no issues. He was back in my arms.* I kept running my hands along his chest and legs.

"Come here!" Donald drew me into his lap. "Let's do this properly." His arm wrapped around the back of my neck. His lips were warm. I could feel his body vibrating. We both shook with pent-up energy. The last month had pinched at us, tweaking fear and excitement. Now something had to give.

Donald pulled up my shirt and tore my bra aside. His lips went from one nipple to the other, sucking, biting, and pulling. I felt waves of pleasure shooting down between my legs. Helpless, I moaned, squirming.

"Oh, it's coming!" Donald returned to kissing me. His fingers wandered up my skirt. Running up and down the centre of my panties. Up, circle, down, up, circle down. I bit his lip in desperation.

His fingers were warm as they parted and entered me. Slowly moving in and out. Then circling up. Stroking over and over again. "God, Donald!"

He added his thumb, circling counterclockwise over my clitoris.

"Ahhh." Spasms racked my body. Donald looked into my eyes, ensuring I continued to twitch once, twice and a third time more.

"There." Donald finished, licking his fingers clean. "That should hold you until we get home."

I kept looking at him, no words coming out, staring at the grin on his face. My breathing was laboured. "My... God..." I finally got out.

Donald laughed, putting his hand on my thigh. He removed my clothing and then his. When he climbed on top of me, I was warm and ready. Already primed from the previous orgasm, I came again and again.

We drove in silence through the Montreal traffic. It lightened up on the 15 North. Finally, we took our exit ramp.

CHAPTER 47

"Oh my God, Donald... puppies!" There was a sign stuck on the side of the road in front of a driveway.

"You want a puppy? Let's go see." He opened the door and I followed him towards the farmhouse. A litter of German shepherd puppies chased each other and wrestled in the front yard. A smaller puppy noticed us, trotting over. I picked him up. He licked my face, not really struggling in my arms. "This one, Donald. I want this one."

The puppy nipped Donald's finger. "Of course."

"Excuse me, can I help you?" An older woman came out onto the porch.

"Yes." Donald moved towards her. "We would like to buy a puppy."

The woman walked off the porch. "Okay."

"My wife wants this one."

The lady took the puppy and looked him over. "Sure." She put the puppy down. "He's a good dog. The runt of the litter, though."

Donald paid the woman seventy-five dollars and we left.

"So, I guess he's a male. Now you'll have two of us to love." Donald smiled at me.

I nodded, stroking the puppy's ears. The puppy looked out the window, barking as the world went by.

"I think he's going to be a hellraiser. Let's call him Satan," Donald suggested.

"Satan." I tried the name. Satan turned and began licking my face. *That settled it.*

Donald found our next stop. We pulled up to a mechanic's garage. A few cars outside were for sale. One of them was a yellow 1976 Triumph sports car.

"What do you think, Victoria?" Donald ran his hands along the roof of the car. "Get in." He opened the door for me. "Can we take this for a test drive?"

The mechanic got in and handed me the keys. The car started up beautifully. I shifted into first gear. The car sped onto the road, hitting sixty miles per hour in fifteen seconds. I could feel the pullback as I shifted through the gears and sped forward.

"Do you love it?" Donald asked me through the open window. He had watched me take the car for a few laps. "We'll take it," Donald said after a few seconds of looking into my eyes.

The mechanic and Donald sorted out the paperwork while I played with Satan in the field behind the garage.

It was arranged that we would pick up the car Monday and we took off again towards the country house. Donald made one more stop. Someone had left their canoe near the end of their driveway. Donald stopped, picked up the canoe, and strapped it to the Beetle's roof.

CHAPTER 48

"Happy birthday, Louise!" I hugged her as she got out of the car. "Hey, Theresa." Her foster daughter followed us into the house. "Ready for a fun weekend? Let's get inside. Dinner is almost ready." I ushered them into the kitchen, Donald was somewhere in the house doing whatever it was that Donald did. Satan charged Theresa the second he saw her. He jumped and barked until she picked him up and cuddled him.

A stew was cooking on the stove. Salad and buns were already on the table.

"Can I help?" Theresa asked.

"Sure, why don't you set the table?" I pointed her in the direction of the dishes. I had always liked Theresa, short with an athletic body type, soft-spoken and sweet. Louise had taken over caring for Theresa when she was sixteen years old.

Louise and I had met quite a few years ago, way before Donald. In fact, I had met my ex-husband because of her, hanging around Pigeon Park as it was called back then, at the entrance to the Atwater metro station. Satan's Choice bikers, hippies, and anyone who just chilled hung there. Everyone talked to everyone. Louise and I hit it off the moment we spoke to each other. Two adventurous spirits, we had hitchhiked across Canada many times. In those days there were crash pads, hitchhikers were safe, and it was fun to travel. We had made our way across Canada from Montreal to Vancouver at least four to five times. Mostly reformed, Louise now worked in computers and lived in a quiet part of town.

"That smells good." Louise plunked herself into a chair.

I mixed her and then myself a vodka and orange. "Here you go, birthday girl."

She took a long drink. "What have you and Donald been up to?"

"Not a whole lot," I said, not missing a beat. "Mostly, we've been up here enjoying the summer."

"That's good. It must be nice to have Donald back."

I turned to smile at Louise. "It really is. It really, truly is."

"Hey, did I hear my name? Are you guys talking about me?" Donald walked in, stopping to give me a kiss on his way to the table. "Happy birthday, Louise."

"Thanks, Donald. It's good to see you two so happy. I hope you can stay out now and marry Victoria."

Donald turned to her and said, "That's the plan Louise."

We had a great time that night. Louise and I drank while Theresa and Donald listened to us tell stories about our wilder days.

The next morning, we slept late and enjoyed a big brunch. The day got hotter and hotter so we jumped into the lake. Satan followed us, taking to swimming instantly.

Life was finally in perfect synch for us. Donald was satisfied with his job gone well. I was happy there were no more jobs being planned.

I pulled out the Saturday paper to read while we all sat on the lawn eating lunch. Louise and Theresa looked at the paper beside me.

The news was a lot of the same. Then, on page four, the headline read, "Teller Kidnapped Extortion Paid." I looked at Donald, my eyes not giving away any clues. We read it silently while commenting on the other side of the paper and its news.

"So, Louise, do you want another drink? I'm heading inside to get myself one."

Louise and Theresa looked at him. "Sure, Donald. I'd love another," Louise said.

I turned the page of the newspaper.

"How about you, Theresa?"

"Sure, Donald. Thanks."

Louise and Theresa turned their attention back to the paper.

We drank and ate late into the night. I had made Louise a birthday cake with all twenty-three candles. Theresa was the first to go to bed. Louise and I stayed up talking until she passed out on the couch. Donald basically carried me off to bed. I was so drunk I let him have his way with me any way he liked.

Sunday, July 10, 1977. We all got up and I made a big breakfast. It was nice to have the two extra people filling up the house and adding to the fun.

After breakfast, Donald and Theresa jumped in the lake. Louise and I sat on the beach working on our tans. We waited until we were too hot to stand it and then we jumped into the freezing cold lake, too.

Donald and I splashed each other. Theresa tried to splash Louise but Louise refused to be splashed. She got out after a few minutes and went back to her book.

"What the bloody hell?" I grabbed my foot. I had felt a rock open my skin as I stepped on it.

Donald rushed right over.

"It's my foot. I think I cut it."

Donald picked me up and brought me to the shore. He lifted my injured foot. Blood was gushing from it. I began to feel queasy.

"This looks kind of bad, Vic," Donald said, helping me hop onto the porch.

"I know, I feel dizzy." I lowered myself into a chair. Donald grabbed some bandages and covered my foot.

"Maybe you should go lie down, Victoria." He helped me hobble into our bedroom. "Here, just strip." Donald helped me out of my wet bathing suit and tucked me into bed.

"You don't have to stay with me," I told him.

"No, I want to, Vic." He smiled down at me.

"Go, I'll be asleep soon. That sun has made me really drowsy."

"All right." Donald kissed my forehead. "I'll be in to check on you soon."

CHAPTER 49

"Victoria, get up! You have to get up—the cops are coming!" Louise was shaking me.

"What?" I couldn't think. My mind was still groggy from my nap.

"The cops are coming over the bridge!"

I rolled out of bed, naked. Frantically, I pulled up a pair of jeans I found lying on the floor.

"What are you doing?" Louise asked.

"The cops won't let me get dressed once they get here and I'm not being interrogated naked. Help me find a shirt."

The front door blew open.

"Here." Louise handed me a shawl. The phone rang and Louise ran over to answer it. I heard her say, "No." Later, she told me Carol had called and asked, "Is everything okay up there?" Then a cop smacked the phone out of Louise's hands, shoving her towards the kitchen table. Theresa moved quietly to the table without being told. I was told to sit with them as well, still only dressed in my orange shawl and jeans.

The cops began fanning out, searching.

"Why do you come in yelling?" Louise asked, clearly more curious than afraid.

"Because we want to distract everyone in the house," the nearest cop answered.

There was a loud smash and the sound of a cop shrieking. Satan bolted out of my bedroom. "Satan!" I called. He clearly had scared the cop silly as he ran out from his hiding spot under the bed. He ran over, whimpering, ears down. I picked him up, stroking his head. "It's okay, boy." I sat him in my lap. My mind began to catch up. *Where the hell was Donald? Did he get away? The cops clearly didn't have him. They would have brought him in, as well...*

I heard the whirl of a helicopter. Then gunfire erupted. "Come out with your hands up," some cop boomed from the helicopter's megaphone. Then more gun shots. *Donald!* Shots popped off repeatedly.

"Is he dead?" I asked Louise over and over again.

Each time she responded, "I don't know, Vic. I don't know."

It was worse when the gunfire stopped. The silence loomed, heavy with uncertainty.

"Get in there." Two cops hauled Donald into the house, tripping him. I watched him fall on his knees. The cops lifted him up and dragged him to our bedroom. I couldn't hear what they were talking about, but after a few minutes I heard boots run up the stairs to the attic.

"We found it!" a cop shouted down.

He must have hidden the money in the attic.

After the cops found the money, their whole mood changed. They cuffed Donald to a chair outside and started congratulating themselves. In those days, girls were not handcuffed so we were able to move around freely and sit on the grass outside.

The hours that followed were unbelievably surreal. I found myself offering to make the cops drinks. The day was growing hotter, so each accepted and I began mixing gin and sevens. I could see the sun beat down on Donald. Each time I passed him, I tipped a drink into his mouth, alternating between gin and water.

"Make sure you get the Rice Krispies box," Donald whispered to me as I leaned down. I nodded my head slightly.

Walking back into the kitchen, I looked at my options. Satan was hiding under the table; I knew what I had to do. I gathered up some dog food and put it in a box, along with the Rice Krispies.

The cops were getting us ready to leave. I picked up Satan and then the box. Theresa and Louise were getting into their car. The cops were letting them leave. They only wanted Donald and me. I handed Satan to Theresa and the box to Louise.

"What's that for?" The cop holding the driver's door asked.

"It's for the puppy," I replied.

The cop closed the door. Louise and Theresa took off.

I was put in the back of one cop car and Donald in another. The cops drove back to Montreal in a convoy, sirens blinking, going 100 miles an hour. It was the shortest drive I had ever had on Highway 15.

CHAPTER 50

"Have a seat."

I was again in the basement of the Montreal police service headquarters, the dingy walls and bad air once again encasing me.

"We've counted the money twice. It seems there is $2000 still missing."

I looked up at the cop.

"We already collected the money from the garage," he added.

"I have no idea where the money is. Donald doesn't tell me things like that." I raised my gaze back up the cop.

"Are you sure that's the answer you want to give? If you don't give us the money, you'll have to go back to Tanguay to finish your sentence."

"I don't know where the money is." I leaned back in my chair.

The cop in front of me stared, trying to intimidate a confession out of me.

I had already put together that the money was in the Rice Krispies box. I didn't know for sure. Technically, I was telling the truth.

There was a knock at the door. My interrogator stepped outside.

"Donald says if you want to tell us that's okay," the interrogator said when he re-entered the room.

I snorted. "Sure, he said that."

"No, it's true. He did." The cop laughed. The one thing about Quebec cops is they have a sense of humour. He signalled to another cop. Donald was brought in, still cuffed.

"Donald" I jumped up. A cop shoved me back into my chair.

Donald grimaced. "It's true, Victoria. I did say it. If you want to tell them, that's all right. Figure out if $2000 is worth going back for eight months. Your parole is not up for another two weeks." The cop started pulling Donald out of the room before he finished his sentence.

"Okay, Donald."

Once again, something inside me clicked into place. "I'll get the money, but you can't come inside when I get it. There can't be charges for anyone there and I want a three-hour visit with Donald."

"Is that all?" the cop asked.

"Yes." I nodded my head.

"We can accommodate that."

I was taken back to a cop car. I gave them Louise's address and we drove slowly through the city.

When I knocked on the door, Theresa opened it. "Don't worry," I said before she saw the cop car.

Theresa let me through the door. Satan ran over to greet me. Louise came out of her bedroom.

"I just need the Rice Krispies box. The cops aren't coming in. I made sure there will be no charges here. You guys are completely in the clear."

Theresa went to the kitchen and got the box. I put Satan down and dug inside. Sure enough there was a roll of twenty dollar bills plus some tens. "Thanks, guys. I'll be back later."

"Of course," Louise said. "We'll be here." I nodded and headed back to the car.

The cops just about tore the money out of my hands. They counted it twice. "Do you have any money?" The cop in the passenger seat turned to me.

"No, I'm totally broke."

"Here." He flipped me a ten dollar bill. "Take a taxi home." The cop in the driver's seat started up the car and we made our way back.

CHAPTER 51

Donald was waiting for me in an interrogation room. He was seated on a chair sitting directly in front of a wall with a bar along the top. The cops had cuffed his left hand high above his head to this bar. How he endured it, to this this day I still don't know. I ran to him and gave him a hug. Then I eased myself onto the chair next to him

"Victoria…" Donald used his free hand to hug me back. He leaned over, kissing the top of my head.

"Are you okay?" I searched his face and arms. I didn't see any cuts or bruises.

"Yeah, Vic. They didn't beat me up." He laughed. "Come here." He took my face in his free hand and kissed me on the mouth. "Everything's going to be okay, Victoria. Trust me. I'll fight this and be out in no time. No one saw my face."

I looked straight into his blue eyes. "Sure." I kissed him to stop him from talking. I felt terrible. Time slowed so that the minutes felt like hours. Each cut a raw edge at me, cold and tainted. I don't really remember what we talked about.

"It seems like you don't want to be here, Vic," Donald said.

"No, that's not true! I want every second I can get with you. Who knows how long before I see—"

This time he cut me off with a kiss. I couldn't convince him otherwise. He read me like a book. He knew I was putting on my armour because he was going away, and I was losing my right arm.

Not long after, our three hours were up. Donald was uncuffed and recuffed to be taken upstairs to the cells. I was put into the back of a taxi, left to fend for myself. I made my way back to Louise's. I was weary. Every bone in my body ached. My throat wouldn't swallow. Everything shut down.

Theresa put me in a warm bath and tried to comfort me. Tears burst out of me the second my skin touched the warm water. "It's going to be okay, Victoria," Theresa said softly.

I curled my knees up to my chest, sobbing, rocking myself back and forth. I had no words, no thoughts. I didn't even really hear myself cry. I replayed our final kiss over in my mind, sobbing harder.

"Please, Victoria, calm down." Theresa tried to touch my arm. I jumped back.

Louise walked by the bathroom door. "I don't know what to say," Theresa said to Louise.

"Oh, she's just crying for herself," Louise said in passing.

I screamed at her, "I am not!"

CHAPTER 52

I watched the sun come up the next morning. Everything was still. I had exhausted myself crying. Now my chest felt empty, an open space for the morning cold to find. I heard Louise and Theresa begin their day. I didn't get up. I listened to bits of their conversation, though.

"Should I wake her up for breakfast?" Theresa asked.

"No, let her sleep," Louise responded.

Theresa went to work and it became quiet again. Around noon there was a loud knock followed by Janette's greeting. She barged into my room. "Victoria…" she gave me a hug. For a moment she didn't seem to know what to say. "Let's get up and get something to eat." She pulled me out of bed and made eggs.

"Thank you." I pushed away my half-eaten breakfast.

"What's the plan for today? You must have things you need to get done." Janette cleared my plate.

"Yes." I had begun a list of them in my head. It all seemed unbearable. "We should go to the cottage and get our stuff."

"Sure," Janette agreed.

I got up and sat on the couch. Janette didn't push me. She sat down and started watching TV.

"Okay, I'm ready." It was 3:00 p.m. The hottest part of the day was over. It was a bad time to go. Montreal afternoon traffic was just starting to thicken. Slowly, we seeped out of Montreal. The highway drive dragged on. We reached the cottage around 6:00 p.m. I could hear laughter coming from inside.

"What is this?" I asked the landlord. He and his guests were sitting down to dinner. "We paid until the end of the summer!"

"Just a moment." The landlord turned to us and moved a little ways away from the table. "You are going to have to move your stuff. I'll be staying here for the rest of the summer."

"You can't do that. I told you the house is paid for until the end of the summer." I took a step towards the landlord.

"I really don't care. It's too bad. Pack up your stuff and get going," he sneered.

I glared at the gleam on his balding head. His stomach was expanding, and he was in need of a shave and a shower. "It's too late to get that all done tonight," Janette pointed out.

"Fine, spend the night in that bedroom. You can finish packing up tomorrow. I want it all gone. The cops told me you wouldn't be coming back" He turned back to his guests.

Janette and I had to share a bed that night, the same one Donald and I had slept on all summer. Janette slept soundly, snoring and occasionally muttering.

Donald never snored...

I lay in bed, once again staring at the wall. My thoughts drifted back to Saturday. It had been a perfect day. Anything felt possible. Donald and I were ready to get on with the rest of our lives. The last two years were about to become nothing more than unhappy memories. Neither of us saw the cliff before we went over. *What had happened?* I began to wonder about Shorty and the other two guys. I had heard they had all been arrested, but nothing since. I had also put two and two together. Red would forever be the red-headed rat in my eyes. Only he could have sent the cops our way. Peter didn't know where we lived. Shorty had visited us a few times, but I knew he would never have ratted. I woke up at sunrise after a few hours of sleep. I got up. There was no going back to sleep. I moved quietly, packing my clothes. Janette was dead to the world. I didn't need to worry about waking her up.

I was able to get a lot done before the rest of the house woke up. I poked around for some breakfast. By noon, Janette and I were on the road, leaving behind the summer memories of Donald and me at the cottage.

Over the next few weeks I continued to stay with Louise and Theresa as I got back on my feet. I changed Satan's name to Brother. It was nice to have his constant companionship. I found it hard to leave him every night when I went to the bar to work. A job I had found quickly. I spent a lot of my time talking to patrons. Brother was the only thing on my mind, filling the void Donald had left behind.

"Victoria." The owner of the bar approached me.

"Yes, Mike?" I looked up from wiping the bar.

"This isn't working out. I'm going to have to let you go."

"But why?" I was taken aback.

"Well, the customers are complaining that all you do is talk about your dog." Mike gave me a look that read, *I'm not interested in your sob story.*

"Oh." What could I say? It was true. I didn't really want the job, but I needed the money. Brother was having health issues. He couldn't keep any food down. I had taken him to two vets before I was referred to Sainte-Hyacinthe veterinary school.

Sainte-Hyacinthe was the vet school for most of Quebec. It was located forty-five minutes outside of Montreal. Difficult-to-diagnose cases were referred to the school. I drove down with Brother sitting on the seat next to me. The vet said I had to leave him there and they would call me with the diagnosis. The next day I received a phone call from the vet. He very calmly told me Brother had been born with something wrong with the nerves in his throat. This was why he could not hold his food down and it kept coming up. He could have lived maybe a year more, slowly starving to death.

I couldn't do that to him. I asked the vet to put Brother down. I didn't go to see him one last time. I wasn't there when he passed. To this day I still regret it.

CHAPTER 53

Life had to go on. My loneliness didn't matter. I spent the next few days going through the help wanted ads. One in particular caught my eye:

DRIVERS WANTED: $300-$500 A WEEK

That interested me. Three hundred to five hundred dollars a week was a lot of money. Most jobs didn't pay that. When they did, it usually meant you were doing sales work. I didn't want to do sales work, but this was too much money not to call and at least see about the job.

"Hello, Data Courier."

"Hi, I'm calling about the ad for drivers in the paper. Is the position still available?"

"Yes, I'll transfer you to Joe now."

I heard the line being transferred. "Joe speaking."

"Hi, Joe. My name is Victoria. I'm calling about your ad in the paper. Is it a sales position?"

"No, it's not a sales job. It's a courier position. I'm looking for drivers," Joe assured me.

A driving job... Could I get this lucky? I knew Montreal like the back of my hand, and I could drive like a son of a bitch. "Are you sure it's not a sales position?" I repeated.

"It's absolutely not a sales job," Joe insisted.

"Okay."

"But," he chimed in, "if after a few months you want to bring in some new business and sign up new clients, we pay commission for that."

"Aha! So this is a sales job!"

"No," he assured me. "You'll never have to do that."

I went for the interview the following day and was hired on the spot. I was to be their only female courier. In those days, courier jobs were based on commission. We set out around 9:00 a.m. from our homes to pick up packages, then we worked as long as we wanted. I worked all the time. Once my CB radio was installed in my Volkswagen, I was never alone in my car. Being the only girl in the business made being lonely difficult. I never lacked for male attention. I made a good amount of money fast, and I never wanted to go home.

I had to visit Donald. I had put it off for a month. Then I couldn't wait any longer. I dragged myself to Parthenais. I felt my skin crawling, looking at him from behind glass, picking up the cold, sticky telephone.

"Hey, Victoria." Donald smiled at me.

"Hi, Donald."

"How are things? You said in your letter that you got a new job?"

I nodded. "I did. I'm a courier now. I like it. I just drive around the city all day, picking up packages and taking them to the address on the labels. Oh, yeah"—I grinned—"and I talk to the guys on the radio."

"The guys?"

"The other drivers and the dispatcher, Paul. Everyone has a CB radio in their car. I get to start work from home. I pick up packages and go into the office when I'm ready and finish my day when I'm done. It's all done by commission." I raised my eyebrows at him.

"You must be making a killing." Donald smiled but it didn't reach his eyes.

"It's easy to save up." I didn't bother mentioning "for us." He was still in the pretrial phase, but we both knew he wasn't going to get out anytime soon. Bail had been denied as we expected.

Theresa had spent the summer working at the Royal Bank. When she got caught up in our raid, the police had to inform the bank, who promptly fired her.

I felt terrible. Then it dawned on me: Theresa had worked in the Royal Bank mailroom.

I walked over to my boss. "Hey, Joe."

He looked up from his paperwork. "What can I do for you, Victoria?"

"I wanted to ask you a question."

"Sure." Joe put down his pen.

"Would you hire someone who really, really needs a job? And, is a really, really awesome person?"

"That would depend if I also thought this person was awesome. I take it you have someone in mind?" Joe smiled at me, his eyes half closed, kind of glazed-looking.

"Yes. My friend's daughter just lost her job in a bank mailroom. She would be perfect as a walker."

"Send me her resumé and I'll see."

I doubt Joe bothered to look at Theresa's resumé. He had a big heart and a laid-back attitude. He liked Theresa right away; all the guys did.

CHAPTER 54

I ended up working a lot of nights with our dispatcher.

"Hey, Paul." I sat down on his desk.

"Hey, Victoria." He shuffled some papers to make room for me. "All done your route?"

"Yep." I looked in Paul's eyes and he smiled at me. "Did you do anything interesting today?" I licked my lips.

Paul swallowed. "Nothing. Want to catch dinner tonight?"

"You know I do."

I liked Paul. He was tall with long black bangs. Not handsome, but he had an aura of calm around him. He never seemed to get upset and he didn't care what people thought. Paul always wore a purse. He was teased mercilessly by the other drivers. He never cared.

"Dispatch, I have a major problem!" It was Steve, one of the other drivers. His voice sounded panicked as it came over the radio.

I could hear sirens in the distance.

"Ten-four, Steve. What is your issue?" Paul's voice was collected and cool.

"This… taxi cab rear-ended me!"

"All right." Paul was taking notes. "Do you want me to get you a tow truck?"

"Yes, but that's not the end of it." Steve took a deep breath. "The taxi pushed me into an unmarked cop car."

"I see." Paul's tone didn't change.

My blood pressured went up just listening to Steve. I could barely handle a traffic jam. But Paul was unruffled, a quality I've always been attracted to. That is the reason I felt drawn to Paul. I certainly didn't like his messy black hair and lankiness.

He was always there, just like me, letting me waste time chatting at his desk. Paul was unhappily married with two small sons. He and I often went to dinner after our long, hard days, allowing us to avoid the rest of our lives.

"So, you want to head out for some dinner?" Paul asked.

"Sure."

At dinner Paul sipped his wine thoughtfully. "I can't wait to get out of Montreal," he said finally.

"Yeah?"

Paul nodded. "Just drive into the sunset and never look back." He smiled at me.

"That would be nice."

"We could do it together." Paul put his hand over mine, considering my eyes. When he looked up at me I saw the same look of affection I saw in Donald, but Donald's eyes were so much bluer. I had tried not to think about Donald. He was like a phantom limb, a constantly nagging pain. I knew Paul was in love with me and that I was not in love with him.

In those days, Paul like most men, didn't speak about his wife. Not the way he might today. He told me in so many words and through his actions that he was unhappy. He made it clear he was ready to leave her.

"We could head out west." I took his fantasy a little farther. "Go to Vancouver. You can get another dispatcher job and I can be a courier."

"Really?" Paul's face lit up.

"Sure, why not. My family is all in Vancouver."

Paul brought up going out west the next day. "You know, Victoria, I don't think the Volkswagen will make it to Vancouver. We would have to use my car."

"Of course." I loved Paul's big blue car. Paul drove a conservative car; it was in his nature to be conservative. That's why I liked him. No danger there.

I found my visits with Donald harder and harder. We had less and less to talk about. My work was my life and Paul was at my work. It was a world Donald was not a part of.

CHAPTER 55

"Donald!"

"It's good to finally see you, Victoria."

He didn't mean to imply I had been neglecting him, but he couldn't help it. "I know I've been busy. I haven't had as much time to come here."

"No, you're working. That's good. Still enjoying it?"

"Yes, I got Theresa a job at Data as a walker downtown. She's enjoying it and is a hit with all the drivers."

"I thought Theresa was working at RBC." Donald's expression became blank.

"She was, but they fired her after the raid." I forgot I hadn't told him that yet.

"The cops told the bank?"

"Yes, it's the law or something."

"Pigs. Tell her I'm really sorry about that." Donald shook his head in disgust.

"Are things okay inside, Donald? Is your head on straight?"

"Yeah, it's going well. Mom visited once. It's doing time, the same time over and over again."

"Did you get your court date yet?"

"Yes, I go to trial in November and then, normally, there are two to three more times that I may pass. It won't be until next year that I find out what the verdict will be," he replied

Donald was pleading not guilty. He always pleaded not guilty. I knew they had him dead to rights. The raid on our summer house was just a small part of the Montreal police service's investigation.

It was stupid, stupid, stupid. Beyond stupid. Peter, the youngest, had taken his share of the money. He went out the next day and bought a new truck, paying cash. He then decided to cross over the US border. In those days, crossing the border wasn't a big deal. Peter must have been looking ridiculously suspicious. The guards pulled him over. I'm sure they were expecting drugs or guns. They found the money. Peter had no explanation for it. What Peter had was a big mouth that wouldn't shut once he started talking.

I had forbidden Donald from letting Peter come to our house or know our phone number. I was right. Peter told them where to find Shorty and the red-headed rat. Peter even remembered to mention Red's suicide-by-cop plan. Plus the fact that I turned down the offer to drive. I guess I was the only one to have a funny feeling about Peter. Red had welcomed Peter to Red's new girlfriend's home, fool that he was.

Each time the red-headed rat went home, he would call his girlfriend from a payphone near their duplex to see if everything was okay. That's the word he used: okay. As long as his girlfriend answered 'yes' he would go upstairs to their home. He was out when the cops rang the doorbell. They waited inside until he called. They told his girlfriend not to warn Red or they would rape her, a tactic they had used at the country house to get Donald to produce the money. I imagine they used it a lot back then.

What could she do at that point?

A simple code word would have sent the lifer running and the Montreal police service sitting on their hands. Donald and I always used code words; communicating secretly came as natural as breathing to us.

The cops waited behind the duplex's door. They struck Red from behind, disarmed him and hauled him off to jail. I think they should have just given the guy what he wanted. My life would have been so much simpler.

Shorty was a true friend; he had been there right from the beginning. Shorty was smarter than most criminals. He took out a wall in his house, put the money inside and then dry-walled it over. He planned to use the money in a few years when the heat had died down.

When the cops came for Shorty, he lied through his teeth, taking the beating of his life trying to convince the cops that Donald had ripped him off. Shorty wanted to keep the money so that he could pay for good lawyers for Donald and the others. Shorty never ratted. He also never thought that the red-headed rat would give Donald up. Again, if the rat had gotten his wish of suicide-by-cop, our country house would have never been ratted out. The rat gave in because the cops threatened him with their old stand-by: "Do what we say or we'll rape your girlfriend. Poor Shorty. The cops believed him, and thanks to the red-headed rat, they then raided us. Only to find that Shorty's money was not with us. The cops beat Shorty some more and took a sledge hammer to Shorty's newly plastered wall.

CHAPTER 56

"I'm sorry I haven't had time to come but you never write me letters anymore, Donald." He was still in Parthenais, so we remained separated by glass.

"No, because I know you're too busy to read them and reply…"

I had never liked the ambivalent side of Donald. "That's not true. I write you at least once a week, just not daily!"

"And I don't want to hear any more about your new job," Donald interrupted me. And I don't want to hear how you're the only girl there besides Theresa, and that your dispatcher is in love with you."

"I can't help if he loves me. I don't love him," I shot back

"You write how much he talks about running away with you and you always play along."

"Because I have so much keeping me here." I gave him a dirty look.

Donald stood up. "Fine, replace me. Take him out west and never come back." He slammed the phone down and walked away.

He was right; we were right. I had nothing here. I could start fresh in Vancouver. My parents would help me, and I would never have to make another prison visit.

Paul and I began sleeping together after that. It was firm in my mind that I was leaving, and I didn't want to be alone.

Donald wrote me one last apology letter, but I never wrote back.

"My parents would probably let us stay with them and help us get back on our feet."

"Really?" Paul stood up. "This could actually work." He paced. "We'll need to save up for a few weeks, but we could really pull this off."

Paul and I decided that we would leave in the middle of October. Paul planned everything, including not waiting for his final pay cheque. He would leave it with Steve. Steve would cash Paul's cheque and send it to me as a money order. That way Paul's wife wouldn't know where he had gone.

Tuesday, October 11, 1977, was the day we picked. We would work our last shift and leave right from the office. Drive into Ontario and spend the night. I enjoyed our shared conspiracy and the distraction it gave me. I had always gotten the men I wanted. But, sneaking away and not coming back felt exciting.

Tuesday morning the rain was pouring down in Montreal. I began my route like usual, arriving at the warehouse just after 10:00 a.m. Paul still wasn't in. I kept unloading my parcels when a taxi pulled up. Paul stepped out, wet and miserable-looking, carrying a suitcase.

"Paul!" He looked at me. "Paul, where is your car?"

"Gone."

"What do you mean 'gone'?" I followed him inside.

"She didn't pay the lease. All these months, she didn't pay."

"Your wife didn't pay who?" I asked.

"My wife has been keeping the money for the lease payment. She'd been planning on leaving me." *How ironic,* I thought.

It turned out Paul's wife was as unhappy as he was. She had pocketed the monthly lease payments Paul gave her. The car had been repossessed earlier that morning.

"We're taking my Volkswagen?" It was more of a statement than a question.

"I guess." Paul sat down at his desk.

I went off to call my parents to let them know I was coming in my Beetle. My brother answered the phone. "Hello?"

"Hey, Chris. Are Mom and Dad home?"

"No, they're out. What's up?"

"Can you tell them we're still coming but we'll be late? We're taking my Volkswagen."

"Your orange hunk of junk you told me about?" Chris chuckled.

"It's not junk, Chris."

"Yes, it is. I bet you fifty bucks it doesn't make it over the Rockies."

"I'll take that bet. Tell Mom and Dad I'll see you in a few days. Don't forget to have my money waiting!"

"Sure," Chris said and hung up the phone.

CHAPTER 57

I was a little nervous about driving the Volkswagen cross-country. Yes, it was old, but it had always been reliable. It was small, Paul was lanky, and I had my stuff and Donald's with me. We were fighting, but I still believed he would get out one day and we would be together. We had broken up and gotten back together before. I knew it was only a matter of time. For sure once Donald was out, we would be together. I couldn't stay out of his arms. Now he was inside, and it was too painful. We had our few happy summer months and now he was gone. I needed space to wait and time to heal.

Paul had packed the Volkswagen. We had confirmed with Steve to pick up Paul's paycheque. We said goodbye to Joe and then there was nothing left to do but leave.

I drove, and we spent the night. In the morning we ate quickly in a diner and drove again.

"Paul, take a picture of me." I pulled to the side of the road beside the Ontario sign.

"Sure." Paul took my photo with the Punch buggy. Paul had dressed carefully that morning. He dressed carefully every morning. Today his boots matched his jeans, which were cuffed just so. His long face and shaggy hair bothered me. In the few days we took to reach Vancouver, I began to see Paul without the aura I had seen at Data. His steadiness didn't seem so impressive. His calm was actually apathy. Each province we drove through, we talked less and less.

"You're getting colder the farther west we go, Vic." Paul looked straight ahead.

I didn't say anything and kept driving. *No shit, Sherlock.*

Climbing the mountains, the Volkswagen began to choke and sputter. We drove that last day, praying we would reach my parents. Late Sunday night the Volkswagen rolled into a parking spot in front of my parent's house and promptly died.

Chris paid me fifty dollars the next morning.

"Victoria." My dad approached me.

"Dad!" I smiled at him.

"Who's this handsome lad?" My mother asked. "He looks just like your father."

My whole body cringed. I look at Paul's long face and pointed chin, then to my father's warm smile and bushy beard. They didn't look anything alike. "Mom, Dad, this is Paul. Paul, these are my parents, Geof and Maiya."

"Nice to meet you." Paul extended his hand.

CHAPTER 58

We stayed at my parents' house the next few weeks. They insisted we not sleep together. I slept in a bedroom upstairs and Paul was put in the basement. I really didn't miss sleeping with him. My parents bought me a Datsun F10, blue and boxy. Chris begged me to give the Volkswagen to his friend for free. I eventually agreed. But a week after we arrived, I found a note on the VW's windshield. It said simply, "I will buy this car for $200 and a phone number."

I had bought the VW in Montreal for $200, and I needed the money now more than ever. I sold the VW that night and it was gone the next morning. Chris whined but I truly didn't care. Even back then, things were starting to line up for me.

With my new car, I found a job at Pink Lady's Courier. It was like any other courier except after three months, I would have to paint my car pink.

Once I had a job, I found a place and my parents helped me with the first month's rent. The second week of November, Paul and I moved into our apartment.

"You should come apply at Pink Lady's. They need a dispatcher." Things between Paul and me had grown tense.

"Sure, Victoria."

"Just make sure you come tomorrow after my shift. They don't allow dispatchers and drivers to date. Don't mention that we're living together."

Paul nodded but didn't look up from the TV.

"Have you talked to Steve? He really should have sent the money by now."

"I know. I'll call him tomorrow." Paul turned the TV up.

The next day, I went about my morning shift. Paul was supposed to come for his interview that evening after I got home. But that's not the way things happened.

"Right this way, Paul. We'll see you in a minute."

I looked up in horror at Paul. He smiled dumbly at me. *God, he's ugly,* I thought to myself. *This is the man I'm living with? Why didn't you listen to me, Donald? Why did you trust Peter? This should be us in a new apartment with a new life!*

Paul's interview was over in a few minutes. He left; I finished up my shift and went home. The door was locked at home and the apartment was empty. I looked around, my eyes landing on the wastebasket. A piece of paper hung over the rim. It had my signature written out ten times. The last few looking confident and authentic. My mind wouldn't process the information. A Western Union slip with my forged signature was in the basket, just lying on top.

"That rat bastard!"

I drove to the train station. I knew that Paul's train wouldn't have left yet. I parked in the parking lot and made my way in. I saw Paul sitting in the restaurant. He was in a booth with his back turned. I could tell it was him because of his greasy hair and his long, funny, duck-shaped neck.

A brilliant idea popped into my head. I walked back over to the ticket counter. "Excuse me, Miss," I said to the girl at the desk. "Did a guy by the name of Paul B buy a ticket and pay by cheque?"

The ticket girl looked at her files. "Yes, he did."

"Okay," I said. "Just so you know, that cheque is going to bounce." I walked away, leaving the girl stunned.

When I walked back into the restaurant, Paul didn't see me. I made my way down the aisle to his booth. Then I slid in on the other side.

"Victoria!" Paul jumped and went completely white.

"I found the note you left. It must have fallen in the wastebasket," I said sarcastically, looking at him.

He didn't say anything. His mind must have still been processing how I found him. It had been a fairly simple process of elimination. I had called the bus station and there were no busses leaving that evening. He was too cheap to pay for air fare and that left the train. Plus, when I called, there was one leaving that evening for the east.

"You know what? I'm not mad. I would have liked if you had been man enough to tell me in person instead of sneaking out like a little child, though." I started to get up.

"Is that all you came to say?" Paul asked.

"Pretty much. I just wanted you to know that I know." I stood up fully. "Oh, and if you change your mind, I will be at the apartment." I thought to myself: *Am*

I just saying that? Or do I really want him back? I was coming to realize Paul was just a rebound from Donald.

Paul never came back. I lay in bed every night, wondering what was the point of all this. The fact that Paul was ugly is what made me pull away from him, but it also made his leaving all the more upsetting. Because Paul had come for the interview and then never gone back, people at work asked me where he was. I had to tell them he had gone back east. Most people at work knew he had left me. My three-month period was coming to an end at Pink Lady. I was bored in Vancouver. The people were quiet and the streets were quiet, unlike the hustle and bustle of Montreal. I missed being with all my friends.

The house felt cold and empty without Paul watching TV. I was never home. I stayed out as late as possible, so I could fall asleep as soon as I walked in the door.

Louise had sent me a letter just before the Super Bowl. She was unhappy with her job in Montreal and needed a break. She finally caught me at home one day.

"My God, Victoria! I've been trying to get a hold of you all week," she said.

I sat down on the chair beside the phone. "Yeah, I've been busy."

"You're never home." Louise laughed.

"I'm not happy. You just left your job. Now is the perfect time for a break. Fly out to Vancouver and we can drive back to Montreal together."

"Oh." She paused. "Okay, but I want to go through the US. I'll book a flight for right after New Year's."

"Done," I agreed.

Louise and I had hitchhiked all over when we were teenagers. We made more than a few trips across Canada. We always had a good time. Now I would see the US with her. I knew the trip would help me keep my mind off Donald.

CHAPTER 59

"How was your flight?" I said, greeting Louise at the terminal.

"Fine." We grabbed her luggage and headed out of the airport.

"Did your parents buy you this?" Louise asked as she got into my car. "Sure beats the Volkswagen."

"Yeah, they did. Nice of them, eh?" I turned the car on.

"This is going to be fun, like our glory days. No jobs, no men, no BS…"

"Don't even mention men, Louise." I shifted the car into gear.

"Did you hear Paul's in Toronto now?"

"Good for him. Bloody coward…" I shook my head. "I must be cursed. I swear I'm cursed."

"Life isn't that much better in Montreal. The clubs are filled with nothing but men who just want one-night stands."

Louise settled into my apartment that night and the next day we began moving my stuff to my parents'. Dad said he would send it to me when I got back to Montreal. He pre-paid me for my coming paycheques from Pink Lady.

At the time, my father was building his business as a psychic. When I was younger, we lived in South Africa and my father worked as an engineer. He tracked satellites for the South African government. My father loved astronomy. It would come in handy when we moved to Canada some years later. Two years after we arrived in Canada, when I was sixteen, my father decided to try automatic writing. I don't know what prompted him, but he had an intense spiritual experience. My dad channelled a spirit named 'Arry Platter. He sat down opposite me in a chair and closed his eyes. Suddenly, he started scribbling like mad. Ten minutes passed if I recall correctly, and then he opened his eyes and looked down. Appearing puzzled for a moment, Dad then got up and held the paper up to a mirror. He had written backwards. I found this incredible but strange. He had just been introduced to a Limey spirit whom my dad would channel from that day forth. The spirit had a British accent, which made the name "Harry" sound like 'Arry. My father changed that day. He stopped drinking. He and my mother started The Hermetic Order of Campo Santo in Montreal. My dad used his knowledge of astronomy to become a famous astrologer and psychic.

When I was living in Vancouver in 1978, he did a lot of astrology forecasting. His big claim to fame came when CBC created a TV show called *Beyond Reason* in the late '70s. Before that, he had published several books and cassettes.

Before we left, my dad gave Louise and I a tarot card reading. I still remember mine.

I shuffled my dad's tarot cards and handed them back to him. He closed his eyes for a moment before laying out the cards.

"When you get to San Francisco," he began, "you will have an amazing encounter with a young gent with a very pronounced limp." My dad paused. "You will never be in danger, but it is a story you will talk about for the rest of your life."

I waited for my dad to continue. He never asked his clients questions; they sat and listened because he was that good.

"It also looks like you will come into contact with a Porsche." He looked at me. "And race it."

I nodded my head. Many other things were said but those two have remained in my memory. I wish Dad had recorded our session.

Dad pulled an envelope from his jacket pocket. "Take this and only open it in an emergency."

CHAPTER 60

It took Louise and me twelve hours to reach our destination. San Francisco is a beautiful city and in the late '70s, it was the place to be. The bay and tall buildings were a backdrop to a scene of hippies, tourists, immigrants and everyone else in between. Being Canadian was especially good. The locals knew about our prime minister, Pierre Trudeau, and the FLQ crisis. Everywhere we went, we were treated like rock stars. People paid for our meals, bought us drinks and catered to us. All we had to do was say we were Canadians and let them hear our accents. It was unreal.

Louise and I planned to stay in San Francisco for a while, so we rented a cheap room and found work delivering dog food samples. On the mornings that we felt like it, Louise and I got up early and met up with the random assortment of San Fran types to collect our quota for the day.

San Francisco is a vertical city. It's nothing but stairs with topped iron gates, and everybody has a dog. From 7:00 a.m. to 3:00 p.m., we walked up and down the stairs, knocking on people's doors, asking, "Do you have a dog?" If they said yes, we took their information and handed them a sample. Then we said, "Someone will be in touch with you soon to see how your dogs like the food." We were paid cash at the end of each day that we chose to work, somewhere between fifteen and thirty dollars.

At night, Louise and I enjoyed our Canadian celebrity status, drinking and playing pool.

"You're pretty good." A tall dark man approached me one night. "Wanna play?"

"Sure," I replied.

"Regan." The man stuck out his hand.

"Victoria." I took my hand back and chalked my pool stick. "Want to make it interesting?"

"Of course," he said.

"Loser buys the next round of drinks?" I asked.

"Works for me." Regan and I went back and forth in a close game. He was sure of himself. He reminded me of Donald. I won the game.

"You won." Regan stepped back from the table.

"Yeah, I knew I would."

Regan laughed. "I like you." He pulled me to a booth where another man sat. "This is my friend, Ron. Ron, this is Victoria."

"Nice to meet you, Victoria."

I took a sip of my drink, and Louise made her way over.

"Regan, Ron, this is my friend, Louise."

Ron stuck out his hand. He smiled the way men do when they like what they see. "Pleased to meet you," he said.

"You, too." Louise took his hand and sat down beside Ron. Regan put his arm around me. The night went the way I expected. Regan and I played pool a few times while Louise and Ron talked. At last call, we all walked out together. Ron took Louise home and I took Regan back to our small room.

"You're beautiful." Regan brushed a strand of hair from my face.

"Thank you." I leaned forward, brushing my lips to his. I deepened the kiss. Regan moved me closer, his hands moving up my legs, over my stomach to my breasts. His thumb circled my nipple. "Oh," I moaned. I pulled off his shirt. His chest was well muscled and warm. In that moment, I lost myself. The heat of my arousal mixed with the warmth of the alcohol I'd consumed. My mind shut down and I let the waves of pleasure wash over me.

Regan's smile grew bigger. He laid me on my bed. "I'm going to blow your mind," he said, pulling off my pants. His breath was warm against my skin. Regan was eager to taste me. His touch was direct and intense. It lacked Donald's finesse and his patience.

Just like that, my mind went back to Donald. Regan was good, but he would always be second best to The King. "Come here." I pulled Regan to me, guiding him inside of me. We moved and rocked. Donald never left the back of my mind.

"Well, I guess we're not working today," I said to Louise the next morning. Regan and I had driven over to Ron's. The sun was high in the sky when we woke up and it had risen higher yet.

Louise shook her head. Her long blond hair swayed in front of her face, looking a little dull in the sunshine. We were both hungover.

"What do you do?" Ron asked,

"We are dog food sample delivery specialists," Louise replied, sipping her water. Ron and Regan laughed.

"I know what you do. I've had you people come here." Ron didn't appear to be hungover; Regan, neither. It seemed unfair. I felt as if my body was filled with lead and my mouth had sand in it. After Ron fed us, Louise and I went back to our room to sleep some more. Regan and Ron went to do whatever it is they did during the day. We all agreed to meet back at the bar later that night.

That's how our next few days went: Louise and I worked until three, came home, napped and were at the bar by nine. Ron and Louise hung out while Regan and I ran the pool table. We won a lot and drank our winnings.

One very successful night, Regan and I staggered out to the car. "We're too drunk to drive," I told Regan. He laughed. "No, I mean it." Somehow, we kept each other standing. Regan looked at me.

We all drove drunk in the '70s. The government didn't make us wear seat belts or motorcycle helmets, and nobody cared if you drove drunk. So, saying we were too drunk to drive meant we were barely conscious.

"No problem," Regan said finally. "I know a dude who has a place down on the beach. We can crash there."

"Lead on." I felt safe with Regan. If he said he knew people and it was cool for us to crash, then I trusted him.

Under the stars and moonlight, Regan found the house. The sliding door was unlocked. We stumbled in, made it to the living room, and passed out in each other's arms on the carpet.

I woke up the next morning, smelling bacon. I left Regan asleep and followed my nose into the kitchen. A man stood in front of a stove frying bacon. "Hello?"

"Hi," he replied.

"I'm Victoria, Regan's friend."

"Cool, I'm Mike." Clearly Mike didn't think it was strange to have a random girl spend the night. "Where are you from?"

"I'm Canadian, from Montreal."

"Really, you're Canadian? Have a seat." Mike ushered me to the table. "Do you want some breakfast? I've got bacon cooking. I'm going to make eggs."

"Sure." I smiled; it was good to be Canadian.

"Jesus Christ!" The kitchen door swung open. I looked up from my plate. A man entered and stood in the doorway. "I had a hit and run on the beach last night."

That's funny, I thought. *I left my car on the beach.*

"I hope it's not a blue Datsun F10 with BC plates," I joked. The guy's face went red like a stoplight. I knew at that moment it was my vehicle he had hit. As he moved forward, I noted the very pronounced limp, and my father's words from his reading came back to me.

I woke Regan up. Of all the people in San Francisco, which had a population of 677, 661 people in 1978, somehow a guy with a limp hit my car. As I ate breakfast, my mind kept going over and over the fact that I had randomly slept at Mike's house and overheard his friend's confession. What if Louise and Ron had been with us? Then we might have gone home with them. What if we hadn't drunk so much? Then Regan and I would have probably driven home. What if Regan had chosen somebody else's place to crash at? How could my father have seen all of that in his cards? Life is a mysterious path you walk.

Unbelievable, my mind said over and over again.

The driver turned out to be an unemployed dishwasher. He and Mike hiked back with Regan and me to my car.

"Oh my God, the trunk!" I ran to the car. The trunk had been broken open, exposing the majority of Louise's and my stuff. "Everything is still there," I assured myself, amazed that nothing was missing.

The tail light of my car was smashed, as well as the back right panel. Mike and the dishwasher banged out the dents, fixed the trunk lock and covered my broken tail light with red-and-white paper so the brake lights still lit up red.

CHAPTER 61

Knowing it would soon be time to leave San Fransciso, Louise and I decided to try our luck in South Lake Tahoe. I love to gamble. We rented a cheap motel and headed to the casinos. I decided to play the slots.

"Hey, Louise! I won!" My slot machine paid out a rush of coins. I put another coin in and pulled the handle. The machine dinged again. Winner!

Louise looked over. "You've got a hot machine. Spin it again."

I did, and I kept winning. There came a point when some big men in suits noticed. One walked over. "You have to leave now. This machine is broken." He tried to come between me and the slot machine lever.

"What do you mean it's broken?" I asked.

"Let's go, Victoria." Louise tugged my elbow.

"Fine." I gathered my coins into a bucket. About $100 all in quarters. We left in such a hurry I didn't bother exchanging my coins for bills. "Look at all this, Louise!" I poured out the money on the bed, admiring the pool of metal that formed.

The next morning, I went to a different casino, ready to win. I lost all my money by dinner time. I went back to the motel and looked at the emergency envelope. *This is an emergency,* I told myself. I opened the envelope. "Thank you, Dad!" Inside was $300. I went back to the casino and lost that, too.

Louise and I went to leave the next morning. There was frost on the ground. It was February, but it was also California. A frost plug had popped out of my car. I found it underneath. I had to ask the motel kitchen for a pot of boiling water to thaw my radiator. It worked. I pushed the frost plug back in and it held. It actually held for the rest of the car's life.

Louise and I headed back to San Francisco. The fifty-cent toll took our last two quarters. We arrived at Ron's duplex a sad sight. Ron laughed from the top of the stairs at us. "How was Lake Tahoe?" he asked, motioning for us to come up.

We spent the next few days staying with Ron and delivering dog food. But our hearts weren't in it. We were ready to move on. So once we had enough money, we left San Francisco.

CHAPTER 62

We left San Francisco in the late afternoon. The night before we had said our farewells to the city. We stayed all night at the bar drinking with Regan and Ron. Our late lunch/early dinner fuelled us. We set off down the coastal highway, watching the sun set. We listened to the sound of the waves, driving in silence. We reached Los Angeles late that night.

Looking for a motel, we learned there were some places tourists should not stay. The wide-eyed owners of the motel we tried to check into sent us on our way. He told us white folk did not stay in this part of town. Alarmed, we drove as far away from that area as quickly as we could. In the end, we spent the night on the side of the road.

The hot sun woke me up early. We drove the twelve hours to New Mexico straight, barely stopping in Arizona to eat. After a restorative night in an actual motel bed, we headed into Mexico for the day.

Getting into Mexico was easy. Again, we were treated to free meals and drinks. Not because we were Canadians, but because of Louise's long blond hair. The men in Mexico went wild flirting with her, trying to touch her hair. We were bought more tequila than we could drink.

"Are you Americans?" a deep voice asked behind us as we were cruising the market.

Louise and I turned at the same time, saying in unison, "We're Canadian." A tall sexy man stood there with a wolfish grin on his face.

"Well, that's even better," his friend said. "I'm Greg and this is Steve." We all shook hands.

"What are two lovely Canadian girls doing in Mexico?" Steve asked.

"Sightseeing, shopping. What are you two Americans up to?" I emphasized the word "American."

"We're roadies with the Charlie Daniels Band. We have a gig in California tomorrow. Everyone is staying at a hotel back in New Mexico. You girls should stop by tonight."

Louise and I looked at each other. "Sure." We found out where they were staying and after a little more flirting we went on our way. Louise and I finished up our shopping for souvenirs and headed back to the border.

The Datsun still looked decent. The dents from San Francisco were hardly noticeable, and you had to look hard to notice the tail light was paper. The car was packed to the brim with our stuff. And the car looked lived-in.

Mexico is easy to get into but not so easy to leave. There were a few cars ahead of us at the El Paso border. At the front of the line were several nasty-looking border guards. One of the guards had a massive German shepherd on a leash. The dog strained towards the poor couple currently having their car torn apart.

"There had better not even be a roach in here," I hissed at Louise. I didn't smoke but Louise did. It was the '70s; almost everyone did.

"There isn't," she assured me.

"There had better not be." I watched the next car drive up. Two men slowly got out. One of them moved too quickly. The dog lunged towards him. *Christ, this is like something from a bad prison movie.* That thought made me think of prison. Which made me think of prisons in Mexico. Finally, I thought about what would happen if they found something. Horror stories I had heard through the grapevine flooded my mind. *What if they asked for a bribe? Or planted something?*

"Get out of the car very slowly," the border cop ordered as the Datsun crept up. Turning the car off, I inched open the door. "That's far enough." The cop stopped me. "Do not move a muscle." The cop with the dog approached me. The dog was pulling on its leash, going up on its hind legs. My whole body froze. I loved animals. It had been less than a year since I had been forced to put Brother down, but I was afraid of this dog.

He snarled at me, I could see his teeth the entire time he sniffed me. The border guard had a tight grip on the leash, but if I moved and the dog lunged, I would be losing skin. I could feel the dog's slobber fly onto my bare legs. It took forever but finally the dog moved on to Louise. I watched her stop breathing.

"Move over here." The cop pointed farther behind the car. They opened the hood and popped the trunk. Their German shepherd walked around and around. I could feel myself sweat in the hot desert sun. I had no spit to lick my lips with.

They let the German shepherd loose in our car. He went back and forth, from side to side. Then he jumped out.

"There's nothing here," the dog handlers said to the other guards.

The first guard waved us back to our car. "Enjoy your stay in New Mexico." The guards waved us off, already eyeing the car behind us.

CHAPTER 63

We found the hotel Steve had told us about. A big semi sat in the parking lot. People came in and out of the cab attached. Louise and I got out, looking around for Steve and Greg.

"You made it." Steve smiled at me. I didn't see Greg anywhere.

"Of course we did." I smiled back at Steve.

He finished loading the gear into the semi, then drove it to a different part of the parking lot.

"You drive a semi?" I asked.

"Sure do, I carry all the instruments for the bands." Steve replied. "Come on, I'll take you guys up to the room and introduce you to the band."

"Cool!" Louise said. Louise has always loved musicians.

We followed Steve to a room on one of the upper floors. Steve introduced us to the band. Then we all settled in to party. That night, we drank with the band and roadies. Everyone was wandering back and forth between the hotel rooms. Steve and I stayed together. I had brought a bottle of tequila over the border. I shared it with Steve.

It's true what they say about drinking tequila. One minute you're sober and the next you are blind drunk. NO warning.

"Let's go to my rig," Steve suggested.

I looked at him, and then at Louise, who was now talking to Greg.

"He's good people," Steve assured me.

I elbowed Louise. "Yeah, sure, go. I'll see you in the morning Victoria."

"Okay." I followed Steve to the semi. He climbed in first, settling into the sleeper cab. I got into the driver's seat.

I was about to move into the back cab when Steve said, "Is that your car?" He pointed to my blue Datsun with Canadian plates.

"Yes, sir," I replied, a bit puzzled.

"You're not in the guest parking area. You'd better move it." I hopped down and jumped into my front seat. I threw the gearshift in reverse and spun into a backwards wheelie.

I saw the motorbike in the rear-view mirror too late. I held my breath. The bike wobbled, but it didn't fall.

"You know you clipped that bike." Steve let out a sigh.

"I know. Good thing it didn't fall down." I laughed. I climbed in beside Steve. He kissed me sloppily. It didn't go any farther. We were much, much too drunk.

The next morning, I hated life. I hated every living being. I hated the light, the heat, everything. My hangover was so bad that the memory of it comes back every time I drink tequila.

I staggered out of the semi to the hotel restaurant. Louise was already sitting at a booth, looking almost as hung over as me.

"Coffee?" the waitress asked.

"Yes, please!" I took a sip of the cup. It burned my tongue. I put it down. "Ready to get out of here?" I asked Louise.

"Sure," she said. "Are you okay to drive, though? You look like shit."

"I feel like shit, Louise, so just grab a couple of coffees to go and hopefully it makes us feel better as we drive."

CHAPTER 64

We drove along Route 10. The desert turned into scrub land, then prairie and then lush green farmland. The air became more humid. It helped with my hangover, as did the coffee.

I looked down at my gas gauge; it was getting just below an eighth of a tank. We had just passed the Texas border. There was a small gas station off to the side of the highway. The gas station looked like it had seen better days, but the bell still rang when I drove over the signal wire and up to a pump. I waited for an attendant to come serve us.

I heard sirens going off in the distance, getting closer. "I wonder what that's about." I turned to Louise.

"I don't know." She stuck her head out the window, looking in the direction the sirens were coming from.

Cop cars came in from all sides, forming a circle around us. Everything is bigger in Texas: the signs, the cars, the cattle, and the men. Several cops jumped out of their cars, guns drawn. Not one of them was shorter than six feet. "We have you surrounded. Turn off the car and slowly get out with your hands up."

"What the hell?" I looked at Louise.

"Why does this keep happening to us?" Louise hissed at me through her teeth.

I looked at Louise. "I don't know." I looked her straight in the eyes. "Get out of the car slowly and don't say anything. I'll handle this. We didn't do anything wrong." We both slowly stepped out of the car.

"Put your hands on the car," one of the cops shouted. "Sir, did the description say that the bank was robbed by women?" the cop asked the sheriff.

"Did you just say there was a bank robbery?" I looked at the cop.

Well, this is too ironic. Donald's in jail and I'm still getting arrested for bank jobs.

"Yes, there was a bank robbed up the street. The getaway car is a blue Datsun, just like yours," the sheriff informed me.

"Did the description of the car include Canadian plates?" Louise asked the cop behind her. I kicked Louise. She never knew when to be silent. These giants were armed and maybe they liked Canadian women, maybe they didn't. Pissing them off was just going to get us taken in.

"No…" the sheriff responded. I watched him sit back in his car and talk on his radio. The conversation seemed to go back and forth. It was a few minutes before the sheriff stood back up. "Let them go. Dispatch confirms the robbers were men and that they weren't driving a car with Canadian plates. My apologies." The sheriff moved towards us.

"An honest mistake, I'm sure," I said as I looked at the sheriff

Louise didn't say anything. She just kept looking at me and shaking her head.

"Have a nice trip." The sheriff tipped his hat to us. "Get in. The car was reported seen closer to Fort Stockton. Let's go!" The cops jumped in their car and sped off, lights and sirens going full force.

"That was weird." Louise sat back in the Datsun.

"I know," I responded.

"It's weird because that is not the first time I've been taken down with you for a robbery." Louise flipped down the car mirror and fixed her hair.

"I know. Only this time I had nothing to do with it." I signalled to the gas attendant, who had finally come out when the cops left. "Fill it up, please!"

CHAPTER 65

"Hey." Louise pointed to a Porsche behind us. The grey Porsche pulled up beside us. A young guy, our age, with shaggy blond hair, was behind the steering wheel. He revved his engine a little, raising his eyebrows at me suggestively. I knew what he was trying to say. This guy wanted a race. I smiled at him and pointed my fingers. "Let's race!"

"Really, Victoria?" Louise laughed.

"Why not? He's kind of cute, I think." I sped up as fast as I could. The guy let me get ahead of him. He followed close for a few minutes, then sped ahead of me. I sped up, and he let me pass again, laughing. We went back and forth for another ten minutes. Louise and I would laugh and wave when we passed him. He honked when he passed us. I could tell he was impressed. Just before we hit the outskirts of San Antonio, he signalled for us to pull over at a restaurant.

"That's some fancy driving for a Canadian!" The driver stepped out of his Porsche.

"Why, thank you." I smiled.

"Why don't you ladies let me buy you some dinner?" The driver was lanky and kind of skinny for my taste.

We paused.

"The restaurant here has the best rib-eye steak in the city," Blondie encouraged.

"Why not." Louise walked up to him. "I'm Louise." She pointed at me. "This is Victoria, and you are...?"

"Lyle. So, what brings you this far south?"

"Seeing the sights on our way home." Louise smiled.

"Where is home?" Lyle pulled out each of our chairs at the table.

"Montreal," I responded.

"That is an awfully long drive from BC," Lyle drawled.

"You know your Canadian geography." Louise giggled.

"I'm in computers. Our company is expanding into Canada right now."

"What kind of computers? I'm in school for IT training." Louise leaned forward, beaming at Lyle.

What followed was a conversation I only half understood. When the waiter brought our food, there was a pause in their techno babble. They started up again before dessert came.

Lyle paid for our meal with a crisp $100 bill. We followed him to a hotel. Lyle opened his trunk to grab another $100 bill. He then booked two rooms. One for me and one for them.

The hotel room was nicer than the ones we had been staying at lately. It had a big bed. Donald would have fit perfectly in it next to me. But Donald was back in Montreal, at Parthenais; I was here in Texas on vacation. *I should be having the time of my life.* Regan had helped me forget when I was in his arms. Seeing Louise and Lyle together stung. Lyle was Louise's type: sophisticated, worldly, well connected and well off. Life with him would mean nice hotel rooms and fancy meals. That didn't mean anything to me now. I would be happier in a tent on the side of the road with Donald. I didn't know how long Donald would be inside, but at least living in Montreal I could start visiting him again. I had to admit I missed him a lot.

I poured myself another drink from my tequila bottle, emptying it into the flimsy hotel plastic cup. I threw the bottle across the room. The bottle didn't shatter, just fell to the floor limply, spinning on its side. A surge of anger swept through me. *The damn thing didn't break.*

Lyle and Louise drove in his Porsche to the Alamo. I followed in my Datsun. The terracotta walls of the Alamo cooled the air.

"That's interesting," Lyle remarked, peering through the glass display case. I couldn't fake being interested. Spending a lonely night in a hotel room sucked. Watching Lyle and Louise twitter and smile highlighted what a third wheel I was.

Lyle pulled out a fresh $100 bill to pay for lunch. He was heading north, and we were still heading east. He gave Louise his business card with his home phone number on the back and they said their goodbyes.

CHAPTER 66

We drove through to Fort Lauderdale. Florida was a much different place. People there were rich, beautiful and didn't care who knew. California was filled with hippies and people trying to get famous. Fort Lauderdale was pools, beaches, bars and sex. Like most tourist towns it was too expensive to find a room to rent downtown. Like San Francisco, Louise and I planned to stay a while. We were able to find a place but it was in a tacky part of town, far from the beach.

"This place is it!" Louise grabbed a seat at the bar, turning to look at all the people partying in the Ocean Mist Bar.

"What can I get you ladies?" the bartender asked.

"Two vodkas and orange please," I replied.

"A screwdriver, I like your style." Two tall boys came over to flirt with us, ordering us another round of drinks as soon as the bartender brought us our first.

"The service here is horrible," Joseph, one of the two complained.

"We got drinks at the bar no problem." I smiled.

"Of course you did," George, the other one said. The guys didn't have anything interesting to say, but they were sexy to look at. The drinks they bought us went a long way.

"Attention! If anyone knows how to waitress, we are in desperate need, so please come to the front. Again, if you know how to waitress, please come to the front."

"We know how to waitress," Louise and I said at the same time. "Sorry, boys!" I jumped up.

"Thank you for the drinks," Louise added.

"Make sure you bring me another scotch." Joseph grabbed my hand.

"Of course! See you soon."

"Please tell me you two know how to waitress." A man in a casual suit stared at us.

"Okay, we know how to waitress." I smirked back.

"A sense of humour…" The man shook his head. "What are your names, ladies?"

"Victoria."

"Louise."

"Great, I'm Ross. Let's see what you girls can do. Annie!" He snagged a passing brunette. "Take these two to the back and show them what's what."

"Of course, Ross." She smiled sweetly. "Come along."

Just like that, we became waitresses at the Ocean Mist Bar. The tips were excellent that first day. We needed bank accounts, so we picked a random eight digits, the same amount of digits in an American social security number. After you had the number, you only needed a cheque and a smile to open a bank account.

CHAPTER 67

My conscious mind focused on the sunlight, warm air, and body heat all around me. Everyone was happy. I was happy and having a good time with them. But nothing ever melted the cold core of my heart. I tried not to think of Donald in Fort Lauderdale, so I didn't connect my subconscious misery with his being gone. Misery that got worse when I didn't have a distraction. Misery that came out even stronger when I drank. My surface reflected my setting. The different sides of my mind ground against each other. They rubbed my insides raw.

Money was easy to come by in Fort Lauderdale, selling booze or sex. We made our money waitressing in a bar but panhandlers, street kids, hitchhikers and hustlers from around the country made their way there to make money in less straight ways. Drugs were everywhere. By 1978, the Fort Lauderdale gay scene was in full swing. Down the road on the next corner was a tea house that was the centre of Fort Lauderdale's gay scene. Louise and I would often drop in there on our way to work at the Ocean Mist.

The Ocean Mist was the bar for everyone, locals, and tourists. They all came to drink and swim. Our days revolved around the bar and the tea house. Louise and I would work all night, then go home to sleep. When we woke up in the afternoon, we headed to the tea house to hang out with the boys, before we went back to work at the Ocean Mist.

"Hello, ladies." A tall blond boy walked over. He had shaggy hair, light blue eyes and dimples.

"Hello," I responded.

"Oh, accents. Where are you two from?"

"Montreal," Louise and I said in unison.

"Exotic. I'm Pete."

"Louise."

"Victoria."

"Pleased to make your acquaintance." Pete sat down on a deck chair beside me. Louise and I had gotten to work early so we could work on our tan.

"Hey, Pete!" a few of the gay tea house boys shouted and waved.

"Friends?" I asked.

"No." Pete waved back. "Coworkers."

"You work at the gay tea house?" Louise leaned forward. "Do you dance there?"

"I do every afternoon." Pete had a grace about him. I could see him performing alongside the other gay tea house boys. This wasn't just some cheap strip show they put on. The boys really knew how to dance; they wore kimonos and everything. Patrons of the bar would watch while they sipped their tea, deciding which boy they wanted to spend the next hour with privately.

"You must really know how to shake it," I teased Pete. "You guys are very popular."

Pete blushed a little and grinned.

Around 4:00 p.m. Pete went off to work and we got ready to start our shift. The three of us joined back up after we had all finished our work. Pete introduced the rest of the dancers to us.

Sunrise would be soon. "Hey, guys, I was wondering if I could stay with you for a couple of days. The place I was supposed to stay at fell through," Pete said. It was time for us to stop drinking and go home. Louise looked at me.

I nodded. "You can stay as long as you like if you split the rent with us."

That night and for many after, Pete stayed with us. We unofficially adopted him. He slept in our apartment and shared meals with us. We worked the same hours, meeting after work to drink before heading home. Pete did well for himself. He looked young, sometimes very young. Yet he handled himself and hustled better than anyone else I saw on the street. Louise and I made a game out of speculating what Pete's true age might be. We teased him night in and out. He only smiled.

"Vic, I think you've had enough." Louise took the glass away from me.

"Screw you." I grabbed the glass back. Pete caught my elbow so I didn't land on my ass.

"Okay, Victoria. Finish your drink and let's go home soon," Pete said softly to me.

"Fine!" I shoved Pete away. My whole body itched. It was too warm that night. I was sweaty, and sand stuck to my feet and legs. "Just leave me alone. Walk back to the apartment if you want." I glared at them.

"No, we'll wait for you, Victoria." Pete was watching me.

"I don't know why you have to get like this, Vic." Louise sucked her teeth.

"Like what, Louise?"

"You're unbearable when you're like this."

"Like what, Louise?" I repeated.

"This!" She gestured at me. "Drunk and miserable."

"Oh Jesus, Louise. Like you're any better."

"Whatever." Louise stormed off. Pete kept silent. He knew how to handle me when I drank. I knew I was being a bitch, but I really didn't care. I drank more to feel better but only ever ended up passing out.

In the morning, Louise and I made up. We always did after a fight. By breakfast we were best friends again.

March in Fort Lauderdale was crazy. Spring break meant tons of drunken coeds sweeping into town. The Ocean Mist kept Louise and me so busy we went straight home after work. I didn't notice if Pete came or went. He was mostly out, making the most of the money to be made.

"Enough wondering, I want to know how old he is." Louise was suspicious of Pete. Seeing him among all the spring breakers he had looked even younger.

I shook my head. "Okay." I finally relented. Louise fished Pete's wallet out of his pants. The shower had just turned on; Pete wouldn't be out for a bit.

Inside, we found his birth certificate. He didn't even have a driver's license.

"He's fifteen! It says he's fifteen and from Georgia."

"Put it back!" I threw Pete's pants at her.

"You're fifteen?" Louise asked Pete as soon as he left the bathroom. "What's it to you?"

"I saw your birth certificate. It says you were born in 1963 that makes you fifteen."

"How did you see my birth certificate, Louise?" Pete began gathering up his clothes. "Did you go through my stuff?"

Louise didn't say anything.

"Who the hell do you two think you are? You can't go through a person's stuff." Pete began breathing heavily. I had never seen him mad before.

"I'm sorry, Pete. We didn't mean to upset you." I took a step forward.

"You went through my wallet, didn't you?"

"We didn't think you would get so mad." Louise followed Pete to the door.

"Well, you were wrong." He slammed the door, and from that day on he avoided us.

I drank after Pete left. He had been calm. Good at handling bad-tempered drunks. I'm sure it was a skill he often used at work. Louise and I fought almost constantly. Three months of living together was taking a toll on us.

Late one night at the beginning of April, I was mad at Louise for something. I fumed through our shift and all the way back to the car. Louise was giving me the silent treatment, making me angrier.

"You know what?" I slammed my door and turned the car on. "I'm going to run all the stop signs tonight."

Louise's face paled a little. "Please don't," she said quietly.

"I'm going to do it!"

Louise didn't say anything after that. I remember getting out of the car even more furious. I don't remember the drive home. I didn't kill us or crash, but I know we had at least one close call.

"What the hell is wrong with you?" Louise opened the apartment door.

"Nothing is wrong with me." My head was buzzing. I could feel myself trying to let out the pressure with angry outbursts. "You're the one who is all Miss 'Look at me and my long blond hair.'"

"What does my hair have to do with you trying to kill us tonight?"

"I did not try to kill us. We are here, safe and sound," I shot back.

"You know what, Victoria?"

"No, Louise, but I'm sure you are going to tell me."

"You're jealous of me." Louise narrowed her gaze.

My eyes went wide. I shoved past her into the bedroom. I grabbed her suitcase and pulled out Lyle's card.

"What are you doing, Victoria? Stop!" Louise followed me into the bathroom.

I tore the paper up over and over again, then I flushed the sweaty paper stuck to my fingers down the toilet. "There. Now you'll never get a hold of him."

"Screw you, Victoria. I'm done. I'm done with you and your bullshit. I'm going home."

"Good riddance!" I yelled back at her. She locked me out of the bedroom and packed her stuff. In the morning, she called a cab and caught a bus back to Montreal.

I stayed another month but even I became sick of myself. I loaded up the Datsun and headed home.

CHAPTER 68

Driving back to Montreal alone had given me a lot to think about. What was I leaving? What was I going back to? Our few months on the road had been a good way to kill time. At some point, I was able to forget about the nagging loneliness that lay on the surface of my subconscious. I knew Donald was in Montreal, and I knew I would see him, but I didn't know when. My move out west was supposed to mean something, change things. But nothing had changed. I didn't feel any better in Vancouver, Paul was not Donald, and no one could really replace him. I had lost interest quickly and my cold nature had sent Paul on his way. Now I was heading back with only a suntan and a few good stories.

I didn't worry about Louise. We had been fighting and making up for years. In numerology we are a 33/6 pair. It means that we have had many past lives together. Oddly enough, it was the same combination my parents shared. I watched them fight and make up my whole life. I knew we would find our way back to being friends again soon enough. I also figured the only bearable straight job I could get was to be a courier. I called Louise before I got back to Montreal and, just as I thought, we revived our friendship and I ended up staying with her for the next two weeks before getting my own place. I went straight for the Help Wanted ads.

"Magenta courier," a man answered the phone.

"Hello, my name is Victoria. I'm calling about your ad in the paper. Is the position still available?"

"Yes, but…"

"Great!" I cut the man off. "I've been working as a courier for the past year."

"Really?" the man asked me.

"Yes, I worked for Data courier here in Montreal and The Pink Ladies in Vancouver."

"And you enjoy the work?" the man questioned.

"Well, I know Montreal like the back of my hand and I love to drive," I said with genuine enthusiasm.

"Okay, well, Victoria, let's set up a time for an interview."

I arrived at Magenta Courier at 10:00 a.m. on the dot. I walked through the door and sat down to wait. A man had followed me in. He glanced at me and did a double-take. Then he looked at me again. I watched him shake his head and walk quickly into the back.

A few moments later, another man arrived; he looked at me, looked around and then practically ran into the back room. The first one could have been a random weirdo, but a second guy doing this was strange.

A third and fourth man did the same thing. They looked at me, and then ran into the back. I was beginning to wonder if they had ever seen a woman before.

"Victoria, I'm Frank. I'm ready for your interview; please follow me to my office."

I followed Frank into his office. Everything reminded me of Data. I had a good feeling about this. "Thank you for taking the time to see me. I'm really excited about the job."

"You said that you've worked courier in the past?" Frank was looking at me thoughtfully.

"Yes, as I said on the phone, I worked for Data Courier here and then at Pink Ladies in Vancouver."

"Your move out west didn't stick?" Frank queried.

"No, not at all. I'm meant to live in Montreal. I grew up in Montreal." I leaned back in my chair.

"You said that you love to drive. Do you know the city well?"

"Yes," I replied.

Frank nodded his head. "You know, Victoria, when you got here, each of my guys ran back here to tell me there was a woman out front. I've never seen my drivers so excited. I came out here thinking I wasn't going to hire you on account of you're a woman, but we really need drivers and you have too much experience not to hire you. And your personality makes me think you will be a good fit. Can you start on Monday?"

"Of course!" I shook Frank's hand.

I guess Joe at Data Courier must have been a more progressive guy, because I had been the only female courier there until I got Theresa hired and no one ever said anything about it. Good thing Magenta was in such desperate need for drivers.

On my way out the door, I saw one more driver walk in. I looked him directly in the eyes and smiled. He jumped a little and nodded his head at me, then retreated into the back.

CHAPTER 69

"Hey, Donald." I picked up the telephone as he sat down on the other side of the glass.

"Hey, Vic." He reached his hand out to cover the glass.

"I was worried you wouldn't come back again." He laughed.

"What do you mean? I was here last week."

"I know. But you've been so all over the place lately. Running away to the west coast with a married man," he teased. "Then you were making your way through the states sightseeing. I figured you would be off on your way back down to Mexico or something."

We both laughed, half seriously. "I've been all over the place these last few months, but I need to settle for a while. No more killer German shepherds for me. At least not for a long while. Besides, I have a new job working courier."

"Congratulations! I know you really like that kind of job." Donald's face lit up.

"'Like' is a strong word, Donald, but it's nice to be driving again. I was sick of working as a waitress."

"Too many women…" he mused. Donald looked at me. "Are you happy to be working with just men again?"

I blushed. "I'm just happy to be driving. It's nice to work in my own car, alone."

"Mm-hmm." Donald sank back into his chair.

Our conversations were starting to become minefields. We both agreed that I was justified in running off after our last fight. We both acknowledged that we loved each other and wanted to be together. But the sentence Donald was expecting would be twelve years. His trial was over and he had been found guilty. Since the teller had never seen or met him, it was interesting how she pointed him out in court when asked to do so. When I asked Donald how that was possible, he replied, "She just said what the cops told her to say and the jury believed her." He then added, "My sentencing date is June 29th. Most likely I will get the twelve years The Crown is asking for. Either way I'll be glad to get out of Parthenais, that's for sure."

Neither of us knew where to start the conversation we really needed to have. So, we put it off.

I went into work the next Monday to have a new CB radio installed in my Datsun. They gave me the number twenty-six.

All the drivers were nice to me. At least they didn't whisper about me in front of me. It didn't take me long to win them over. Magenta was a big operation and there were two crews of drivers. I fell into the one with Robert. Robert had been Driver 26 before me. He had taken some vacation time and wasn't back by the time I started. I don't know exactly what he did to make Frank mad, but Frank thought he would punish Robert by giving his number to a girl. Robert was pissed but took it like a man. He was now number four. It turned out to be the beginning of one of my best friendships.

Debbie was back in my life. However, I was shocked by her change in lifestyle. I knew she was emotionally messed up when it came to men. She was a lot like me in how emotional she was, but when she turned twenty, she became even worse. I don't know if it was the accident or loneliness that prompted the change in her, but I could relate to the latter. While I had been travelling in the US with Louise, she had taken up with some friends of hers on the Main: the prostitute's home of choice. She had also sued for the accident. I don't recall how, as it had been a stolen car, but I know she had a lawyer and ended up getting some compensation. While waiting for her money, someone talked her into hooking. I was appalled. I asked her how it came about. She told me, "Vic, every day this same guy would offer me forty dollars for a roll in the hay."

"Are you kidding me, Debbie?" I said wide-eyed.

"No, Vic, and one day I just said 'What the heck?' and went across the street to the rooming house everyone used. I told him no blow job and no kissing. He lay on top of me and entered me. He came within thirty seconds and paid me. Vic, it was the easiest money I ever made."

"Still, Debbie…" I said back to her. "Now you've followed in your mother's footsteps, just like you said you'd never do."

"I know," she said, "but it's just until my money comes in."

Luckily, her money came in that week and we both rented apartments right next door to each other in a gorgeous newly built building on Gouin Boulevard in

Pierrefonds. She met a married man named David who promptly left his wife and helped her spend the $25,000 she received.

"Are you crazy, Deb? You bought him a Harley Davidson! How much was it?" I asked shocked.

"Five thousand dollars," she replied sheepishly.

"You nut bar," I said.

"I know, I bought it off our friend George and paid by cheque 'cause, truly Vic, I could never take five thousand cash and part with it."

"Well, it's your money, Debbie, but remember, if you spend it all, I don't want to see you go back to selling your body."

"I won't," she promised.

I worked at Magenta daily and spent a lot of time on the weekends with Debbie. My older son Emmett had come for a summer visit so a lot of our time was spent around the outdoor swimming pool at our apartment complex.

Debbie was getting more and more agitated with David. They came back from a three-week vacation in Newfoundland, and I found out she had spent far too much money and was nearing the end of her cash. I warned her again. One night she got far too drunk and stoned and destroyed her apartment from floor to ceiling. She was evicted the next day.

On August 23, 1978, Debbie found out that not only was she stone broke, but David had taken his bike and returned to his wife. She went down to the Pointe and found him. She begged him to return. According to rumours, as I did not witness this, he laughed in her face and kicked her. Knowing Debbie, I have no doubt they got into a physical altercation. Later that day, she bought a gun, put it to her head and pulled the trigger.

I called her mother the next day and asked, "Have you seen Debbie?"

To which her mother replied, "Debbie is dead. She shot herself last night."

Stunned by the news, I could barely believe what her mother said next: "Do you know where she kept her bank accounts?"

Holy, I thought. I told her mother in no uncertain terms that Debbie had no money left and hung up. I called Carol right away, who was just as stunned as I was, and I left her to break the news to everyone else who knew Debbie.

Danny flew in from out west for her funeral. I was way too pissed at her to attend so I took my son and drove to Florida and went to Disney World. All I can say to this day is, "Why, Debbie? Why?"

CHAPTER 70

After Debbie committed suicide and I returned from Florida with Emmett, I put my son on a plane and sent him home. School was about to start for him. I went to visit Donald, who had, by now, heard the news.

"Why, Vic? Why do you think she did that?" Donald asked, his voice pained.

"Her emotions, Donald. I know exactly how she felt. She was rejected. She's been rejected all her life and this was just another stab in the back—from her mother to all her relationships, she's always felt rejected. Her jealousy was her insecurity, just like it is for me. But I have you—I found you and you made me feel whole. Even in one of her letters to me while I was in Tanguay, she wrote that she wished she had someone like you for herself."

"It's true, Vic. She even said that in one of her letters to me," Donald replied quietly.

"Yes, it takes a real man to handle emotions like hers and mine." I smiled at him with tears in my eyes. He said nothing but his eyes told me everything.

"Why didn't you go to her funeral?" he asked next.

"I couldn't, Donald," I told him. "I can't explain how I felt, how mad I was. My best friend just upped and left and said nothing to me." I understand it now, but then I didn't.

"I think if you ever left me, I would feel the same way. I can only hope that she's happier now."

He looked at me for a long time and finally said, "Vic, don't ever let your emotions get to you so badly that you copy her. I will never leave you. I may be in here, but I'll hold you up through any thoughts that would take you permanently away from me."

As I smiled back at him, I looked at the clock and saw that our time was up. "I'll be back next week," I said, and I kissed him goodbye.

CHAPTER 71

Life went on and in Montreal it grew more interesting as the seasons changed. Magenta Courier was split into two teams. It was more a personality thing than anything else. My Magenta boys would meet to go skiing and camping on the weekends. A lot of Fridays the crew didn't wait until 5:00 p.m. I didn't ski. None of them could explain to me why they enjoyed sliding down a hill on two pieces of wood. I sipped vodka and orange in the nice, warm lodge, instead.

"Two-forty-nine, 26," I said as I clicked on my CB.

"Go ahead 26," Joel our dispatcher radioed back.

"Joel, something is wrong with my car. I've just broken down. I'm going to get a tow and start again on Monday."

"Okay, 26," Joel responded. "See you Monday." Joel was our dispatcher; he lacked Paul's calm, but he was still experienced and a good dispatcher.

I clicked off the CB, my work done.

A few minutes later I heard Michael come over the radio. "Two-forty-nine, 16. I have a flat tire."

"What's your status, 16?"

"I'm going to work on the tire, but I might be done for the day."

"All right, Mike. Keep me posted." Joel was starting to get a little suspicious.

"Ten-four, over and out."

Brent was next. "Two-forty-nine, 19. I have a problem. It seems my engine is overheating,"

"Is that so?" Joel now knew we were pulling a fake-out so we could take off early and go somewhere. We were actually all going skiing.

"Yes, I'm pulling over on the side of the road waiting for the engine to cool down to take a look."

"Have a good weekend 19…"

"Two-forty-nine, 4. I'm going to go help 19." Robert cut dispatch off.

"Great. Good luck with that. See you all on Monday." Joel was pissed—you could tell by his voice. We would all pay for it next week by not being given much work. Those who didn't join us would be called first for pickups. He'd get over it, though. He always did. After all we were sub-contractors not employees. It kept work tolerable for me.

CHAPTER 72

I had my own place, but most of my time was spent with Louise. It turns out I was right. Theresa wasn't picking up the phone because she had started seeing David, another dispatcher at Data Courier. She had been staying over at his house and they had fallen madly in love. To this day, Dave and Theresa are happily married with two beautiful children.

"Victoria, this is Maria, my new roommate," Louise said when I dropped by her place one day. "She's Mario's sister. Manny introduced us."

"Nice to meet you, Victoria." Maria smiled at me.

"You too, Maria."

"Victoria is working at Magenta Courier," Louise said.

I nodded my head.

"You like the work, don't you, Vic?"

"I do, Louise. It's nice to just drive all day. You know I love to drive"

"Maria needs a job. I was wondering if you might be able to help her get a job with you. It worked out so well for Theresa at Data Courier."

We all laughed. "Sure, I'll talk to Frank. I think I've broken him in enough that he'll be cool with hiring female drivers from now on."

Maria gave me a quizzical look.

"Well, it's a funny story…" I said.

Turned out, Frank had no problem hiring another woman. Maria had her own car. She knew how to drive, and we were still in bad need of new drivers. Maria was like me; she got on with the guys in no time. She was friends with both cliques. The Jew Boys, as we called the other clique, were known for smoking a lot of hash. Maria and I began hanging out when the guys weren't around. We would go out to the bar with Louise or others and spend our off days shopping. Maria always seemed to have a little bit of extra money, and not just because she was living cheaply at Louise's.

"Hey, do you do something extra on the side?" I asked her one day. "You always seem to have a little extra money."

"Well, yeah, I deal a wee bit of hash," she replied.

"It doesn't seem that hard. I never see you doing any extra work."

Maria laughed. "It's not."

That settled it for me. Making an extra $100 to $150 a week seemed like a no-brainer to me. I often went to the Maiden Head, a bar in Alexis Neon Plaza, with Peggy and others I knew. There was already a hash dealer working in the Maiden Head. I decided since I knew so many of the people who came to the bar from the outside, the bar would be the perfect place to start dealing. Not wanting to be disrespectful, I approached the resident dealer.

"I just wanted to let you know that I'm going to start dealing hash here. I know it's your turf, so do what you have to do, but I'm going to be dealing here from now on as well."

Bob looked at me and laughed. "Chill out. I don't care if you deal here. Good luck."

I didn't need luck. I have a mind built for crime. It had come naturally with Donald and his robberies; drug dealing was just as easy. Quickly, I realized the secret to successful dealing is quality product. I shopped around until I found a supplier who almost always had good stuff. I didn't go looking for people who already had a dealer. I waited for word to get around about the quality of my hash, then people would come to me. Most of them would never leave. They kept coming back for the product and my prompt customer service.

I grew to earn more than an extra $100 a weekly quickly. It was nice to have the extra cash to buy new clothes or pay for a round at the bar.

Things progressed quickly in the spring of 1979. Louise met a fellow named Bob and moved to Toronto with him where he lived and worked. Theresa was basically living at Dave's house, so they made it official. That left Maria in need of a place to stay. I was ready to leave my apartment, so we rented a duplex in LaSalle together.

CHAPTER 73

"You look really happy, Victoria!" Donald was waiting for me in the visiting room already.

Donald was now at Archambault, a maximum-security prison north of Montreal. We had contact visits and, for this, I was thankful.

"Thanks, Donald, I am. My move into my new duplex with Maria went smoothly." I settled myself into a chair.

"I got a letter from Roman. He has some plan to get out. He brought up the Shawbridge Youth Detention Centre." Donald's eyes seemed to go unfocused as he remembered that time in his life.

"Right, that's how you two met. You were both sentenced together."

"We escaped in 1968 in the middle of spring. We were running down a road trying to hitch a ride and this older women stopped."

I made a face. "You guys were thirteen and sixteen. She took you home with her and made you both men."

"She sure did, Vic. She even taught me a few of the things you like so much." Donald winked at me.

"Interesting how it is so much better when boys are raped," I commented. Donald gave me an amused look and continued on talking.

"How's the side business going?" Donald raised his eyebrows at me.

"Business is good," I told him.

I seemed to have two lives now. One with Donald during visits and one where I created my own. His was a series of repetition and mine was a series of waking up and wondering what life was all about.

Life changed with Maria once we lived together. We still worked together so I saw her at work all the time like always. But now she didn't want to go shopping with me and rarely went to the bar at the end of the day. In the months before, we had spent most of our free time together. It didn't make any sense, so I asked her about it.

"I can't be seen with you as much now that we live together. I don't want people to think we're a couple."

Are you kidding me? I thought. I was the most boy-crazy girl that anyone knew. I always had a boyfriend. The thought that people might think we were a couple never occurred to me. I don't know why it occurred to her.

Our relationship changed after that. I focused more of my efforts on my side dealings and Jonnie. I met Jonnie like I met every other guy—by chance. He had seen me, liked what he saw, and came over to talk to me. We had a lot in common. Jonnie lived in the same neighbourhood as me. He also had the same side job. He was a decent lay, but that's about all he was good for. Most of our nights began in my bed. He would undress me, taking his time. I like men who take their time kissing, the ones who are thorough lovers.

A few hours would go by. Then Jonnie would get up to take care of his night-time clients. I would roll over and go to sleep then to work the next morning.

Just like I met Jonnie by chance, I met Irene by chance. She was also my neighbour. She didn't have a job in common with me, but we did have a boy in common. She lived with Jonnie on the other side of our laneway. Irene and I also shared a similar sense of humour.

Jonnie had told me he lived with his mother, and that was why we could never go to his house. I believed him. I honestly didn't think too much about it. That's why I was more amused than mad when I found out he had a girlfriend.

Irene decided on the best way to let Jonnie know that we knew. She told him that weekend a special guest was coming. Irene planned an extra special meal. Jonnie spent all of Saturday cleaning up the house and getting ready for their extra special guest. Irene called me throughout the day and we giggled about the coming evening. I walked through the door at 6:15 p.m. sharp. Oh, the look on Jonnie's face when I walked through the door! He went white, then he looked from Irene to me and then back at her. Jonnie's face then went red and he didn't say a word. He ran into their bedroom and slammed the door. Irene and I both burst out laughing. Supper was superb.

They didn't break up, but I think Jonnie had learned his lesson. A few weeks after the special dinner, Jonnie had his stash stolen. I'm sure he blamed me. It was definitely not me who took it, though. I was robbed a week later, and I suspected him right back.

I kept my bedroom door locked from the outside with a padlock. It was nothing personal, but I was a business person. The flaw in my logic meant that when someone climbed through my bedroom window, they could only get into my room. They stole my hash, scale and my camera, then trashed my room, leaving behind broken glass and muddy footprints. Maria and our other roommate Steve, who had moved into the third bedroom to lighten the rent, didn't know anything was wrong until I came home. That was it. I knew Maria and Steve had nothing to do with my being robbed. But I needed to live on my own again.

CHAPTER 74

"You're moving again?" Donald raised his eyebrows at me while he sat on the other side of the table in the visiting room.

"You've read my letter."

"Yeah, that's terrible about your place being robbed."

"The new place in Ville-Émard is nice. I like being on my own." I smiled at him. "It's the next best thing to living with you." I took Donald's hand in mine. "It's on the ground floor. The front room has a large window looking onto the street. It's a lot like our Evelyn Street layout. The kitchen goes out into a small yard and into the back lane. It was a good deal for rent, and I have plenty of privacy."

"I can't wait to see it, Victoria." Donald squeezed my hand.

He thinks he's going to get out any day now. Yeah, he might see it... if I'm still living there in a decade!

My life took on a kind of routine. In the mornings I drove to work, went home for dinner, and then out to the bars to deal. The more I dealt, the more I came back in touch with friends from my past—the ones I had hung around with, or met before Donald. We all got into trouble, falling away and reconnecting when someone got out of prison. Part of the reconnection process was helping a friend who needed to get back into the game.

Albert was one of these friends and dealers. He and I knew each other through my ex-husband. In fact, many of those I reconnected with were from introductions made during my marriage. When he got out of prison, we reconnected. He bought some hash off me and recommended me to a few friends. One day, he showed up at my door and asked me if I could do a deal for him. I agreed. He asked to use my phone. He called his client and handed me the phone. The guy asked me for a couple of different types of drugs

I, of course, replied, "I can get you anything you want."

"Great," he said and I handed the phone back to Albert. Based upon what happened next, I felt that I was set up with this call.

CHAPTER 75

"Good morning. May I speak to Victoria?" a woman's voice said on the other end of the phone, a few mornings later.

My intuition kicked in. "No, she's not here. She's at work." It was obviously a lie, but something didn't feel right.

"Do you know when she will be back?"

I thought for a second. "She should be home at 5:30." I knew I wouldn't be home at that time as I was working the night shift now.

We hung up. I felt strange; I couldn't put my finger on it. I went to the front door and drew back my front room curtains. They were green, just like the ones Donald had gotten me. I smiled every time I looked at them, drawing them open each day before I left. It was my last ritual before I closed the door.

That's weird, I thought when I returned from work around midnight. My curtains had been open when I left home. Now they were closed. I moved cautiously around my house. I didn't see any other vehicles. I waited a few minutes to see if anything moved. Then I checked to make sure there were no other lights on in my house. I approached the door carefully. A business card was stuck in my doorway. I took it and my heart skipped a beat. "Please call us," it said. Below was Detective Jerry's phone number. I felt better knowing it was cops. My first thought had been the robbers who trashed my last house.

"Oh my God!" I hopped back into my car. I drove to a payphone. I didn't know who else to call at this hour, so I called Maria.

"Hello?"

"Hey, Maria. It's Victoria."

"Hi, Victoria. What's up? It's rather late."

"The cops raided my place. They left me a note on the door. I don't know what to do. Can I spend the night at your place?"

"Sure, Vic,"

I drove over there. I didn't sleep that night. I was too freaked out.

"What am I going to do?" I asked Maria the next morning.

She didn't seem all that fazed. "What would they have found?" she asked.

Thinking about it, I answered, "They for sure found my scale. I doubt they would have bothered tearing apart the basement. So maybe seven grams of hash. The note said I should turn myself in. This is a nightmare." I rolled my eyes. "Maybe I should turn myself in?"

Maria thought for a moment. "I don't know what else you can do, Vic. If you turn yourself in, I can meet you after work and pay your bail. Seven grams of hash is such a small amount."

"Assuming I get bail…" I muttered. I picked up her phone and dialed the number from the note.

"Detective Jerry speaking," he answered on the third ring.

"Hello, Detective. This is Victoria calling you. You left a note on my door last night."

"Excellent, Victoria." He didn't miss a beat. "I've been waiting for your call."

Great. "I'm ready to turn myself in."

"Come to Montreal headquarters on Bonsecour. Do you know where that is?" he asked.

Do I ever, I thought. "Yes, I'm a courier, so I know the place," I replied.

"Good. I'll see you here tomorrow at 9:00 a.m."

I hung up the phone. "That's settled."

"You're turning yourself in?" Maria asked.

"Yup." I sighed.

"Cheer up. At least its pay day tomorrow!" Maria punched me in the arm.

Famous last words.

CHAPTER 76

I drove myself to the police station while Maria went to cash our paycheques. All day I had repressed the memory of the last time I turned myself into a police station expecting bail. *What a dumb kid I had been!* Thinking that if I just didn't tell my lawyer, no one would know about my past arrest.

"Next!" The sergeant at the desk checked me in. I gave him my name.

He filled out some paperwork and put me in the cells upstairs to wait. I didn't know what to expect. I was placed in an interrogation room, just like last time. Detective Jerry arrived and sat down. He asked me the usual questions, which I responded to with "I don't remember." Detective Jerry didn't waste a whole lot of time. After the third "I don't remember," he charged me with trafficking and brought me to the room that we waited in until it was time to pass court. A very familiar room, indeed.

A few hours later, a cop took me to an adjacent room. Maria had hired Sidney Leithman. He was already waiting inside. If I knew then what I know now about Mr. Leithman, I would have settled for a public defender.

"Hi, Victoria. I'm Sidney Leithman, Maria retained me on your behalf."

"Nice to meet you, Mr. Leithman."

"I've read the indictment and it looks like this is your first offence."

"It does?" I asked, cutting him off.

"That's the way it looks, Victoria." Sidney looked at me. "Is that correct, Victoria?"

I nodded my head.

"Good. They found the scale in your house. Unfortunately, it was dirty, so it was admitted into evidence. There is also the hash, but that's it. Play stupid, plead not guilty, and I will have you out of here in a few minutes."

"I can do that." I went back to the holding cell to wait. Buzzers were going off in my head. He had looked through my files and nothing had come up. The cops hadn't mentioned anything to my lawyer. I did the mental math. There was no gain to be had by saying anything. This was Quebec in the late '70s, so it was entirely possible for those files to have been misplaced, or even destroyed accidentally. Then it would have no bearing on this hearing. Even if they found out later, that would mean right now I would get out on bail. And worst case scenario, the cops had just forgotten to tell my lawyer and I could play dumb like last time.

"Docket number 776," the court clerk read out. "The Crown versus Victoria Gray. Possession with intent to traffic."

"How do you plead?" the judge asked me.

"Not guilty, Your Honour."

"The Crown on bail?" The judge looked at the other lawyer.

"We are allowing a signature bail," the Crown replied.

"Any objections?" The judge looked at my lawyer.

"No, Your Honour."

"Return to court for the preliminary in thirty days."

That was it. I signed myself out. It was over, and I was out. Maria used my paycheque to pay Sidney, so I was out but had no money.

It turns out something miraculous had happened. My previous criminal record had disappeared. It was never mentioned again. Even though they had taken my fingerprints, nothing showed up. It was a bloody miracle. I went before the judge thirty days later, pled guilty and was fined $1000. It should have been a slap on the wrist. But it ended up being more of a handcuff. I had to keep dealing in order to make the money to pay the fine. The lawyer Maria hired for me was one of the best. So he was ridiculously expensive.

"Hey, wow." Maria had followed me into the house.

There was stuff strewn all over the floor. It wasn't the worst post-raid mess I had seen. Nothing was broken. I had left my scale out in the open. The hash they found wasn't hard to find.

"Yeah, give me a moment." I opened the door and went into the basement. The basement was unfinished; wood, and random stuff was spread out from the staircase. It looked like the cops had barely been down there. I walked over to a pile of wood near the back wall. I moved aside some heavy beams. "It's still there!" A pound of hash peeked out at me. I gathered it up and went back upstairs.

"It looks like you got off light." Maria laughed. She had started to pick things up.

"Yeah, I would have a lot more than a fine." I tried to tidy up the room. But no matter what I put where, nothing fit anymore. "Come on, let's go for a drink." I grabbed my coat and keys.

"Hey!" Peggy waved us over to our regular table at the Maiden Head. The bar was busy today. People smoked one cigarette after the next, so the air was thick with smoke. They talked loudly; the men bragging about their latest conquest, and women about their latest date. We all gossiped, laughing and drinking. This was my home. A woman sang in the back, accompanied by a piano. The waitresses were all dressed as medieval wenches. One brought me my usual vodka and orange as soon as she saw me.

"Hey." I slipped in next to Peggy and Maria followed in behind me.

"How was your day?" Maria asked Peggy.

"Fine." Peggy took a sip of her drink. "Every kid starts to look the same by the end of the day."

I laughed. "Just make sure you stab the right kid when you collect their blood."

"Thanks for that." Peggy shoved me. "Where have you two been? I thought you would have been here a while ago."

My shoulders sagged.

"I had to pick Victoria up after her court hearing," Maria told Peggy.

Peggy looked at me.

"The cops busted my place the day before yesterday. They found my scale and some hash. I had to turn myself in. Maria got me a lawyer and stayed for my case." I signalled a waitress over and ordered another drink.

"That's a bummer."

"Yeah. I have to go back later and clean up my house."

"I don't know if I could stay there." Peggy looked at Maria. Maria didn't say anything.

"I really don't want to. A house is never the same after a raid," I groaned.

"Yeah." Maria handed me my fresh drink. "Hey, listen, maybe we should find a place again. My lease is almost up and I'm ready to blow the joint."

"That's not a bad idea." I took a sip of my drink. We all sat silently, enjoying the atmosphere.

Maria and I moved in together quickly after that. I couldn't stand being in my house in Ville-Émard anymore. A house was dead to me after it had been raided.

The whole place felt like it had been contaminated. I didn't want to tempt fate and stay in a place where the cops knew exactly how to find me.

CHAPTER 77

Donald sat facing me, smiling. His hair looked a little shaggy and his face unshaven. "I got your letter."

I smiled back at him.

"It sounded like you had a close call."

I nodded. "Yeah, it was just a fine. I'll have it paid off in no time," I assured him.

"I know you will. I heard from Dougie things are going as planned." Donald's whole face lit up when he talked about work. "We have a plan now, and I think I might need your help with something soon."

"Sure, Donald, anything."

"Thanks, I'll let you know soon." Donald looked deep into my eyes. "I'm going to set you up and make sure you're taken care of for life."

I nodded. I knew what Donald was talking about, but I didn't have a lot of interest. Roman was in jail now, too. He wrote me letters about all the things he was doing to get himself sent to a minimum-security prison. Roman had a plan. By getting sent to minimum security he could get himself into classes and jobs. The more you worked the system in minimum, the sooner you got out. Donald had never once said anything about how he planned to get out early.

"Have you heard from Roman?" I cut Donald off.

"Yeah, I got a few letters." Donald looked at me puzzled.

"Did he mention what he's been up to?" I pressed.

Donald looked harder at me. "Well, he mentioned he's applying for that program—the one for guys serving big bits. You sign a contract and are sent to the Federal Training Centre in Laval. You have to slave in the kitchen for eighteen months. According to Roman, his classification officer is ready to submit his papers."

"In his letters he sounds really excited," I added.

"I'm sure he is. The screws like the guys who sign up. It will be easy for him to get out from there." Donald sat back in his chair.

"Have you thought about joining?" I leaned forward, emphasising the word "you."

"No, Vic, it's not for me. I've got a lot of things going on right now. Like this job. I need to focus. Can you tell Dougie…"

I didn't push Donald further. There wasn't any point.

CHAPTER 78

Our duplex on Gervais Street was easy to settle into. I continued to work at Magenta, but now I had to step up my dealing. Out of every $100 I made, I stuffed ten dollars into the insulation of the fridge. Clifford, my long-time drug dealer, was starting to sing the praises of cocaine. He told me it was so easy to deal, it practically sold itself. I started to carry and sell a gram here and there. It just happened; it had to happen. I had to pay off that fine.

"Are you just getting in?" Maria was eating breakfast at the kitchen table.

"Yes. Nice of Frank to give me the night shifts still, eh? It's easy money. I mostly run parcels for IBM from St. Laurent to Place Ville Marie." I grabbed some orange juice on my way to the shower. "I had fourteen runs to Ville-Marie last night."

"It's the middle of the night. That seems like a terrible time to be making deliveries." Maria put her dishes in the sink.

"It's not that bad. No traffic, I can go fast, no chitter-chatter with clients I don't like. Plus, it pays more."

"Sure, Victoria, I just do not know how you do it." Maria headed out the door. "I'll see you at work."

"On my way as soon as I shower."

After my shower, I went back to Magenta. I worked until I was sleepy and then went home to my bed. I woke up in the late afternoon. I made my lunch/dinner, and headed over to the Maiden Head. Maria and Peggy would always be there waiting for me. We would drink and hang out until I was ready to work. At 6:00 p.m. I turned on my pager and waited for jobs to come in. Faxes had yet to be invented. I doubt people had even dared to dream of something like email. But, business was basically the same; you just needed more people when you had less technology. Big companies still needed to send documents and parcels in the middle of the night. I spent my nights running errands for IBM and other companies that didn't just work in the Eastern Time Zone.

I kept working in the morning because I still wasn't ready to go to bed. I needed to be exhausted. That way I could guarantee I would fall asleep the second my head hit the pillow. That kept me from having too much time to think about Donald before I fell asleep.

Without realizing it, I created my own trap. My life became an endless cycle of working, sleeping, hanging out, repeat. I avoided unwanted thoughts, but I also avoided being able to think about any other way of life.

"I am so bored." I walked around my house. It was Saturday, so I wasn't working.

"Okay." Paul, my co-worker, and friend, had dropped by to visit. Watching me from the couch as I paced, he asked, "What do you want to do?"

"Let's go out."

"Out where, Victoria?"

"I want to get a motorbike." I had toyed with the idea of getting a bike for the last few weeks.

"Do you even know how to drive a bike?" Maria said from the kitchen.

"No, but I'll learn."

"I'm sure you will." Maria walked to the door to see us out.

"Yes, I will, Maria."

Paul laughed at me, but he didn't comment.

It wasn't hard for the salesman to help me find a bike. I wanted one and I wasn't leaving without one. "This is a nice bike." He pointed to a Kawasaki 250 LTD "It's fast but light, easy to hold up. Here are your gears." The salesman showed me. "One down, four up. Here's the brake, the clutch and gas."

"I'll take it," I told him.

Paul drove the bike home for me. I had already bought the perfect outfit. A black leather jacket with fringes and all. I practised riding my bike enough over the next few weeks to feel confident. That Friday night, I dressed up and took the bike out for a spin. Everyone was looking at me. In those days not many girls rode bikes. People stared long and hard.

CHAPTER 79

Looking back, I think of myself as an idiot. Mostly because it never occurred to me to be afraid.

It was now December 1979. "Hey, Vic, are you all ready for the pickup?" Donald asked me at our next visit.

"Yes." I looked at him. "It'll be done tomorrow. Don't worry about it."

I knew enough of what he needed done and I didn't need to know more. The next day I drove to an address. A nondescript house in a nondescript part of town. When I got there, a man put several sticks of dynamite in the trunk of my car. I never touched it, but I did see it was leaking. Next, I drove the dynamite to an equally unremarkable house. A different guy took the dynamite out of my trunk. I don't know where the dynamite went after that. I do know it ended up in Archambault. Some guard brought it in as he had been instructed. The dynamite was hidden somewhere in the prison. Most guards would do anything for a decent amount of cash. From what I hear, this is still the case—not with all guards, but some. Inmates seem to know how to find them. Maybe it's the guards that find the inmates. Donald knew where the dynamite was stashed. The plan was for Donald to leverage his knowledge of the dynamite to get sent to Cowansville. Cowansville is a medium-security prison, which meant it would be much easier to escape from.

The warden was not impressed by Donald's stunt. He sent Donald to Cowansville on December 20, 1979. What else could he do? A bomb threat is a bomb threat. My suspicion is that when Donald was planning the operation, or after it was complete, he confided in other people. The wrong person heard and cut their own deal. On January 16, 1980, Donald was put in segregation. Another word for the "hole." The first chance the warden had, he found an excuse to write Donald up. The warden accused him of standing too close to the fence. He was shipped back from the hole in Cowansville on February 7, 1980, to Archambault. Here, life, according to the reports made against him, was very bad. I believe that false reports were made so there was an excuse for the next series of decisions. Donald was taken back and placed in segregation at the Laval institution on August 14, 1980. His case was presented for a transfer to the special handling unit, or SHU. He was kept in the hole until February 16, 1981, and then transferred to the SHU the worst place in the entire Quebec prison system. He remained there until July 1982.

I was allowed very few visits while he was in the SHU. I can tell you this: rats came up in the toilets and he had to feed them some of his sandwich to keep them away. The guards, if you wish to call them that, peed in the sandwiches. The bars above the cells were walked up and down by the screws, as they dragged their batons along metal. Donald was allowed in the yard one hour a day. The other twenty-three hours, he was locked up with no windows and no contact with anyone. If you add up the time he spent in the hole at Laval and the time he spent in the SHU directly afterwards, he was in segregation for a total of twenty-three months. I have a letter in which he wrote about suicide. I could only hope, at the time, that he followed the advice he gave me when Debbie died.

Life had to go on even with Donald being isolated in the SHU. It was a bitter pill to swallow. *If he would just stop… If he would just put his energy into trying to get out early, instead of trying to escape!*

CHAPTER 80

One Monday morning, a few months later, I was on my way to work. All the guys were on the CB twittering to each other

"Did you hear about Mike?" they all asked each other. They were all talking fast, and I only caught snippets of their conversation. Something about cars. When I got to work, Mike wasn't there. Bill told me why.

"Did you hear about Mike's car?" he asked me.

"No. His Pinto?"

"No, his Chevy Vega." Bill emphasized the last two words.

"My God, no! His race car, the one that he's been working on forever?" I gasped. Bill let that sink in. "Go on. What happened?"

"Well, he picked it up from the garage on Saturday. It was all ready to go. He parked it on the street in front of his duplex—"

"No!" I cut Bill off.

"Yes. He woke up in the morning and it was totalled. Someone crashed into it in the night and took off." Bill's mouth twisted in a half-cocked smile. "That's some bad luck."

"I'll say. I really wanted to drive that car!"

Bill's eyes looked over my head. "Hey, Mike. How are you doing, buddy?"

I turned around. Mike did not look good. His eyes were bloodshot and his mouth looked mean. He mumbled something that sounded an awful lot like "Fuck off."

I gave him my best shining smile. It had no effect.

"I just want this day to be over." Mike tossed his boxes and envelopes into their pile. He grabbed the next stack to be delivered. Then he left, slamming the door. I felt for the guy. It was a nice car. He had spent so much time, money, and energy on it. Mike planned to race with that car. He was the best driver I knew. He was even better than I was.

It took Mike a few weeks to cool off. He started consoling himself at Maria's and my house, complaining endlessly about city life.

"I can't live like this!" Mike finished his beer. "I feel like I'm trapped, trapped like a rat in a cage."

"I hear you, Mike." My feelings on straight life and straight jobs hadn't changed.

"There's no space in this city. Everyone lives right on top of one another. I'm sick of neighbours. All this bullshit can just—"

"So, what are you going to do?" Maria grabbed a beer for herself and another one for Mike.

"I'm thinking about hitting the open road. Trucking. That way I can be gone weeks at a time. Spend my days just driving, seeing the country."

"That does sounds nice, eh, Maria?"

"Yeah, Victoria. No neighbours would be nice. Did I tell you the landlord sold the place and is moving out? I'm not excited. Our walls are paper thin." Maria took another swig of her beer.

"See?" Mike gestured with his hands. "This is what I'm talking about. I don't want to hear my neighbours doing it upstairs. I don't want to hear anything. I'm sick of the noise, the lights, all of it."

He had a point. Truck driving was appealing. What was more freeing than the open road? I could just go and come back when I felt like it.

"I was thinking I might use my insurance money to put a down payment on a semi." Mike looked at me. "I only have enough for half the down payment. I was wondering if you wanted to come in with me. We could be partners. Take turns driving, get there twice as fast. At least think about it, Victoria. I know you're unhappy here, too."

"I'll think about it, Mike. I'll think hard on it."

Really, it was a no-brainer. Nothing was keeping me here. The kids weren't here, Debbie was gone. I didn't care if I saw my friends every day, and I still didn't know when I would see Donald. If I hit the road, when I was home I could do whatever I wanted. I wouldn't have to work. Plus, Frank would take me back no problem. I was good at my job; people always took me back. I called Mike the next morning. We arranged for my half of the down payment.

"You won't regret this, Vic. I know this is going to be great," Mike said from the other side of the phone.

"I'm sure it will be," I told him.

Mike had called me to tell me the time of our appointment to finalize the semi sale.

There was a knock at my door. "I have to go, Mike. There's someone at the door."

"Okay."

I went to the door, and my landlord was on the other side. He was flanked by a couple. They were short, square, and dark-skinned. Indian maybe, definitely immigrant. "Is Maria here, too?" our landlord asked.

"Yeah, let me get her." I opened the door to let them in.

They stood in the living room, talking about the house. I heard the landlord say, "These have been great tenants. We have always gotten along."

"Maria!" I banged on her door. "The landlord is out here."

Maria opened the door. "Why?"

"The new owners are here to look at the house and meet us."

Maria shook her head and we went into the living room together. They had migrated to the kitchen. The new owners were poking around the cupboards, looking at the floor, behind the fridge.

"Maria and Victoria, this is Mr. Singh and Mrs. Singh, the new owners."

"Nice to meet you." I extended my hand. We talked for a few more moments and then they left.

"This is going to be... interesting," Maria commented before she headed back into her room.

The new landlords moved in without a whole bunch of fuss. They seemed like the kind of people who kept to their schedule. They ate at a certain time, left for shopping at a certain time and had sex at a certain time. I tried not to be home during that time of the day. I don't know what was worse, the sound of four thrusts or that it was only four thrusts. *Poor woman.* I had a hard time looking either of them in the eye without thinking about their Thursday afternoon appointment...

Before long, Maria and I began to notice something was off with the landlords. They didn't really talk to us, or acknowledge our presence, except when it was time for the rent. They always seemed to be looking in on things in our lower part of the duplex. I tried to tell myself I was being paranoid, but I wasn't. I came home early one day, and the garage door was open.

"Maria... come in, Maria," I said into my CB.

"Maria here. What is it?"

"Did you leave the garage door open when you left?"

There was silence for a second. "I don't think so," she responded.

"Okay, well, the door is open. I'm going inside."

"Okay, Victoria. Let me know what's up."

"Will do, over and out." I hung up the radio, closed the car door and took a breath. I don't know what I expected to find. I walked quietly through the house. I heard someone rummaging in our kitchen. *Great, we're being robbed!*

"What the hell do you think you are doing?" I exclaimed.

My landlord almost fell off the chair he was using to look above our cupboards. He didn't say anything for a second. He narrowed his eyes. "You are a bad tenant!"

"Why are you going through our stuff?"

"You are a very bad tenant. You make so much noise in this kitchen. You are banging cupboards. All I hear is you and that girl talking and yelling and carrying on." The landlord was starting to move towards the door.

"*I* make so much noise?" My eyes went wide at the guy. "What about you and your Thursday afternoon sex? I hear every thrust you make. Thank God you're so quick. I can't stand the sound of the bed creaking."

The guy's face went completely red. His breathing stopped, and his jaw clenched. "Well, I have never in my life been so insulted!" The landlord blew past me and out the door.

What followed over the next few months was the predictable series of battles. First, they would up the ante, and then I would find a way to top that. I was always able to come up with something they couldn't top. Mike had purchased the semi and I was learning to drive it. Mike and I had left Magenta and had found an agent who supplied us with jobs. When we were in town, the semi stayed in my driveway. It fit perfectly, with the exhaust pipe level with our landlords' front window. I would let the semi warm up for a good two hours before I would take off.

In Quebec at that time and I think still now, being a landlord is taken very seriously. There are strict procedures to follow. Coming to the end of the yearly lease, we were given our ninety days to decide to renew or find a new place. Out of spite, we waited. When sixty more days had gone by and I was bored of tormenting them, we gave notice that we were leaving. I packed up my stuff again and found a place to store it. The semi would be my home now. I'd crash the few nights I was in town with my friends and then hit the road again.

CHAPTER 81

"Finally!"

Mike climbed into the driver's seat. We had finished loading up the tar paper and were ready to set off. Mike started up the truck and we pulled away from the loading zone. "We're on the open road now, Victoria." He winked at me. "There's no going back."

"What's to go back to?" I replied.

It turns out I am not a trucker. It was by far one of the most boring things I've ever done. I kept a journal. I wanted to have something to read should I ever forget how awful trucking is. I could only sleep so much. Loading was awful. A few weeks after we started, someone didn't strap the load down properly. Tar paper blew all over the road. Neither of us noticed for a few miles. Mike and I spent hours cleaning that shit up. When we arrived at our destination, the owner threatened to refuse the load because of the condition the tarpaper was in.

I told the guy, "If you don't take this, we'll dump it in the driveway and leave."

He saw I was serious and unloaded the cargo. That owner became our first complaint.

That was not the worst thing that happened, not by a lot. Our friend Maurice, who I have known forever, mortgaged his house and bought a brand-new semi. We had the same agent and would often head the same way on our travels through the US. Maurice was incredibly organized. He kept all his papers and certificates in a folder. He had to have a McNally map—no other map was good enough. His permits were kept alphabetized. We met up at a weigh station. He was in line behind us. I checked our papers for permits for the next state; everything was in order.

"The fellow behind me doesn't have a permit for this state," I said jokingly. Surely Maurice would have this permit; he never made errors. I was simply joking, knowing he would find it funny.

Unbeknownst to me, he had missed getting this exact permit. He had to pay the fine and wait while they figured it out. He was pissed at me and I felt terrible.

It wasn't long before karma got me back. Mike and I had picked up a load of lumber and were driving through the States on our way south. Once again, someone didn't properly strap down the load. Some very helpful policemen noticed our load was loose. They followed directly behind us, waiting for lumber to fall off our truck. When the wood fell, it landed squarely on the hood of their cop car.

Sirens flashed, startling both Mike and me.

"Shit!" Mike looked in his side mirror.

"What?" I asked, as I looked in mine. "Shit!"

A cop got out of the car and sauntered up to the truck. "Could you get out of the vehicle, please?"

Mike and I both stepped down.

"You two do realize that you're carrying an unsecured load? A piece of your cargo fell on our cruiser." The cop started going through the paperwork Mike handed him.

"No, officer. I'm very sorry. I would never have intentionally driven with an unsecured load." Mike was sweating a little. We were already going to be late for our drop-off.

"You're going to have to come with us down to the station." The cop took Mike by the arm. "You're under arrest for traffic safety violations."

"Please, we're already running late. Can't you give us the fine to pay so we can be on our way?" I asked.

"We can discuss this at the station. You are not under arrest"— the cop turned to me—"but you can come with us to clear this up." The cop ushered me to his car.

Back at the station, we waited while the cop talked to the other cops. After a lot of pleading on my part they agreed to wake up the town judge. The judge let us off with a fine, delaying us three hours.

Mike and I didn't last much longer as truckers.

When we had been sold the truck, the bill of sale said the mileage was listed in kilometres, when it was actually listed in miles. That meant the truck had a lot more wear and tear on the engine than they claimed. Mike and I bought the truck with the plan to work across Canada. The only way you can get through the Rockies is with a Jake brake. The salesmen assured us the truck had one. Turned out it didn't have one. To honour the terms of our original bill of sale, the dealership would have had to overhaul the engine. That would cost them at least $5000. Plus, to install a Jake brake would have cost the dealership a bunch more money. I told Mike to act like we would buy a new one and offer them the deal. Get a Jake brake installed and an overhaul on our engine or give us back our $12,000 deposit. I gambled that they would go for the deposit, and my gamble paid off. Mike almost blew it. For a moment, he agreed a new truck might be better. I kicked his shin hard. That jolted him back to his senses. We followed my script and left with our $12,000.

Mike and I went back to Magenta. I found a new place. Being on the road and not having a home was almost as bad as the work itself. I am a gypsy by nature, but I am not a nomad. I need a home to come home to.

CHAPTER 82

July 1982, Donald was taken out of the SHU and told he was going to be transferred to Millhaven. He was brought back to Archambault just in time for the riots. I missed Donald more than ever. The thought of his transfer gave me hope. Millhaven would mean contact visits again. I'd had to make do with staring at Donald through glass since his failed leaky dynamite stunt.

THREE GUARDS KILLED IN ARCHAMBAULT RIOTS

I almost dropped the paper when I saw the headline on July 25, 1982. The article said that three inmates had tried to escape and had taken ten guards hostage. They slaughtered three prison guards. One of the guards was disembowelled. The article went into detail about how the guards rescued the ten other officers who were taken. The article repeatedly stated the guards had not fired their shotguns at the prisoners, only above their heads. Tear gas was used. The story briefly mentioned that most of the prisoners were outside having yard time when it happened. These prisoners had to spend three nights sleeping outside.

I tried to get word about Donald, but it was a week before I heard from him directly. I called the prison a few days after the riot, and I was finally told Donald was alive. He had been one of the prisoners forced to sleep outside.

A week later I was able to see Donald.

"Oh my God, Donald. Thank God! Are you okay?" I almost leaped through the glass, I was so happy to see him.

"Yeah, Vic. I was outside the whole time." Donald sank into the chair. "I'm still on track to transfer to Millhaven in a few weeks. It can't be soon enough. The guards are out for blood right now. I've never seen it this bad before."

I looked more closely at Donald for bruises and cuts.

"I'm on my way out, and I'm not causing trouble right now so I'm left alone." Donald shook his head. "I need to get out of here, Victoria. I've never been out in the cold like that. We were living like animals, sleeping on the ground. I would have given anything to be able to hold you and have you warm the cold out of my bones."

A tear slipped down my cheek. "Those first few days when I didn't know if you were alive or dead were the worst."

"I'm okay, Victoria. I'm not going anywhere. I'm coming home to you," he said, waiting for me to look into his eyes. "You'll see, I promise."

When I visited Donald, all we could talk about was how nice it would be to have contact visits again. Since Donald had first been sent to the SHU, we'd had to talk between glass. That wouldn't change until he was transferred to Millhaven, which happened on August 24, 1982.

CHAPTER 83

"**Victoria!**" **Donald wrapped me up** in his arms. I could feel his warmth invade me. It had been too many months since Donald held me. Still, it felt like a lifetime ago.

"I've missed you so much." His face was buried in my shoulder, smelling my hair. I felt the gentle brush of his lips on my neck.

"I've missed you, too." I stroked Donald's hair. It felt so strange. I had thought about this moment, dreamed about this moment the whole time I had been bored on the road.

"You feel the same." Donald leaned down. He kissed my lips and everything stopped. My whole body went warm. My breath caught. We both enjoyed the gentle kiss, the soft brushing of our lips. Slowly savouring the energy buzzing between us. Neither of us said much on that first visit in Millhaven. It was too much to finally be able to hold one another again.

Life went on like it always does. I saw Donald when I could, and I hung out with my courier gang. Mike, Doug, Andy, Robert, Brent, their girlfriends, and I were always up to something. Days went by, sometimes a week, without my noticing. Everything was the same one day to the next. Some nights my bed was empty, and others I shared it with the boyfriend of the month. I never really felt different, though. The change in people, my schedule, buying myself new things, none of it moved me. At my core I always felt the same. Numb and purposeless. I wondered about life all the time. What was the point of doing the same old thing every day?

CHAPTER 84

"Hey, Victoria!" Donald gave me a big hug. He was jumpy today. I could tell he hadn't been sleeping well. "Did you bring it?"

Donald had asked me for something on our last visit. "Yes." I passed him a few white pills. He quickly swallowed them, and I passed him some more.

"Thank God."

"You know those will only work if you bleach everything."

"I know, Vic. Someone is in my cell cleaning it right now."

"It's just worm pills, Donald. Why didn't you ask the nurse?"

"It's too embarrassing." Donald's shoulders sunk a little.

"Well, what would have happened if the guards walked in as you swallowed those pills? They wouldn't have believed it was worm pills."

Donald shrugged his shoulders.

I shuddered a little. When we first started living in Verdun, I had discovered the hard way that Donald had worms. The image of them wiggling back inside of him as I exposed them to the light of day still haunts me.

"Don't say it, Vic," he warned me.

I took a big deep breath and then nodded my head. "Fair enough." I kissed his cheek. "I still think you're sexy."

"Thanks, Victoria." He kissed me a little deeper. "I've missed you, wifey."

Lately, Donald had taken to calling me this. "Is that so, hubby?"

"It is." Donald smirked the smirk that started all of this. I couldn't say anything, so I just kissed him.

"I'm going to quit my job for a while," I said when we broke the kiss.

"Yeah? What are you going to do?"

"I don't know. I was thinking about going on unemployment. Just to give myself some time to figure things out." I pushed my hair out of my face.

"You do whatever you think is best, Victoria. I want you to be happy. If you're not working then you'll have more time to write letters and visit me."

I went on unemployment. I sat around at home, I went out to the bar, I didn't really deal drugs. I became more and more listless. The longer I was on unemployment, the less I could see myself going back to work. The longer I was away from work, the more anxious I felt. It became a vicious cycle I didn't know how to break. Pierre Trudeau made the decision for me. I had been an independent contractor at Magenta. With the new law that passed, I no longer qualified for unemployment. I had to go back to work. But first, I had to tell my landlord that I wouldn't be able to pay the rent. I was going to have to break the lease.

"Thanks for seeing me." I had gone down to the landlord's office to see him face to face.

"Of course. What can I do for you Victoria?" He was a big man with a happy face.

"Well, my unemployment has been cut. I won't be able to pay next month's rent. I have to move out and break my lease."

"Thank you for coming to tell me this in person."

I looked up at him a little surprised.

"Most people would have just left. They wouldn't have explained—they would have just taken off and left me on the hook. I appreciate you coming down here to see me."

I nodded. "It's the right thing to do."

We said our goodbyes and I began to drive home. I checked my mailbox in the hallway and pick up my mail, not looking forward to reading it. I had a few letters from the unemployment office. They were my back unemployment cheques. Somehow, they had still sent me my unemployment. I called my landlord and told him what happened, and I managed to stay in that apartment. It occurred to me that whenever I needed money, it seemed to arrive, sometimes in the most mysterious ways.

CHAPTER 85

Summer finally came to the city. So much of my life didn't change. I had quit Magenta and gone back. I was once again hating my straight life. Both my children were spending the summer with me.

I had saved up, and, together with my friend Sandra, we rented a summer house near Lac-Brome. Our house was right on the lake, with the town a few miles away. After Sandra and I put my kids to bed, we took off in search of some excitement.

"This place looks interesting." Sandra pointed to a bar on the side of the road. It had lights strung up on the patio. People were inside and outside the bar, music blasting out of the speakers. I pulled off to the side and we made our way in. All kinds of men were in the bar and they all looked at us. Sandra ordered at the bar for both of us.

"Hello, there." A shorter man turned to me.

I looked over at him. Beside him stood a giant, brown-haired, man with hazel eyes. Everything about this tall man screamed sex. "Hi," I said back to the shorter guy.

"I'm Bryan." He turned to the bartender and signalled to bring another round.

"I'm Victoria." I smiled back, trying to catch the taller guy's eye.

"You must be new around here. I haven't seen you before." Bryan had that look. He was already eyeing me up for his bed.

"I've rented a summer house with my girlfriend Sandra." I elbowed Sandra. "Sandra, meet Bryan. Bryan, this is my friend Sandra."

Sandra waved. "Hi!" Then she went back to talking to the guy on the other side of her.

"Are you going to be here all summer?" Bryan was inching closer and closer. I could see his tall friend looking around the room. The guy bent down to whisper something in Bryan's ear. Bryan nodded. The tall guy was about to walk away. "Armand, this is Victoria. Victoria, this is my friend Armand."

Armand barely looked at me. He smiled and left in a hurry.

Bryan became a lot less interesting now that Armand was gone. I started to look for a way out of the conversation and find the next guy I wanted to talk to.

Then Armand came back. He sipped his drink and finally looked at me. When he smiled at me, my whole body melted.

"Victoria…" Bryan brushed my hand to get my attention. I could see he was more than a little drunk. "Victoria, would you like to go take a walk with me?"

I took a deep breath. Armand had gone back to talking to the guy beside him. "You know, Bryan, I'm really much more interested in your friend."

Bryan stopped for a moment and then he laughed. I don't think this was the first time a girl had asked to speak to Armand instead of Bryan. "Armand…" Bryan elbowed his friend.

"What's up?" he asked Bryan.

"Victoria, here, said she would rather speak to you than to me. My feelings were almost hurt for a second," Bryan added, a little whine to his tone.

"Really?" Armand looked at me again. "I guess that's just bad luck for you, Bryan." He pushed Bryan away a little so he was standing right in front of me.

"Hi." Armand looked down at me.

"Hello," I said back.

"Do you like bikes?" Armand asked me.

"Yes, I have a Kawasaki. What do you ride?" My hand brushed against Armand's.

"I have a Kawasaki 1100 in the parking lot if you want to go for a ride." Armand took my hand.

"Are you kidding? I'd love to go for a ride." I tugged his hand towards the door. Sandra and Bryan followed us. Armand's bike was out front. It was shiny white with red trim. I left Sandra the keys to my car with a big grin.

He fired up the bike, and I got on and gave him directions to the country house.

The roads were dark. The moon shone down, and you could see the lake through the trees. The wind was cool, blowing in our faces.

At my house I asked him, "Do you want to come in?"

"Of course. Lead the way, Victoria."

He turned the bike off and set down the kickstand. He waited for me to get off and then followed suit. "Let's see what you have to offer." He put his hand on my wrist.

We walked towards the house. My nerves were on fire. The vibrations of the bike and warmth of Armand as I held on to him had caused heat to pool through my body. Armand leaned down and kissed me. His hand went to the small of my back, pulling me up onto my tippy toes. He pressed into me. My breathing became deep and my knees felt weak. Finally, he pulled away. "That's just a taste." He smiled down at me.

We went inside, I checked on the kids and they were both dead to the world. We headed straight for my bedroom. Armand liked to take his time; he was in no rush. We kissed, sitting on my bed, slowly taking our clothing off, piece by piece. Kissing each patch of new skin that became exposed.

"Here." Armand fluffed a pillow. "Lie down." He moved me where he wanted me on the bed, pinning my wrists before gliding on top of me. Armand placed a knee on either side of my hips, looking down at me.

I reached up to pull him closer.

"Not yet." Armand pinned my wrists again. "I want to look at you."

"You like what you see?"

"Very much so." Armand kissed my neck and worked his way down to my breasts. He sucked while he slowly entered me. I arched into him uncontrollably. "Like what you feel?" Armand nibbled at my earlobe.

I moaned; I couldn't answer. He was starting to set a pace with his hips that was all-consuming. Each wave washed over me, my heart beating in time with his. We were both working, moving in the same direction.

Armand shifted his hips ever so slightly and I felt him hit me at a new angle, a higher angle, once, twice, and on the third time I released. Every muscle in my body clenched and unclenched. I clung to him, my nails digging into his shoulders. Finally, my chest stopped heaving.

Armand laughed.

"What?"

"We're just getting started." He leaned down to begin again.

Armand spent the night and didn't go home in the morning. At dinner he was still with us, and that night we went to bed together. On Sunday, we made plans to meet the following weekend. He waved us off back to the city and then took off on his bike.

CHAPTER 86

Armand was in my thoughts all week. Life didn't stop because it was summer. I had to go back to driving and Donald. We had a standing visit each week.

"Donald." I kissed him before we settled down.

"It's so good to see you, Victoria." He leaned his head against my forehead. "You smell so nice." He cupped my chin and kissed me, his hands roaming wherever they wanted. I could feel my skin respond to him, but the sparks didn't reach my bones.

"I need canteen money, but you have to buy artwork from me. Go to the front desk and ask for the picture I have up there in your name. Then fill out the paperwork and wait while they go and get it."

"Really, Donald? Since when do you do artwork?" I suspected he had someone else do it for him but remained silent. "I would rather just put the money in your canteen account," I said.

"They won't let you do that. The screws want you to be productive. You can't just have people give you money. They have to buy your artwork." He looked at the door, his jaw clenching and unclenching.

"You don't know what it's like in here, Victoria."

"Yeah, I do. If you hate it so much, why don't you get out? Roman's nearly out. Why can't you be like him and work at getting out?"

"Get off, Victoria. I don't know what you want me to do."

"Get a better prison job, don't cause trouble, don't take chances and don't get mixed up in other people's crap."

"That's not fair. I can't do that!" Donald's whole face went red.

"Why not?" I stood up now.

"Because, Victoria, I just can't. You have to stand up for yourself in here. It's a different life, if you look sideways at someone there is confrontation".

"Well, then you can rot." I signalled to the guard that I was done. Unfortunately, I had driven one of my friends, Carol, and I couldn't just leave; I had to wait for Carol to finish her morning visit, take a break for lunch and then go on to her afternoon visit. I read some of the magazines in the waiting area, but it didn't make any sense. *How could Donald be like that? How could he not want to get out of prison?* I missed Donald during the week, but our visits didn't make me feel any less lonely.

"Finally." I stood up when Carol came out. We walked out and didn't really talk. Carol could see I was pissed and it wasn't hard to guess why.

CHAPTER 87

Armand was waiting for us when we got back to Lac-Brome. He was holding a big, dark blue inflatable raft for my two boys. They loved it. Right after dinner, they took it to the lake.

"That was really nice of you." I ran my fingers over Armand's hand.

"I'm sure you can find some way of making it up to me tonight." We both smiled.

The next few weeks were pleasant. Armand was over every weekend and when I went back to the city, I skipped that week of Donald's visit. The boys were in town and I was busy. It was an easy excuse. I did feel guilty. My time with Armand helped distract me. The following week, my friend Wendy and I went up to Millhaven in her brand-new light-coloured Honda.

Donald was happy to see me. He had a big grin on his face. Our fight was no longer on his mind. As far as he was concerned, we were both over it because I was there visiting. Nothing had changed for me. The humiliation I saw Donald go through every visit infuriated me. He didn't think to be embarrassed, but I was embarrassed for him.

"Sit down." Donald looked like he was going to jump out of his skin. "There's a prison social coming up."

"A prison social?" I asked.

"Yes, you and other guys or girls can come for dinner. It will be like a date for us."

"Like a date." I repeated back to him. I really didn't want to fight with him. I smiled. "That sounds like it could be a good time."

"I know!" Donald said.

Donald continued. "If this goes well, it means we can get approval for our trailer visits."

"You mean we can finally spend the night together, Donald?" I kissed him. I trailed my hand down his chin, over his chest, my fingers dragging down to his stomach. I stopped with my hand right above his crotch.

"Jesus, Vic!" His hips lifted, trying to make contact.

"Does that excite you, Donald?" I lowered my hand an inch.

"You know it does, Victoria." Donald yanked me into his lap. I laughed.

It felt strange thinking about having sex with Donald after so long. After my last visit I had gone back to Armand and enjoyed the summer weekends. Armand wasn't the most generous lover, but the things he could do to me... Donald was incredibly giving, but it had been seven years. How could things ever be that good again? I was a different person. I had gone on to have experiences with other men. I missed Donald dearly, however. My life still felt pointless without him.

I drove myself up to Millhaven this time. My friend Blake had been released from Millhaven after eight months and sent to Warkworth. He was back living with his wife by 1988. Funny, Blake had twenty-five years to serve, less time served in Parthenais, so that meant twenty-three years and nine months while Donald only had twelve. *How much more of that sentence would he have to serve? Would Donald find a way to add more charges?* I asked myself these questions as I drove.

It was a quiet drive. Bath, Ontario, is about three-and-a-half hours from Montreal. It's mostly forest. I drove with the windows down and radio on. I had put on a dress, nothing special.

Inside the prison, I went through the mandatory pat-down and then to the prison gym. The gym was filled with tables in rows. Hundreds of men and woman milled about. You could see each clique visiting with their own.

"Victoria!" Donald walked over wearing his signature smirk and kissed me. The guards milling around the gym didn't take notice.

The food was what you would expect in prison. Meat that was dry, and mashed potatoes that stuck like glue to your fork. But no one ate. Each man focused all his attention on his date. One of the dates at our table was tall, dark and Québécois-looking. She had bangles of all kinds on each wrist. The woman giggled loudly and looked around the room as all the other men at our table stared. It was clear she wanted to be the centre of attention. I honestly thought that she looked like a hooker.

Her annoying voice went quiet for a moment. I watched her disappear under the table with her guy friend.

I peeked under the table and could see a pillow and blanket waiting. I looked back at Donald.

"There is one under every table," he told me. "The guards look the other way at these socials."

"I see." I heard rustling under the table. The man must have gotten himself into position because I heard her bangles jingle in time with his first thrust.

Donald's whole body jerked. With the next thrust, he started making a noise like a cat in heat.

Jangle, thrust, Donald moaned.

Jangle, thrust, Donald moaned.

Jangle, thrust, Donald moaned. "Stop it!" I smacked Donald's arm.

Donald tried to stop himself when the next jangle came, but he couldn't. *Who does that bitch think she is? Why on earth does she seem to think it's okay to torment my boyfriend with the sound of her fucking? That trashy bitch!*

Donald moaned again. "Please, Vic, please," he said.

"Please what, Donald?" I looked at him.

"Please, Vic. It's been so long. I need you. Come on, Victoria…" Donald's whole body twitched every time a bangle jingled.

"No, Donald."

"It's been too long, Vic. Please… The guys all have blankets under the tables. Everyone is going to do it."

"I am not getting under this table to have sex with you." I glared at him.

"Victoria, I'm dying. It's been so long."

I looked around the room; a few of the other girls had disappeared and reappeared with their guys. I couldn't let Donald touch me when he was turned on by some slut. Nor was I about to go under a table and go at it. With Donald's luck this would be the one and only time the guards would decide to put their foot down. It was horrible. My skin crawled. "No. Do you want a turn with Jangle Bangle?" I glared at him.

"No, Vic, but—" Donald guided my hand down to his crotch. He moaned uncontrollably with each thrust.

"There is no way in hell I am going to have sex with you in front of all these people, Donald! I don't care how much you beg." I drew my hand back.

"Victoria…"

My stone-cold silence told him not to try any further.

My stuff still needed to be unpacked when I got home from Millhaven. I took a long hot shower with the radio on. All I could hear that night was the girl and her bangles. Over and over and over again. *What kind of a stupid whore wears noisy bangles to a visit? That girl was a pro. She was there to do a job. Each one of the men moaned along with her, even when they weren't doing her.* I scrubbed myself harder.

I didn't go back to see Donald the following week, but I did write him a letter. He wrote back with a date for our trailer visit.

CHAPTER 88

I spent as much of my time as I could at Lac-Brome. Armand was with me, all the time. He was always in my bed, in my house, hanging out.

"Wake up!" I elbowed Armand.

"What?" He sat up.

"I'm late!" I began gathering up my clothes. I rushed around the house, getting ready to pack up what I needed.

"I can't find my underwear. Why is there no clean underwear? There's never any clean underwear!" I plunked down on the bed.

"Here, take mine." Armand handed me a pair of red Hanes underwear. I gathered them up and ran to the shower. I threw on some makeup and got dressed.

I hadn't told Armand where I was going. He didn't need to know. We were together, but we weren't together. He had a marriage he was getting himself out of and I have my past. We didn't really talk about it. We would agree to be exclusive at some point down the road. But not today.

I looked at myself in the rear-view mirror. My hair was nice, blond, a little wild-looking. My skin was tanned. I looked like I had just gotten off a beach. Which wasn't entirely untrue.

Once I parked the car, I drew a deep breath. This was it. Seven years and now it was time. Going through the security motions was a blur. I don't remember getting my bag searched or anything else. Donald waiting on the front steps of the trailer is the first thing I remember.

"Victoria!" Donald swept me up in his arms and spun me around. He kissed the top of my head and then set me down. "Come on." Donald took my hand. His fingers encased mine. I could feel the warmth of his palm spread up my arm. "I'm so glad this day finally came." He planted another kiss on my cheek.

"I know." I really didn't know what to say.

Donald led me past the tiny kitchen into the hallway. "I can make you breakfast in the morning, Vic!"

"Great, Donald. Sounds great." Donald sounded proud of being able to cook something for me.

He set my bag on the bed. The bedroom didn't have a door, just a bed and mismatched dresser. I didn't look very closely at the mattress.

Donald grabbed me. His lips touched mine; his hands went under my shirt. My body responded. Donald's kiss tasted the way I remembered. Slowly, he pushed me back and I fell onto the mattress. Donald climbed on top of me, holding me there for a moment while he looked down at me. His hand went straight for my breasts, moving my bra aside to tug and then suck on my nipples. He was in no hurry, kissing inch by inch down to my waist. He stopped to nibble on my hip bones before pulling down my pants. He paused for a second when he saw my underwear. It was only a second, and then he went back to work.

Donald's first lick almost sent me over the edge. He knew how to lick me: his mouth was just the right temperature, his tongue used just the right amount of force and he kept a rhythm that was all his own.

"Donald!"

"Mmm…" He didn't stop. I shuddered again, then again.

"That's better." Donald climbed on top of me, having just removed his clothes. He was still fit. His arms were muscled, and his chest was strong. I ran my hands over his pecs, reaching up to his chin. Kissing him as he entered me. We moved over and over again until neither of us could get up.

"That was amazing." I lay in Donald's arms. We enjoyed the after-sex glow. I could feel the peace that came over me when we were together.

"Are those men's underwear?"

I snapped back to reality. I looked at him but didn't answer.

"That's kind of low, Victoria."

We cooked. We both cooked. In the past, I always did the cooking and the cleaning. Now Donald chopped and did a lot of my prep work. We sat down over dinner. It felt different together, but not a bad different.

"Listen, Vic, I want to tell you this now, so I can get it out of the way."

"Okay." *Now what*? I thought.

"You know that murder that happened inside that they tried to pin on me? I told you about it back in March." My mind went back to the conversation we had had then.

"Yes." I looked at him. "You were questioned about that if I recall rightly?"

"Well, they're investigating again. Don't worry, though. They don't have a case."

"Donald, you're supposed to get out soon." My voice was high and squeaky.

"I know, Victoria." He took my hand. "Don't worry, it will be okay. Just like last time. I'll beat the charge and I'll be back with you in no time."

It's been seven years... I nodded my head and went back to eating.

Donald and I went back to the bedroom. All night we alternated between talking and having sex. In the dark I couldn't see the trailer's stained walls. The blinds covered the window, so I couldn't see the cell block outside.

"Stay in bed, Vic. I got this." Donald stood up. We had barely slept.

"Okay, if you're sure."

"I'm sure." I heard Donald go into the kitchen. Pots and pans banged. I heard bacon frying, and Donald making toast. He brought the finished breakfast to me in bed. He did a good job. The bacon was cooked just right, and the eggs were perfect.

A bell rang outside

Donald jumped up. "I'll be right back." He kissed my cheek and put on some pants. I got up from the bed and peeked out the window to the stairs. Donald stood with his hands behind his back, shoulders straight, all ready to be counted. He was at the screw's mercy. If the screw wanted, he could search Donald; he could come in and search the trailer. Donald and I had no recourse. It made my skin crawl. In Tanguay, I hated it; I was always uncomfortable. It was humiliating, and a driving force for me to get out of Tanguay as soon as possible. Donald didn't care. Donald didn't know how foreign this would be on the outside. This was his world. Donald had first gone to prison at the age of fourteen. He had been in and out ever since. Now there was a murder charge possibly hanging over him. He should never have been anywhere near that. If he really wanted to get out, he would...

"There." Donald walked through the door and gave me a kiss. "Let's get back to our breakfast before it gets cold."

It hit me then. *He didn't love me enough to try to get out.* I sat back down and tried eating. I couldn't. "Donald..." I got up.

"What?" He jumped up from his chair.

I gathered up my stuff. "I'm sorry, Donald, but I'm going and I'm not coming back." I had tears in my eyes. I looked at him.

"What do you mean, Victoria?" He took my elbow.

"I can't take this anymore. I'm done waiting." I gave him a kiss on the cheek and walked out, waiting for the guards to take me back inside. Again, I don't remember being searched but I do remember the relief I felt driving home.

September 10, 1985, Donald was formally charged with the murder that was being investigated..

CHAPTER 89

It was getting close to fall. The lease on my country house would end Labour Day weekend. Then I would have to return to the city. Armand was now the foundation of my life. I couldn't give him up. I made a compromise. Armand and I rented a place near Lac-Brome. I would have to drive into the city, forty-five minutes each way.

Life in the country was lovely in the summer. You could escape the humidity and heat of Montreal for the cool lake breeze. You didn't have to answer to anyone. You were free to spend your time how you wanted, swimming, barbecuing, or lounging around. When you live in the country all year, it's different. The house we rented was outside of town. My back windows had a view of cows grazing as far as the eye could see. The county was still. The town shrunk when the tourists left. All of the locals were relieved to be done with them until next year.

Armand lived in a quiet place, but he did not have a quiet life. Throughout the summer I learned Armand was in the process of getting a divorce. He was at a point in his life where things were going well for him. He had lots of money and liked to spend it. I knew that Armand didn't have a straight job. He told me that he worked for Dunie, a major drug dealer, not just in Montreal but all of Eastern Canada. I had never heard of Dunie, which was strange, as I thought I had heard of everyone based on the fact that I practically lived at The Red Lion all throughout the '70s and into the '80s. What's funny is the title that many books give Dunie and his crew today: The West End Gang. That name was never used. Most of the guys who frequented The Red Lion worked for the Otis Elevator Company and were in their late thirties to early forties. In the '70s, we affectionately called them the "over-the-hill boys," and more than once I heard the "over-the-hill boys" refer to our younger crowd as "just punks." As our younger group grew older, the two age groups started to mesh.

Any ride on a motorcycle is enjoyable. But cruising through the Eastern Townships in the middle of summer and early fall is the best. Armand drove at breakneck speed down the winding roads, while I looked out at the lake and forest. The day was still warm from the sunshine and the wind felt fresh.

Our destination was a motel, just off Saint Jacques Street. Peg's, I think it was called. Armand pulled into the parking lot. He waited for me to get off the bike. Then we walked into the motel's conference room together. A large table was set up in the middle of the room. Most of the seats were already filled. I only recognized one face at the table: Dougie. Dougie recognized me right away. He looked at me and then at Armand, and then back at me again. I could tell he was as surprised to see me with Armand as I was to see him there.

Armand took a seat near the foot of the table. I sat beside him on his left. There were no other girls in the room. Dunie sat at the head of the table. I could see that he was a man who didn't have to be loud to be heard. With a glance of his eyes and a well-timed eyebrow raise, silence rippled across the table.

I don't remember a lot of what was said at the dinner; I know that I didn't say a word.

The year 1984 had been a successful one for Dunie and his West End crew. I quickly learned that Dunie was a big-time drug importer. Dunie brought his shipments in through the port of Montreal, shipping them throughout Quebec, Ontario and into Atlantic Canada. Armand worked as low as you could go. He was simply a runner. Still, he was earning a good income that would grow dramatically if he was able to move up the ladder.

When I got up from the table, Dunie looked over at me. I gave him a small smile. He didn't smile back. He was still making his mind up about me. Armand took the crook of my elbow and guided me outside where everyone was gathered, having a smoke.

"Hey, Armand!" Bob flagged Armand and me over. "Can you drive my bike home? I have to go somewhere with Dunie."

I knew Bob. He lived with his wife and daughter a few miles from us in his own house. A truly nice house with a hot tub in the front room.

"So, you're going to drive Armand's bike home?" Bob asked.

"I got this." I nodded at Bob

Armand handed me his keys and I hopped on. The bike was pointing in the wrong direction to head back to Lac-Brome. I can do a lot on a motorcycle and most of it I can do very well, but turning a bike around in a small space is not one of my strengths. I had already thought about that. I put the bike in gear and drove around to the front of the motel. I can do wheelies with any car but not a heavy motorcycle. In front of the motel was a little roundabout where people could unload their luggage. When I drove back to the parking lot, I pulled in next to Armand.

"How can you drive that thing?" a short man asked me.

"It's not my fault you're a wimp," I replied with a grin. Everyone laughed.

Out of the corner of my eye, I saw Dunie lean over and whisper something to Armand. Armand laughed and nodded.

"What did Dunie whisper to you?" I asked as I climbed into bed that night.

"He said, 'Even though she doesn't talk much, don't ever think she's stupid.'"

"That's quite the compliment." I kissed Armand.

"Mm-hmm." Armand began to kiss my shoulder, pulling down the strap of my nightgown. He nipped at my neck, his hands roaming up and down my stomach, before snaking around the curve of my hip. Armand pulled me flat against the bed and rolled on top of me. His lips dominated mine. Our bodies rode the surge of passion already building in each of us. Armand was a master with his hips. He timed each thrust to a rhythm that built you up high then shattered you, over and over again.

Late summer turned to fall. The month of November approached with its promise of wind and snow.

Armand was now always busy with Dunie's business. The West End crew was expanding their power. Dunie didn't trust banks and everyone knew it. That meant not only was he the "king" of Montreal, he had millions in cash hidden somewhere. Everyone wanted to take the king's place. The possibility of pocketing a million dollars is motivating, never mind millions of dollars.

"What am I going to do, Victoria?" Armand asked. It had been two weeks since Dunie had been murdered for his millions. Justice had been dispatched for those responsible. Everything was uncertain and, for now, Armand needed to find himself a job.

"I don't know, Armand. I'm going to go back to Magenta. We could work courier together."

Armand shook his head back and forth, weighing his options. "I guess I could. It didn't seem so hard when you did it. I can deal on the side until things are running again."

"Works for me." I smiled at him.

It didn't.

When we moved to the country, I traded my Datsun Micra for a truck. Armand lasted a whole week being a courier. After that first Friday, he quit.

Armand didn't care if he had money, but I did. We were very different people and we were from very different worlds. He was country and I was city. We wanted different things from our lives.

That Christmas confirmed it. We went shopping at Ogilvy's, a massive department store in the heart of downtown Montreal. Each year, Ogilvy's tried to outdo the previous year's window display. It was large enough to fill two massive windows. This year, there was train set that chugged along its little rail board. Santa waved and all of his little animal helpers worked together and moved in unison. The Ogilvy's Christmas display was a big part of Christmas in Montreal. People looked forward to it and gathered for its unveiling. Looking at all the moving parts, I felt such wonder in my heart. Snow fell softly, Salvation Army Santas shook their bells, and people milled about contentedly. This was a perfect Montreal Christmas. All of it made my heart sing.

I took Armand's hand and he jerked it away. I looked up at him. His eyes were darting around, his shoulders were tense, and his chest barely moved when he breathed. He was uncomfortable, and I could tell he hated everything about the situation.

I hated our rented house in the middle of nowhere. I wanted skyscrapers, not cows for neighbours. I couldn't handle the stillness and Armand couldn't handle the noise.

After that Christmas I rented an apartment in town and left the house to Armand. I went to Armand's during the week when I could, and most weekends. The distance seemed to help our relationship. We both appreciated each another more after spending a few days apart.

"That's interesting." I had arrived at Armand's house before him. I looked at the *TV Guide* next to the remote. It was still open to Wednesday, the last time I had spent the night. The previous Wednesday, I had noticed the *TV Guide* was still open to the Sunday before. I had come that Friday and left for the city Sunday night. Armand lived for the *TV Guide*—God help you if it fell off the couch and he couldn't find it. *He's not using the guide when I'm not here; he must not be here.* Bastard. I really didn't like the thought of that. I asked around and Frank told me that Armand was dating somebody new. I cornered him the following Saturday when I knew he would be home.

"What the hell, Armand?" I stormed in. "You're cheating on me?" I slammed the door. Armand jumped up. He looked at me for a moment. I could see he was trying to decide if it was worth telling me a lie. "Don't lie to me, Armand. I already know."

"Okay." His face froze. "I was going to tell you but—"

"But?"

"But I was afraid of how you would react."

"You were afraid of how I would react?" I pushed Armand. "What kind of a coward are you?"

"I don't know, Victoria. I'm sorry. I don't know what to say." Armand stood perfectly still.

"Don't say anything, Armand. Just go to hell." I threw open the door and walked out, not bothering to close it behind me. My mind raced. At that moment, more than anything else, I wanted to make him pay. I wanted him to hurt as much as I hurt. How could he just start seeing someone like that? I had stopped seeing Donald when I met Armand. Our relationship had been that solid to me. But Armand—Armand had no problem going off and finding some whore. *I'm going to make him pay,* I promised myself.

CHAPTER 90

I went to work every day, and started going out again with other friends on Fridays and Saturdays, mainly to The Lorelai. I resumed drinking, after having truly stopped while I was with Armand. I was beginning to recognize a pattern of behaviour. Later, I would realize how my emotions played a big part in this.

A month later, Armand paged me and I answered his page right away.

"Hey, Victoria." Armand opened the door with a hug and kissed my cheek. "Come in, have a seat," he said, pointing to his living room couch.

After I found out Armand had been cheating, Frank had informed me that he'd rented a new house out in the middle of nowhere. It was even more isolated then the one we had shared in Lac-Brome. He also told me that his girlfriend was pregnant.

"Thanks." I sat down. "What's up?"

"Right down to business. I've always liked that about you." He smiled at me, his eyes going soft. "I have a friend who wants five ounces of blow. I figured you were the person to ask."

I nodded my head.

Armand slid a stack of $100 bills my way. "Count it if you want."

"No, I trust you, Armand." I took the bills and put them in my purse. "Well, I'll go pick up the stuff and let you know when it's ready."

"Sounds good, Victoria." Armand kissed my cheek again on my way out the door.

I found a payphone on my way into Montreal and paged Roger. Then I headed to his house.

"Roger!" I smiled at him when he answered his door.

"Victoria, come in."

"Christ, Roger, you're getting scrawny. You need to start lifting weights." I pinched Roger's bicep. I had known him a long time and knew he was one of the drug dealers I could go to.

"Yeah." He laughed. "One of these days I'll find the time, right after I cure AIDS and visit the Louvre."

We went into his dining room, and sat down.

"Here." I handed him a stack of money. "My guy wants five ounces."

Roger put the bills in his pocket. "That shouldn't be a problem."

Roger got up to the phone and made a page. He hung up. His pager went off a few minutes later.

"I can pick up from my guy later tonight. Want to meet up around eight?"

"Sure."

I went about my day. Then it was time to leave to meet Roger. I drove back to Roger's duplex and walked up to the second floor.

"Hey, Roger." Roger wasn't smiling. "What's up?"

"Did you check the money, Victoria?"

"What do you mean did I check the money?"

Roger was sweating and fidgety. "The money is fake. It has the same serial numbers on it. My guys are pissed."

"Are you sure?" I asked.

"Of course I'm sure. They spotted it as soon as I arrived. I felt like an idiot for not noticing."

"You've got to be kidding me." I shook my head. How could Armand do this to me? That rat bastard. I tried to swallow and collect my thoughts. *What was I going to do?*

"What are you going to do, Victoria?" Roger echoed my thoughts. "We have to confront your guy. We can't let this stand. I need it dealt with now."

Armand is an idiot, I thought. "I'll take care of it, Roger, just give me a sec." I paged Armand and waited for him to page me back.

"He's ready to meet. Let's go!" I grabbed my car keys; Roger followed me to my car, another Datsun Micra. I had traded that stupid truck back in for the car I needed.

I drove, listening to Roger go on and on about how we had to make Armand pay. That this wasn't going to stand.

I knocked loudly on the door. Armand opened and invited us in.

"Did everything go smoothly? Do you have it?" Armand asked.

"Did it go smoothly? Armand, did you even look at those bills? They're fake!"

"That can't be," Armand replied.

"Really?" I pulled out the bills and showed him.

Armand went a little pale.

"I'll handle this," I said. "Stay in the house when your friends come, Armand."

"Sure, Victoria."

I waited by the window. Roger disappeared for a minute and then joined me.

I saw a car drive up and park in the driveway. I walked out. Roger didn't follow me. "Roger come on!" I yelled.

Roger stood frozen in the doorway. He wasn't coming.

I squared my shoulders and walked up to the car. The driver rolled down his window. I didn't wait for him to speak. "These bills are fake!" I threw the bills back in the car. "Get the hell out of here! What kind of trouble are you trying to cause?"

The two guys in the car looked at each other.

"I'm not kidding. Get OUT!"

They drove off into the night.

Armand was silent that night. I didn't stay long. I took Roger home. Then I went home. I told myself I didn't care, but I couldn't shake the after-effects of all the adrenalin. The other shoe would drop eventually. You don't try to screw someone over and not have to pay.

Roger paged me. When I went over to his place, he told me he had gotten a call from his guy and it would be a $5000 fine. I didn't have the money. Really, it wasn't my problem. I had been doing Armand a favour. When I told Armand, he stepped up right away. He sold his bike and gave me the money. I gave the money to Roger and I never heard anything else about it. That's how life is in the drug world. Stay honourable and you have no issues.

CHAPTER 91

Halloween had come around again. I had been focusing on my courier work and taking it easy on the dealing. Armand paged me again. This time with the code for two pounds of hash. The meeting place would be the Alexis Neon Plaza.

"That's the third undercover cop car to go by," I said to Carol. I knew Carol from high school. It was convenient that she lived downtown on Fort Street near where the deal was taking place. I watched out the window for a bit and saw another car go by.

"Are you going to go? Armand is waiting," Carol said.

I thought about it. *This didn't feel right. Something was up.* "No, I have a stop to make first."

I walked down Closse Street and went into The Red Lion.

"Victoria," Tom greeted me. Tom was a member of the over-the-hill guys. He was a good-natured guy, and easy to talk to. I often played bullshit with him, a game much like poker except you used one and two dollar bills to call out your numbers. It's not a game I ever see anyone playing today, but it was fun back then to win a wee bit of cash and pass the time.

"Tom." I sat down at the table next to him.

"Something wrong?"

"Yeah." I nodded my head. "I'm supposed to make a deal at the plaza, but I've seen a lot of undercover cop cars heading over there over the last 30 minutes."

"Are you meeting someone you trust?" Tom asked.

"I thought so, but not anymore. I'm beginning to wonder if he's become an informant or owes the cops a favour."

Tom thought for a while. "There's an easy fix." It was Halloween; many of the bar patrons were wearing costumes. He motioned a woman wearing a witches-costume over.

"Yes, Tom?"

"I want you to go Alexis Neon Plaza. Where are you making the deal?" he asked me.

"At the restaurant downstairs. Armand will be at the restaurant."

"Okay, head on over there and take a look. Pretend you don't know what you're doing and be nosy. Keep your mask on."

The woman, Sherilyn, giggled, and left.

"The mall is crawling with cops." Sherilyn reported back.

I slammed my glass down. "That bastard! I'm going to kill him." My escapade with Roger flashed in my mind.

"Well, you have to go."

I knew this and walked over to the plaza. Just as the universe has always taken care of me, the person who was bringing the hash to Armand happened to be walking down the back staircase at the same time I was walking up. I pretended not to see him and mumbled "Cops," as I walked by.

I knew he heard me and I was pretty sure he had seen the undercovers and was getting out of there. The restaurant was on the ground floor; you could see it from the two floors above. I went to the top level and looked down at Armand. "One, two, three, four." I counted the undercover cops under my breath.

I walked down the stairs towards Armand. The person sitting right across from him a few tables over was clearly a cop. I walked right by Armand, pretending I didn't know him.

I was out of my mind with rage. How could he do that to me? He must have set me up on the coke deal, too. He obviously was some sort of informant now.. God! I closed my eyes and imagined all the things I could do to him, as I walked back to Carol's and paged him. No reply.

CHAPTER 92

"A stop order automatically converts into a market order when a predetermined price is reached. This is referred to as the stop price. Therefore, ordinary rules of the market order apply."

I sat in a classroom in Victoria Square, at the Montreal Stock Exchange. Each Friday, different brokers were invited to give lectures on the basics of market trading.

A hand shot up. "Can you explain market order, please?"

"The order is guaranteed to be executed—you simply don't know the price. It can be higher or be lower than the current price reported on the ticker symbol."

I had spent the last four Fridays here, getting a foundation in how to trade. Like all things having to do with numbers, trading came naturally to me. It also held my attention. I could sit in class and not feel like my face was melting off out of boredom.

I hadn't meant for this to happen, but dealing coke had grown into a full-time business. I quit Magenta for good.

I knew it was important to make it look like I was still working. That meant each morning I got up and went to the gym. After my workout, I came home for lunch. On Fridays I sat in on the stock-trading course. Every afternoon, my pager would start going off, and I would make my deliveries.

Six years ago, when I started dealing hash because Maria made it look like an easy way to make money, it never occurred to me that this would one day be my business. I never advertised. I didn't need to. My clients started off as my friends, and when they became clients they referred their friends to me. After I vetted these friends, they became my new clients and referred their friends. It was like a pyramid scheme, but I was making all the money.

Armand was long gone, living out in the middle of nowhere. I had moved on to some good-looking guy who was hot but not much else.

CHAPTER 93

"Oh my God, did you have kids?" I had been walking through the parking lot, intending to do some Christmas shopping in the Dorval Shopping Centre when two misbehaving kids had caught my attention. Their mother had them both by the elbow and was trying to hustle them towards the entrance. The woman had long brown hair and an incredibly familiar face. "You swore you would never have kids!"

Linda turned around. "Victoria? From Tanguay?"

I laughed. "Yeah, it's me." I looked down at her son and daughter. "Looks like you and Ronny had kids after all."

The Linda I knew used to compete with her husband to see who could smuggle in the most hash. She swore she would never have kids, never be tamed. But there she was, dressed like a mom, acting like a mom, with two kids in tow.

"I know, it's funny. My God, how have you been?" Linda smiled at me. "Want to grab a cup of coffee? The kids could use a hot chocolate."

Life has a funny way of coming full circle. There are some people you have karma or destiny with. They pop back into your life when you least expect it. When they come back, it's like no time has passed. After coffee, Linda and I exchanged numbers. Within a few weeks, we were spending almost every day at each other's houses. My time was now taken up by lunches, boating, shopping and chilling at either my house or Linda's.

Thanks to Armand, who had taught me how to ski, when Linda and I went skiing, I could hold my own. Spring went by so fast. I made enough money and traded in my Micra to lease a grey Dodge Lancer. I had also met many of Linda and Ronny's friends and took to hanging out with this crowd now.

"Welcome, Victoria!" Colleen opened the door to her eleventh-floor apartment on Lakeshore Drive.

"Hey April, Jason, Keith, Marleen." I took off my coat and settled on the couch with my purse. "Wayne." I nodded at my rival.

"Victoria! Now the party has arrived!" Jason laughed.

"So, what will it be this time?" I asked Jason.

"I'll take an eight ball," Jason replied.

"I'll take a gram and a half," Keith said next. They went around the circle, giving me their orders.

"Nothing for you, Wayne?" I teased.

"Ha ha, Victoria, very funny." He rolled his eyes at me. One-armed Wayne was my biggest competition. I was only at the party because he had run out. That being said, I genuinely liked Wayne. I was making enough money and I didn't care what Wayne did.

The real appeal of dealing was the unpredictability it added to my day that kept me from getting bored. For example, I headed to the gym around 9:00 a.m. Then I would wait and see who called to go for lunch. I knew I would end up at a party or bar somewhere later that night. But I didn't know where and I didn't know when. I waited for the beep that would send my whole day in a new direction.

"Okay." I took out my little black scale. Drug dealing didn't require a lot of equipment, but you did need a scale, preferably digital, and small baggies. I purchased all my supplies from a store on Sherbrooke Street and Girouard in Notre-Dame-de-Grâce that specialized in things dealers need. That meant they sold scales and the baggies you used to put your coke in. The store had a lot of fake cleaning cans that cops would never think to look in. Finally, the store sold cutting mixture. I considered myself an honourable dealer. I cut my coke as little as possible. Quality and customer service were the hallmarks of my business. I generally delivered within forty-five minutes.

"Thanks." Jason took his blow and placed it on a mirror. He pulled a credit card from his wallet and cut himself two lines. I heard one line go and then the next, while I weighed Keith's.

"SMMMMM!" Jason's eyes got big. "This is good shit, Victoria. Are you sure you don't want some?"

"No, I'm good, Jason," I replied, not looking up from my weighing.

"Come on, Jason, you know Victoria doesn't do drugs," Colleen admonished.

"That's what I like about her. You can always trust a dealer who doesn't do drugs." Colleen did a small dainty line. She licked her finger, swiped the mirror, and then ran her finger along her gums.

When everyone had their blow and I had their money, we all sat down to drink. Partying with people while they're on coke and you're not is different. I could see their twitchy movements. They talked really, really fast about nothing. But it was a good time.

The clock on the wall read 1:00 a.m. The sky was as dark as it gets in Montreal on a cloudy night. "Okay, well, I'm going to go now." I stood, gathering up my stuff.

"Really?" April asked. "You don't want to stay a little longer?"

"No, I'm good." I told her. "I'll see you guys later." I walked out of the apartment and back to my Lancer.

I woke up the next morning at 10 a.m. I did my thing: went to the gym, had lunch, and then turned my pager on at noon. My business hours were from 12 p.m. to 12 a.m.

At 12:02 p.m. my pager went off. It showed that the page was coming from 115, the number I had assigned to April. This was followed by a phone number, so I walked around the block to the payphone. It looked as though I was going back to the high-rise. When I opened the door, I saw that most of the people from last night's party were still there. April, Jason, Marleen and Keith were all in the living room wearing the same clothes they had on yesterday.

"Oh good, you're here!" Marleen looked less enthusiastic and more relieved. She was instantly digging in her purse. "I want an…" She counted out her money. "An eight ball."

"Okay." I set my scale back down on the coffee table.

Everyone else had their money out by the time I finished weighing Colleen's eight ball.

Oh my God, these people have been up all night… and they want more!

Each person did a line the second they got their blow. It seemed to straighten them out. They were no longer jerking around, clenching their jaws, and their noses stopped running.

"Are they still there?" Keith asked.

Colleen looked out the window. "I think so."

April fingered the curtains. "Oh my God, I think it's the cops."

"Where?" I got up to the window.

"There." They pointed to an empty station wagon.

"Where?" I asked again.

"There!" They pointed to the same station wagon. "It's been there all night. It's an undercover cop!"

The car was empty. I had seen it empty last night and it was still empty when I walked past it this afternoon. "Let's not panic," I said as I gathered up my stuff. "I have some more clients to see. When I go down I'll check and see if it's an undercover car."

"Would you?" April looked as if she might hug me.

"Of course, no problem." I put my hand on the doorknob and turned around. "When I go down there, I'll give you guys a big thumbs-up if it's clear."

Everyone nodded, almost in unison.

I walked out the door and up the street. I could see the station wagon a few cars up. I could tell from where I was that it was empty, but I figured I'd better make a show of it. I wanted them to be convinced it was safe. I looked around. Then I walked up to the car slowly. I bent down and looked inside. I could see kids' toys and a few Mc Donald's wrappers. I straightened and looked up. I could just barely see the window I knew they were watching from. I stuck both my thumbs way up and smiled. I saw the window darken as they closed the curtains.

My God, I thought as I walked back to my Lancer. *Is that what it's like? Is that what paranoia is?*

I really didn't understand doing coke. Dealing it, sure—that was easy. But doing it, I really couldn't imagine.

My next stop was Peter's. Peter was a good customer and a businessman. He was particular about everything, including his blow.

"Hi, Victoria." Peter's wife Jeannie invited me in. I walked into the entranceway of their Beaconsfield home, then on to the dining room. Peter was at the table reading his Sunday paper.

"Peter." I smiled at him.

"Victoria." he smiled back. "Let's see what you have for me today."

I put my purse on the table with my scale and my baggies. "I think you'll be happy with this batch."

"I guess we'll see." Peter leaned forward.

Today the blow I had was pure white, and shiny with a pleasant smell. I measured out Peter's eight ball. He put a tiny bit on his hand and sniffed.

"You're right. This is good stuff." Peter pocketed the bag.

"I thought so." Really, I had no idea. Usually, when coke was pure white and had the almost baby powder smell, it was good. But not always. Yellow coke was bad.

Although people who did crack liked the yellow coke. Apparently it cooked better. It was worse if the coke smelled like gasoline. If it smelled like gas it was because it had been smuggled out in gas cans. Someone had explained that whatever the yellow coke was made with was so illegal in certain parts of Colombia, it was a life sentence if you were caught with it.

CHAPTER 94

Part of what made my life so awesome was the place that I lived. It was a little house on Canary Street that cost me $425 a month in rent. It wasn't fancy, but I liked it there. All my friends had Corvettes and Jags, I had a Dodge Lancer. All my friends lived in mansions and I lived in a nice, but cosy house. It wasn't something I thought about consciously, but when I saw this amazing house in Dorval with a for sale sign I couldn't resist. Making the kind of money I did, it was easy to save. I already had $10,000.

The address was 455 Boulevard des Sources. I knocked on the front door. The owner answered right away.

"Hi, I'd like to see the house. I'm interested in buying it." I waited for the man to let me in.

"Of course, of course, come right on in."

The house was as nice on the inside as I imagined. You walked up the front porch and through the front door. A curved wooden staircase led upstairs to a master bedroom, bathroom and two smaller bedrooms. Downstairs, you walked into a living room, then a dining room. Off the right side of the dining room was a lovely kitchen. The back of the house had an extension built on with a laundry room and an office.

The house had real hardwood floors that matched the ceiling panels. In the backyard, there was a built-in swimming pool, a shady back porch, and a good-sized yard.

"I'll take it," I declared. The owner stopped and looked at me. "Will you take $10, 000 as a down payment and hold the mortgage for me?"

The guy didn't say anything.

"I can have the cash to you by the end of the day."

That got his attention. "I'm sorry. What your name was again?"

"Victoria."

The first of the next month I moved in. The house was right around the corner from where I had been living on Canary Street. The mortgage was at eighteen per cent. But, I now owned my own home. Soon I would have a Corvette to go with it.

Right after I made the buy, I went to Ronny and Linda's. I regaled them with my $135, 000 impulse buy and promised they would be the first to come over once I moved it.

"You don't have that kind of money!" Linda exclaimed.

"I do now," I said and grinned wickedly at her.

"Welcome!" I said, as I answered the door, letting Linda and Jeannie in. "I'll give you a tour before the party starts."

After we'd finished touring the house, I took my friends out to the backyard. "I love it!" Jeannie exclaimed, taking her shoes off and dipping her feet in the pool.

"I know, isn't it great? I'm going to go inside and get us some drinks." I walked back into the kitchen to mix up the drinks.

When the girls returned to the kitchen, Linda stopped at the table and looked at the box of photos I had found earlier. "What are these?" she asked, starting to go through them.

"I don't know. I found them in the attic. They're cool looking, eh?" I handed her a drink.

"Yeah, they're from the 1920s. Look at the way the people are dressed." Linda handed a photo to Jeannie. "When was the house built?"

"In the '20s. I guess around the time those pictures were taken. But it's been renovated and had that extension that holds my office added to it." I handed Jeannie her gin and tonic.

"That's crazy." Jeannie pulled a few more photos out of the box. "Did you find any letters? It would be cool if you knew who these people were."

"No, no letters, just those pictures. Check out this pure silver cutlery set I found as well."

The doorbell rang; this time it was Alan.

People came and went all night. They brought me gifts for my housewarming. I made an effort to be a good host. Everyone would be discussing my party tomorrow and I wanted to measure up. People who wanted to buy coke asked me and I would get it for them. Otherwise, I kept it locked in a drawer.

CHAPTER 95

"Here you go, Victoria." Victor my new supplier that I had met through my new friends handed me my new ounce of coke. "It's good shit this time. Not like last time."

"Cool, Victor." I grabbed the ounce. "I'll see you next time."

At home, I started measuring out the ounce, getting some bags ready to sell. The white powder looked harmless. It smelled good, it looked good, but was it good? I moved the powder around the scale. I felt twitchy. All this time I had been dealing this drug and I had never even been tempted to try it. Last week, Peter had been on my case about the quality of that batch. That blow had looked white and smelled nice, too. But he hadn't liked it and it was a wasted trip. On the way home, I wondered how I could know if my product was good. Peter was an excellent client, one I wanted to keep. He appreciated my prompt delivery, flexible hours and, most important, my discretion.

There is only one way to find out, I told myself.

Am I really going to do this? It made perfect business sense to me. If I tried this blow and Peter liked it, then I would know what he liked. I could test the quality of my coke before I sold it. I would always be sure it was good, and not waste my time making wasted trips. I can't stand wasting my time.

I dumped a wee bit out on the glass tabletop. I grabbed a straw. Leaning down, I snorted it the same way I had seen so many of my clients do. The blow hit the back of my throat and burned. It tasted like rubber. I looked around, blinking and snorting.

I blew out a sigh and stood up. I walked to the kitchen and had a drink of water. Then I went back to the blow. My hands were shaking. *This is terrible. My heart is going to pop out of my chest.* I put the blow away. The clock said 10:32 a.m., time to get to the gym. I went upstairs to get my stuff together then had to go hunting for my keys.

"Jesus Christ!" I said out loud to no one. "I'm too goddamn high to drive. I am never not able to drive." I paced back and forth in my kitchen, eyes darting around the room. I decided to clean the kitchen, then the office, then the upstairs. Finally the jitters went away and my heartbeat slowed. My whole day had been wasted.

"Linda, why on earth would you do coke?" I asked her the next day at lunch.

"Did you try it?" Linda sounded shocked.

"I couldn't go to the gym. I couldn't even drive!" I sat back watching Linda's expression.

"You did coke. Why did you do coke?" Linda was trying not to laugh.

"Well, it's simple, really. I sell a product and I need to make sure that product is good quality. This is how I pay my bills. If my clients aren't happy, I don't make any money. I figured that if I knew what they liked, I would know which coke to sell them."

"Ahem." Our waiter cut me off. "You ordered the Caesar salad as usual, Miss."

"Yes." I nodded. I came here almost every day for lunch.

"Go on," Linda urged. She was eyeing me eagerly over her soup.

"I told you, I need to be able to tell if it's good or not." I took a bite; the salad was perfect as usual.

"I don't know what to tell you, Victoria. It just makes life better. Speaking of which, do you have any on you?" Linda pushed her chicken breast around her plate.

"You know I do. I always carry. We'll head to your place after lunch." I smiled at her.

"I can't believe you did coke." Linda shook her head. "Wait till I tell Ronny."

"Okay, okay. Let's not make too big a deal out of this," I said, laughing.

I went back to my normal routine; I didn't think about doing coke again—until my next batch came in. I looked at it as I weighed it out. *Why would I do this again? My day had been wasted,* I remembered. I thought about it. I could never focus on anything for long. That's why I liked dealing. I was always being pulled in a different direction.

Screw it. I cut myself a little bump and snorted it without thinking. The second time wasn't as bad. I didn't feel my eyes bulging out of my head. I could sit and read the next chapter in my astrology textbook.

Summer turned into fall and fall turned into winter, and before I knew it Christmas was here. My drug habit had grown as naturally as my drug dealing. I did a line every time I got a new batch, and Peter never complained again. Then I started doing a line every other day, every day and then twice a day.

"Come on in. What's this?" I let Jason and April into my house. Jason had a large carpet rolled up under his arm.

"Just a little Christmas gift." April gave me a kiss on the cheek.

Jason took the coke. "Just a minute. Let me make this better." He turned to the stove. I tried to see what he was doing but his broad shoulders blocked my view. "Here." Jason turned around and stuck a pipe in my mouth. "Suck on this." He lit the pipe.

I breathed in a massive toke. Instantly, I was in love. "Jason, oh my God! This is just like acid. I loved acid in the '60s!"

"I thought you might like it." Jason took a toke and passed the pipe around.

It's true: I loved acid. My glory days in the '60s were filled with mind-expanding acid trips. I have never had a bad trip. People are always surprised when I say that, but it's true. Just give me acid and let me talk to God. There is nothing I enjoy more.

"My turn." I took the pipe from April, and took another massive toke. Light waves rippled across my vision. Sound became amplified. Everything felt warm and fuzzy. I moved side to side, savouring all the feelings in my body.

"Oh, my turn again." I took the pipe again from Jason.

Ding dong. A gong went off in my head.

"Well, time to put this away. Finish your toke." Jason took the pipe from me.

"Why, Jason?" I asked.

"Trust me, just trust me. People look at snorting and smoking crack differently. One is recreational and the other is an addiction."

"Okay." I went to answer the door. It was just after ten; within an hour the house was full. People drank and talked. They did lines everywhere. It was a really jolly holiday party.

"Wayne!" I smiled at my biggest competition and good friend.

"This is quite the party." Wayne moved over so I could sit on the couch next to him.

"Thanks, Wayne." My head rolled a little to the side.

"You having a good time, Victoria?" He looked around.

I smiled and nodded. "It's a rocking Christmas party!"

"Out of professional courtesy, I left my stash at home. It would be rude for me to deal here." Wayne took a sip of his drink.

"You know, Wayne, it really wouldn't bother me if you did."

"Really?" Wayne's eyes widened.

"Yeah, it's cool." I leaned back in my seat as a head rush came over me.

"I'll be right back." Wayne jumped up and walked out the door. He was back in an instant with his bags, scale and blow. *I guess he meant he left it in his car, not his house.*

It was true; I didn't care if Wayne dealt at my house. I was partying with my friends and having a good time.

If Donald was home, we'd be cuddling together all the time. With him, I had no need for parties, drugs, gambling, drinking, gossiping or such. I never felt that way before or since. We had been content to just be together. I missed that, which was why I kept myself so busy having fun.

"Wow, Victoria, you really outdid yourself this time." Wayne was gathering up his stuff.

The sun was shining bright in the sky. It was starting to hurt my eyes.

Wayne looked at his watch. "One o'clock. I think that's almost a new record."

"I'm pretty sure it is a new record, Wayne." I opened the front door for him.

"I guess I'll just have to try and beat it next weekend."

"Next weekend." I closed the door behind Wayne and walked upstairs to my bed. *At least my party will be the talk of the town till the next one.* I sat down slowly, not even realizing my head was hitting the pillow before blackness closed over me.

CHAPTER 96

A month or so after I started smoking crack, I was staying up all night and sleeping in until late afternoon. My eyes were glued shut and my mouth had grit in it when I woke up.

"Eleven new messages!"

I listened to the first one. "Hey, Victoria, it's Linda. Listen, don't worry—it's not for you. They're chasing some guy, but it's not you."

I didn't like the sound of that.

Next message: "Victoria, it's Wayne. There's been a bust, but it's not you they're after."

What the eff?

Third message; Linda again. "Don't be freaked out by the helicopter. It's not for you."

Helicopter. Now I was up and mostly awake. I stumbled my way into the kitchen for a glass of water. I looked out the window and did a double take. *Why was my fence-side door open?* I slid the patio doors open.. There were footprints on my lawn. I went back inside and dialed Linda.

"Hello?"

"Linda, what the hell happened last night?"

"There was a store knocked over a few streets away and the guy took off. The cops had dogs and helicopters tearing through your neighbourhood. Didn't you get my messages?"

"Yeah, I got them. Thanks for calling."

"No problem. I'll see you soon, Victoria."

Oh, my fucking God. I had a police chase taking place in my backyard and I didn't even wake up. Something crazy must have gone down, and I just slept through it.

I picked up my pipe from the kitchen table and took my first morning toke. I put the pipe down.

Oh my God! There was a police chase in my backyard. I didn't hear a thing. I was asleep. What would happen if I got raided? If I get raided, I won't stand a chance.

I won't hear them coming until it's too late...

The paranoia set in for the first time.

It was worse than what they describe.

CHAPTER 97

I had been in my house on Boulevard des Sources for a year. I had bought a country house last summer; I was still driving my Corvette and had kept my Lancer. My money was being spent faster than I could make it and too much of my stash went up in smoke.

I couldn't sustain my lifestyle. I had to sell something. I picked the country house. It was ugly orange-and-white and tiny, two bedrooms on a lake. I had bought the place on a whim, anyway. I was up in Saint-Sauveur and saw a sales office selling country houses. I went in there and bought one for $15,000 on credit. My credit was still good, even then. You rarely know you've spent too much until it's too late. That's the downside of good credit.

Hanging out with friends didn't cost me any money. It was a good way to keep in touch with clients and advertise my country house. Karate John—let's call him KJ, so this doesn't get complicated in a moment—was one of my clients and friends. I had met him through Ronny and Linda. He and his wife, Chelsea, would have me over almost every day.

Montreal may be a big a city but, really, it's a small underworld.

"I went like this." KJ did a few karate kicks, imitating the Bruce Lee movie playing on TV. "And then this." He fist-punched the air. "And then finally like this." KJ kicked an imaginary line of men. "Almost as good as John A that night at The Mustache."

That caught my attention. "You know John A?"

"Yeah, Victoria. Do you know him?" Chelsea looked interested.

"He used to date my best friend Heather in the '60s. I haven't seen him in, like, twenty years."

KJ looked at me and said, "He lives right around the corner."

"You should give him a call. I'd love to see him again." I looked right at KJ.

"Do it KJ," Chelsea encouraged.

"Sure." He picked up the phone. "Hey, John, come over. There's someone here who wants to see you… Find out when you get here." KJ hung up the phone.

It was true; I hadn't seen John in twenty years. Not since he had gone out with my best friend Heather. They had a child together named Angel. We had all been very young back then.

Ding, ding, ding.

"Come in, it's open!" KJ yelled.

I heard the door open and looked towards the landing. John looked down at me. I had a moment.

Twenty-three years ago, when I was sixteen and Heather was eighteen, we would eat lunch every day at an underground café called The Bus Stop. I don't know if the servers were high, or just a pain in the ass. They never got our order right, and we ordered the same thing each time: toasted ham with ketchup for me and plain bread with ham and mustard for Heather. Without fail, we would be served every combination of those four ingredients except the one we actually wanted, every single time.

On that day, I believe my sandwich was toasted but had mustard.

"Look at that good-looking guy," Heather said, putting down her sandwich.

"Where?" I looked around. I didn't see anyone all that good-looking.

"There." Heather pointed to a man in a suit, sitting across from us in a booth with two other guys. "The one with the goatee."

"Okay, I got this." I walked over to the dark-haired guy. He was interesting-looking, but not what I considered handsome. At least not in the way Heather seemed to think. "Excuse me, my girlfriend wants to meet you. She's right over there," I said, pointing at Heather. She smiled at him.

I walked back to Heather, and John came over as soon as he got his sandwich. The rest was history.

As John stepped into the house, my heart did a very similar take to that day back in 1975 when Donald had gotten into the back of my vehicle. *Oh, shit,* I thought.

John didn't recognize me until I brought up Heather. We then sat and chatted. Talked about the old days.

"How long has it been Victoria, twenty years?"

"Twenty-three, to be exact," I clarified.

"You always did like numbers, Victoria." John sat down beside me. I could feel his body heat. I wanted him, like I wanted Donald all those years ago.

"You know, John, Victoria's selling her country house." Chelsea smiled at him. "Know anyone's who's interested?"

John laughed. "Actually, I do, yeah."

"Do you know someone who needs to get rid of something fast? It's right on the water," I jokingly said, putting my hand on John's knee and giving it a small squeeze.

"It sounds interesting. Maybe you can show it to me?"

"Sure, John. How does tomorrow sound?"

"Tomorrow sounds great, Victoria."

That night when I went home, I felt happy. My mind rested on the image I had of John in my head and the conversation we had shared. Tomorrow, I would take him to the lake house, and see where it went from there. I knew he was married. He had been for fourteen years to a woman named Lucinda. Still, the need to see him again was strong. I didn't think he felt this way about me. I could, however, see what Heather saw in him all those years ago. He was good-looking, charming, low-key, and very easy-going. John was also quite intelligent. He had several black belts in different martial arts and studied the cultures they were from.

I pulled up to John's house in my Corvette. He and his wife Lucinda came out to greet me. I heard John turn to Lucinda and say, "I'm sorry. It's a two-seater."

"But I wanted to come," she said.

"Next time." He waved goodbye and hopped in. "Let's do this."

It was a pleasant drive to the country. The sun was shining and the closer we got to the lake, the louder the birds sang and the more comfortable I felt. We talked a lot about the old days and what we had done over the years.

"Here it is," I said when I pulled up the driveway. The house had a wooden front porch and a path that went right down to the lake. We went inside and I showed him around. "This is the bedroom." I stopped in the doorway, so John bumped into me. I turned around and backed up farther into the bedroom. "What do you think?" I took his hand and pulled him closer.

"It's nice. You could have a lot of fun in here." He didn't let go of my hand.

"The view of the sunset is amazing." I pointed out the window. We looked at the yard outside, still holding hands. "Want to get a drink?" I suggested.

"Sure," John replied.

What happened next happened rather fast. We drove back into the city of Saint-Sauveur and found a patio to have a few drinks. Lots of couples were talking and laughing around us. It made me feel like one of them, a couple. All the sunshine made it hard to look elsewhere, so we spent a lot of time looking into each other's eyes, while still talking about the old days. When I was sixteen, John was secretary-treasurer of the newly founded Montreal chapter of the Satan's Choice motorcycle club. John was from my life pre-Donald. Everything felt simpler, like it was before. Before all the drug dealing and crack, before I had even been married.

"John, I think we should go back to my place to have a few more drinks. Now that you've seen my country house, you should see my city house. I have a swimming pool and everything."

"Okay, Victoria." John got up and paid the bill.

Once again, I gave him a tour of the house. It also ended in my bedroom.

"This is really something, Victoria. You've done well for yourself." John sat on the bed.

"Thanks. I like it better with you here." I walked over to stand right in front of him.

"Yeah?"

"Yeah." I put one leg on either side of his and sat down. I took his chin in my hand and tilted his face up to me, then I leaned down to kiss him. I felt his hands wrap around my waist. He didn't rush. We kissed slowly. John was gentle. I pushed his shoulders down on the bed, letting our waists make full contact. When I took off my shirt, John's eyes widened before he reached up to touch me. He was gentle, accommodating. He followed my lead.

John was over every day after that. My smoking crack never bothered him. Within a few weeks, my house became a meeting spot for John and his friends, many of whom I knew from way back. It was nice to connect to the old Choice members. In 1977, they had patched over to the Outlaws. I was now John's main squeeze. "Can I interest anyone?" I sat down with my pipe and vial of crack. I set the crack on the table and picked up the pipe. I took the pipe and placed tinfoil over the top. I poked a few holes in the foil with a pin, then I sprinkled some of the ashes from my ashtray on top. I crowned all of that with a rock of crack.

"You're going to smoke that?" Carl, one of the Outlaws asked.

"Yeah, you want some?"

"No, I'm good."

Jackie, his girlfriend, leaned a little closer, and I offered it to her as well. "I'm good," she said.

"Okay, suit yourselves." I held the pipe and then held my lighter to the crack on the tinfoil. Within a millisecond, the pipe filled with smoke and I sucked it in. It felt like taking your first deep breath after you've been drowning. Everything slows down; it calms down. I leaned back into the couch.

I opened my eyes and sat back up. Put the pipe back on the coffee table. Carl was staring. John just looked amused. He really didn't care that I smoked. He didn't care about anything. John accepted me unconditionally. Even Donald had demanded I stop drinking.

"Achoo!" Jackie sneezed.

I looked up. "Oh my God, that sounded like a waterfall!" My hearing was turned up to ten, maybe beyond. I heard everything, and I understood it differently. It was as if a part of my brain that I didn't normally use was finally working. I could see and understand how addiction takes hold of people so easily. Once you tap into unknown resources, it's fascinating; at least, I thought so.

Jackie laughed.

CHAPTER 98

My pager beeped, and I looked down for the code: 733.

I love you from John.

I had been thinking of him and he had been thinking of me.

SCREECH! The car in front of me slammed on the brakes. I slammed on mine and my Corvette's ABS warning light flashed. I spun around the car and avoided a collision. "What the hell?" I tried the brakes again and this time they worked. I pulled off onto a side street and sped up. Then I slammed on the brakes. The Corvette took way too long to stop, even by normal car standards.

Something was wrong. Ronny owned the Chevrolet dealership I had bought the Corvette from, so I drove straight there. "Leave the car with me," one of the mechanics said. "I'll take a look and see what's up."

"Thanks." I had returned John's page with the phone number of the dealership. He arrived a few minutes later to pick me up. He drove me home and we made dinner.

The phone rang an hour later. "Hello?"

"You know, Victoria, I'm supposed to call the police when we find a bullet in a car," Ronny said calmly with a hint of amusement.

"What?"

"I'm obviously not going to call the cops, but somebody shot your car with a .45. It's fixed now, so you can come get the car. Is everything cool?"

"Yeah Ronny, it's cool. I'll come tomorrow to pick up the car. Thanks."

I hung up the phone and turned to John. "Somebody shot my Corvette with a .45."

"A .45?" John stood up. "How do you know?"

"One of Ronny's mechanics found it. The bullet took out my ABS. Who would want to shoot my car? I mean, shoot me, sure. But my car? They must have a real death wish. Nobody messes with my car." I went to the window and looked out.

Then I listened. All I heard was a plane flying overhead. One of the few drawbacks of living in this house was that it was under a frequently used flight path.

The next day John arrived at my house and said, "I have the answer to the mystery of who shot your car."

He told me and I couldn't believe what I heard. "Lucinda? Really, Lucinda shot my car?" I walked back into the kitchen. "That little bitch. How did she shoot my car? What the fuck, John?"

"She took the .45 out of my safe and came over. She said she waited till one of the planes flew by and then she shot your car."

"Are you fucking kidding me?" I stared at him.

"No. She's pissed about my 'affair,' as she calls it with you. Listen, Victoria, let me handle it. I'll take you to pick up the Corvette. I've already dealt with Lucinda, and I had to throw away my gun. I want to make this right." He stood real close to me. I could feel his breath on my nose. "Victoria…" He took my hand. I pulled it away. "Victoria…" He tried again. This time I let him hold my hand. "Let's go get the car. I'll pay."

"You know it isn't about the money, John. This is serious."

"I know. Let's just start with that. I'll make this right, I promise."

John was one of the very few people who could handle me. "Fine, but, fuck, seriously?"

"I know." He kissed my forehead. "Tell me what else you want me to do. There must be something I can give you that would make you a little less mad."

I thought for a moment. *That bitch. How could I get her back?* John wanted to handle this. I couldn't go behind his back and take matters into my own hands but I wanted to make her suffer. I wanted her to wake up every day pissed at me because she tried and failed, and I got one over on her.

"I want your air conditioner." *Lucinda hated the heat.*

"Done."

John was good to his word and Lucinda bitched about the heat the rest of the summer. At the time I didn't really think of her as John's wife. He didn't belong to her. He went to me to escape.

I was the one he sent 733 pages to. It was my house that he brought his friends to. In my mind, Lucinda was horrible to him. I hated her. She was a drug addict of some sort; John had told me that much. And she was shrill. I could hear her sometimes on John's end of the phone while she screamed at him and threw things. He wasn't happy there and he made me happy. Why wouldn't I give him a place to stay?

Dealing was getting more difficult. I worked till I crashed and then no one could reach me on my pager. Reliability and customer service had always been the foundation of my business. I still traded stocks, but rarely, as I slept most days. Plus, money was very scarce and I was already behind on my mortgage and credit card payments.

My mortgage was at eighteen per cent. I had decided to keep the mortgage in the previous owner's name. He was on the hook if I didn't pay, and I couldn't do that to him. So, I had an idea. I walked into a credit lending place like I was the queen and sat down and asked the woman to refinance my home. I filled out forms and, as she reached the part about my Corvette, she asked, "How much do you owe on it?" Lying through my teeth, I said, "It's paid for." Do angels look after me? I have never heard of any credit lending place not checking your credit or pulling an Equifax report. They didn't. The next day I was called and was told I'd been approved. I called Steve, the previous owner, and arranged to meet him at the credit lenders' where we signed over the house to the credit company and he received a cheque for what had been owing. I felt pleased that he was off the hook, as I knew that the time was coming where I would not be able to handle this mounting debt and my addiction was causing it.

The next thing to go was my power. Hydro-Québec came to my house.

Wayne had to answer the door. I couldn't. I wasn't high, but I couldn't face the truth. "Please, Wayne, can you bribe him?"

"I'll try my best, Victoria." He got up to answer the door. I heard them step outside. Wayne was gone about fifteen minutes.

"Well, he wouldn't turn it back on. But he did show me how to. You should be good for a while."

"Thank you so much, Wayne. How much did it cost you?"

"Twenty bucks." Wayne sat back down.

"That's it?" I asked in surprise.

"I know." I was good for another nine months.

CHAPTER 99

He's going to love this.

I heard John open the door. He would have just seen that I changed out the bulb in the porch light from white to red. He handed me flowers, chocolates, and a bracelet. "Happy Valentine's Day!"

"Thank you. They're beautiful," I said, burying my nose in the flowers.

"Not nearly as beautiful as you."

I encouraged him to follow the rose petals up the stairs and into my bathtub. I had just finished drawing him a bath. I would let him soak in there for a bit and then ask him to join me in bed.

John came out of the bathroom a little red from his bath. I could see his eyes were half closed.

I lay in bed in the black lingerie I had bought in Ottawa, during a recent visit to one of his brothers. He crawled into bed beside me. "Come here." He pulled me close to him, kissing me deeply. I could feel his breathing getting deeper. His eyes were almost closing. *My bath idea had backfired.* I rolled John on his back and put my head on his chest. He was already asleep. In some ways it was disappointing, but it showed how he did things with no expectations in return. *Isn't this what every woman wants? A man to bring her flowers, give her compliments and be satisfied with that? A life with lots of romance and not a lot of sex?*

I didn't see it coming. I had never experienced such weakness in my life. Not even my emotional dependence on Donald equalled the horrific hold crack had on me. I was able to put the pipe away no problem the first night, but it became harder and harder to do. When I woke up in the morning, crack called me from the closet. When I sat down to eat, I had no appetite. My sleep became erratic; everything revolved around crack.

Addictions run in my family. My father was an alcoholic until I was sixteen. As I mentioned before, it was his spiritual life that created a new path for him.

I can't say how much my dads' addictive tendencies affected my own crack addiction. I can't lay blame as many do. You are responsible for your own life. Liquor didn't do anything for me, but crack did. It was a lot like acid: a warm, cosy feeling. Sound was amplified, your mind went to places it had never been, thoughts came to you that you would never ordinarily have. It was heaven. Until the paranoia set in.

Part of my paranoia came from the amount of crack I was doing. But I was also seeing John less. The biker war had started up.

CHAPTER 100

I hugged the wall to look out my back blinds. I peeked through the slats and saw a bush move. I held my breath. It moved again. When I cast my gaze around the fence, I saw shadows moving everywhere. Who the heck was there and why? Could it be bikers?

Get a hold of yourself, I told myself. *Why would they be here? You're not a biker.* But John was... *What if they don't know he's not here right now? What if they want me to be collateral damage? Are they waiting to ambush him?*

The mind thinks in the stupidest of ways when you are high and paranoid. What I saw in the spirit world on crack and acid was real. Those visions came from a part of the brain we don't normally use. Paranoia feels different. What I saw before the paranoia set in came from a place of truth; it was a part of my spiritual awakening. But paranoia comes from a place of fear: a fear of something happening to John, a fear of being arrested, raided, etc. They are two very, very different things.

No. I moved on from that thought. *But what about Lucinda? If she would shoot my car maybe she would send the Hell's Angels to get me. Hmmm... no. How stupid was I being now? She was angry with me, but she was no rat and would have no contact with the Hell's Angels. However, she did know other folks who would be willing to do her a favour...*

My fence was tall, so I couldn't see behind it. I slid open my patio door and listened. I heard footsteps. *This is it, they're coming to get me.* I leaned against the wall, my whole body shaking. My heart was pumping so hard my chest hurt.

"911?"

"Yes, my name is Victoria and I'm at 455 Sources Boulevard. I think someone is trying to break into my house."

"Okay. Tell me what's happening," the 911 operator said.

"I see men outside my house. They're circling around. I think they have guns."

"Okay, don't worry, Victoria. I have officers on the way."

"Okay."

"Just stay with me on the line until the police arrive." The woman's voice was reassuring

"POLICE!" There was a knock at the door.

"I hear the police," I told the women.

"Okay, open the door and make sure it's them," she instructed me.

I slowly opened the door. "Yes, it's the police," I told the operator.

"Okay, you're safe now."

"Come in." I ushered the police inside and hung up the phone.

"What seems to be the problem?" the taller of the two officers asked.

"I think some men are here to kill me. I saw someone in the bushes behind the house, right over there." I pointed to the left at the vacant property beside my house. "I hear them in the back of my property."

The other, shorter police officer wrote a few things down. "Okay, we're going to go look around and make sure everything is okay. You stay here."

"Okay." I closed the door behind him. I watched the police fan out and disappear down the side of my house. I paced back and forth, waiting. It felt like hours.

The tall cop came back inside.

"Well?"

"We found the men outside. Thank you for calling us. My partner is in the car writing a report."

"Really?" I looked at him in surprise.

"Yes." The cop smiled at me. "You'll be safe now. We made sure no one else was there."

I nodded.

"Is there anything else?"

"No, I'm good, but thank you, officer."

Again, I closed the door behind him. *There really were guys out there. I wasn't crazy.* I played it over in my mind. Somebody had been outside my house, ready to get me... and I called the cops on them.

Oh my God... now they were really going to kill me. I called the cops. I got them arrested. Fuck! What was I thinking?

Paranoia is absolutely horrid. I looked outside again and saw more activity in the bushes. I called 911 again like a true idiot. The cops returned.

"Don't you see them? The guys you took away. They must be sending people over here to kill me," I said.

"Miss, do you know what day it is?" the shorter of the two officers asked me.

"Of course I know what day it is. It's Thursday."

"Okay, do you know what time is it?"

I looked around for a clock. The cop snapped his fingers to get my attention. "Can you tell me what time is?"

"It's late. After midnight."

It wasn't.

They called for an ambulance. The ambulance arrived and the cops said, "Don't fight this. We can do it the hard way or the easy way."

"Easy way? I'm not crazy" I hissed. "I saw what I saw."

"Okay, enough of this," the tall cop said. The attendants came in and asked me to walk to the ambulance.

The psychiatrist was a middle-aged man, of medium height and medium weight. "Good morning, Miss"—he looked at my chart—"Victoria. Do you know why you're here?"

"Yeah, because I thought I saw bikers outside my house. I called the cops and when they came, the cops told me they arrested the guys outside my house."

"That's not what the police—"

"Then I thought that if I got the cops involved, the bikers would be really angry and come back." I cut the psychiatrist off.

"That's not what I have written here in my notes. Based on my notes, I'm inclined to admit you for a few days for observation."

There was no way in hell I was being committed.

"Look," I said, as I smiled at him, "I did some cocaine and I think I did a little too much. I'm fine now, so no need to keep me here any longer."

"Okay, well, do you have a job?" the psychiatrist asked. He looked at me skeptically.

"Of course I have a job. I work for Jack an accountant. I'm a tax-paying citizen—look it up."

"Is there anyone who can verify this? Because the police said they found you distraught and hallucinating."

"Call my son. He's visiting for the summer. He should be at the house. He'll tell you. He came home from his girlfriend's just as I called the cops." I crossed my arms.

"All right."

The psychiatrist left and when he came back, his whole demeanour had changed. "I'm very sorry, Victoria. We've spoken to your son and he's confirmed everything you said. Apparently they told you that so you would calm down. There really was nobody outside."

"I told you."

"Yes, and again, I'm sorry. The cops made it very clear to the attending doctor last night, who made it very clear in his notes, that you were psychotic."

"Well," I said getting out of bed, "don't believe everything the cops tell you. You never know."

He nodded his head.

My son came to take me home. He pulled up to the hospital in my Corvette. Technically, he wasn't supposed to be driving it, but I wasn't in a position to say anything.

"Rough night?" Emmett raised his eyebrows at me.

"Yeah, something like that." I closed my eyes to the bright sunlight. "Can we please just go home? I need you to call John."

"Sure, Mom."

We drove in silence the rest of the way. When we got back, I lay down on the couch. My anger at almost being committed had masked the exhaustion I now felt. "Can you please call John now? If Lucinda answers the phone, don't say it's you. She'll recognize your name."

Emmett dialed. "Hi. Is John there? Yeah, this is Emmett. My mom just got out of the hospital and she wants to see you." Emmett hung up the phone. "He's coming."

My door opened ten minutes later and it was John.

CHAPTER 101

Shortly after I got out of the psych ward, John and his Outlaw brothers were arrested in Ontario. All of the members had been charged and then had their bail denied. The Crown wanted the Outlaws locked up; now they had some of the Outlaws where they wanted them. There wouldn't be a speedy trial.

Before John had been arrested, I had tried hard to stop using. Once he was gone, I gave up fighting it and just tried to cut back. Which was a good thing for my business. I was able to work up a couple of deals. I made money and I had enough coke for myself.

It felt like a good day. I finished my deal and then went about cleaning my house. I vacuumed all the floors, washed the windows, did some laundry, and made my bed. After a few hours, the house was clean, and I was content. I stretched out on my couch the way I had done so often with Donald in Verdun.

Lying still wasn't easy. I wasn't unhappy, but I was lonely. *Maybe I should have a toke. I'm just sitting here.* I knew it was a stupid idea. The coke was my income. I sat up. Then I stood up. Half of me knew I should stop but it didn't know how to stop the other half. I got my stash and pulled out a few grams. I took it to the kitchen and cooked it up on the stove. I grabbed my pipe. *Am I really going to do this?* I took a big toke. It hit me like a wave. As I lay back, a vibrating, warm voice sounded from the stairway.

"We've done all we can to help you. You're on your own now."

I know what I heard and, as I evaluated what that meant, I knew I had made a mistake in taking that hit of crack. I could have done so many other things: gone to a movie, gone over to Linda's, read a book, watched mindless TV, or contemplated the meaning of life. But no, I chose to be stupid. Now I would be up all night, fending off paranoia and anything else crack threw my way. But that voice had spoken with such conviction. The voice felt warm and friendly; I wasn't afraid of it. I knew it was telling me the truth. This was just more proof that someone was watching over me. Little did I know how much or what was to follow. Life would spiral downward.

CHAPTER 102

"Victoria." Mark opened the door for me. There was a party going on in full force in the middle of the day no less. "Did you bring the party favours?"

"You know I did. I always bring the fun." I smirked.

"After you." Mark made a flourish with his arms. I went into the living room. People were scattered all around, talking in groups. I didn't say anything, but people seemed to sense me. Everyone turned in my direction. I set up my scale as the most eager came forward first.

I ran out of customers just before I ran out of blow. I let myself into Mark's kitchen to do a few lines myself.

"There you are. I was wondering where you wandered off to." Mark was sitting on the couch. "You look like you're enjoying the rewards of your hard work."

I don't know why but I felt a little sheepish. I sat down in front of him. I was silent.

"I haven't seen you in a while. What have you been up to?"

"You know, this and that. Lately I've been working a lot from home." I shrugged my shoulders.

"I see." Mark was a nice guy. He was well connected, ambitious, a good listener.

"You know how it is."

"I do." Mark stopped talking.

"I mean, it's getting a little out of hand maybe. I've been thinking maybe I should cut back. Take up meditation."

"You think that will help?" Mark didn't laugh like the few other people I had told.

"I don't know, Mark. I've thought about rehab. There's this place in Toronto I was looking at."

"I think that's a good idea. Why haven't you called?"

"I don't know. I think I'm trying to work up the courage to let go of this life. It's all I've known for a long time and I don't want to have to start from scratch.

I don't know what I want to do with my life. First I have to quit this hold that crack has on me, though"

"Is that it?" Mark stood up and brought over his telephone. "You should call. I'll even pay for it."

I thought about pretending I didn't remember the number but, even high out of my mind I was still good with numbers.

"Hello, I'm calling about a spot in your program." I said, when they picked up. I twisted the phone cord around my hand nervously.

"Is it for yourself or somebody else?"

"It's for me. I'd like to come in as soon as possible."

There was silence on the other end of the phone. "Our next spot won't be available for three more months."

"Three months! I'll be dead by then." I slammed down the phone.

"That didn't sound like it went well." Mark put the phone back.

"Well, maybe it's a sign that I'm not meant to go to rehab. I'll just have to stick it out a while longer. I can kick this on my own, no problem."

"Fingers crossed." Mark smiled at me.

I hated the way Mark was looking at me. Deep inside, I was distraught. My plan had always been to wait until I couldn't take it anymore, then I would ship myself off to rehab. Now I knew that wasn't an option. *What the hell was I going to do?* I wanted a toke more than ever. "I'm going to go to get some air." I stood up. Mark was already talking to somebody else.

I went out to my car and drove home. I couldn't face going back inside.

"Did you hear what happened to Mark?" Ronny said to me one day, a couple of weeks later.

"No." I hadn't been out of the house in days.

"Really? Mark's dead. Somebody took him out. They found his body out on some highway."

"I was just talking to him two weeks ago when I dropped over. He let me use his phone so I could call a rehab centre in Toronto."

"He was a nice guy," Ronny said.

"I don't know what I'm going to do, Ronny. I need to get away. I want to dry out."

Ronny looked at me thoughtfully. "Is there anywhere else you could stay?"

My parents were now living in Edmonton, but due to my addictions I had started ignoring their letters and calls. Eventually, they stopped writing and calling. I didn't want to go live with my parents. I didn't want to go that far west. But west had always been my plan with Donald. Run away from here and never come back. It hadn't worked with Paul. Maybe I wasn't meant to go there forever, just for a time, and go alone. Lorna was the only other family member I would consider staying with. She was also in Edmonton, along with Danny and the kids.

"I think I might go to Edmonton. I can spend time with my kids. Who knows when John and his brothers will be out."

Ronny smiled. "I think that would do you a world of good."

CHAPTER 103

Kenny, a friend I had met through John and his wife Moira drove me to the bus stop. I found a seat on the bus next to a young lad. We chatted about where we were going. My bus ride to Edmonton would take me three days, stopping only to eat and pick up new passengers.

I was drying out from drugs. I didn't feel happy. The boy took care of me. The farther we drove, the more grateful I was to the kid. I promised him my son would have some music tapes for him when we got to Edmonton. At our next rest stop, I called Emmett. When we finally arrived, Emmett did not disappoint. He had brought the kid a whole bunch of stuff. The kid could not believe his good fortune. He must've said thanks to us a trillion times. I thanked him for taking care of me on that long bus drive.

Being at Lorna's was a lot like being at home. She had been the place I stayed when I got out of jail., Her house was the launching pad I used to get myself back on my feet. This time was no different. I found a job right away, driving an RV for a guy who made deliveries to hotels around Alberta and Saskatchewan. The first two weeks were great. I was driving, and I only had to deal with the guy. There were no people to talk to when we picked something up or dropped it off. Tuesday of my second week, he took over the driving shift. I went in back to sleep. I hadn't been asleep long when I heard a loud, annoying voice. I opened my eyes and looked around. My co-worker was driving, a six-pack next to him.

"Hey, you're up!" he greeted me.

"What the hell are you listening to?" I demanded.

He mentioned the name of some motivational speaker.

"He sounds like he doesn't know how to talk." I paused for effect. "Never mind know what he's talking about." I got into the front passenger seat and looked at the guy.

He laughed at my comment. "I know, but just wait for this part…" He held up his finger. Then looked at me when it was over. "Isn't that amazing?" he asked.

This guy was too happy to just be drunk… "Oh my God! Are you doing cocaine?" I looked more closely at his pupils. "You are! Let me off, I want out." I didn't care that it was the middle of nowhere. I wanted off now.

"No, I'm not stopping the RV!" he yelled at me. "I don't know where you get off being so high and mighty. I mean look at you."

"Excuse me?" I asked.

"You heard me. You're an ungrateful, no good bitch!" The guy started to curse. He continued using abusive language, all the while refusing to stop the RV.

I went into the back to drown him out. I counted the seconds until we arrived in Edmonton.

"Okay, we're here. I quit!" I hopped out the RV door.

"Wait!" The guy dug in his pocket. "Here, take this."

It was $500. "Hush money, eh?" I looked at him.

He didn't say anything; he waited for me to close the door and then took off again.

"Better luck next time," my brother in law said to me that night at dinner. "I need to talk to you after supper."

"Of course, Jimmy," I said.

After dinner, Jimmy and I went outside to sit on the porch.

"I know you just quit your job. I think I might know a way for you to make some easy money to help you get back on your feet."

"Okay, I'm listening." I looked at Jimmy.

"I was hoping you could call Montreal and set up an introduction for me. I can give you $7000 right now."

"Really." I sat up in my chair. I knew who Jimmy wanted me to connect him with. "No problem, I'll set it up right away."

"Danny's on the phone," Lorna called me from the kitchen a few days later.

I came downstairs and took the receiver from Lorna. "What's up?"

"Victoria, the cops were just here. They're looking for you."

"Seriously? Why would the cops want me?"

"I don't know, Vic, but you should go. They sounded very serious. They say you witnessed something in Montreal."

Puzzled I hung up the phone.

"What did Danny want?" Lorna looked up from the paper she was reading.

"He says the cops were just at his house looking for me."

"That sounds serious, Victoria. You should get out now."

"It's fine. I'll take a shower and be gone in no time." I walked up the stairs.

"I really think you'd better hurry, Vic."

"Yeah, Lorna, it'll be fine." *But why am I leaving?* I thought. *Why not stick around and find out what they want?* But cops are cops; it was better to find a lawyer and then see what this was all about.

I showered quickly, grabbed my purse and went downstairs. It had been less than half an hour. I still had plenty of time before the cops get here. "I'm going out the back," I said and waved goodbye.

"Seriously, Victoria. Get the hell out of here!" Lorna almost pushed me out the door.

Metal flashed as hands holding guns popped up the second I stepped outside. "Put your hands up! We have the house surrounded."

Fucking overeager Albertans. The Montreal police service would have still been at least fifteen minutes away. "Okay, I'm cooperating." I put my purse on the ground and raised my hands. One of the cops rushed me and hurried me into handcuffs. "What's this about?" I asked the cop driving me to the station.

"The Montreal police are waiting for you. You can speak to them when you get there."

What the hell are the Montreal police doing here? What could they want from me? In reality, there was a long list of things they could want me for: possession, distributing, trafficking, maybe even asking about John's arrest?…

"Murder? This is about a murder?" I shook my head. I hadn't seen that coming. "What the hell are you talking about?" I asked the female officer in front of me.

"You are wanted in connection with Mark's death."

I shut up. There was nothing to be gained from saying anything. There was no use being cute or witty with a murder charge hanging over your head. "I need to go to the bathroom."

"Okay." One of the Edmonton detectives in the room moved forward.

"I got this." The female officer took my elbow. She ushered me towards the bathroom. Like always, she followed me inside and waited just in front of the stall.

I'm not sure how she thought I was going to escape in a building surrounded by police.

When we came out, several officers were staring at us. "What?" I asked.

They didn't look at me. "You followed her into the bathroom?" the Edmonton detective asked.

"They always do." I laughed.

The Montreal cop shrugged her shoulders.

"That isn't allowed here," the Edmonton detective told her.

I was put in a holding cell while all the paper work was filled out. Our plane tickets had to be booked. It was later in the afternoon. I wasn't sure when we would be able to leave. I didn't love the idea of spending a night in an Edmonton jail. I knew the Montreal cells way better than I wanted to. I didn't want to add jails in other provinces to the list of places I've spent the night.

"So how did you find me?" I asked the cop when we finally started towards the airport.

There was silence for a minute. "Your mother suggested we look at your ex-husband's home," the male cop driving told me. "Before we went there, we put a tap on his phone. He called you as soon as we left."

That bitch! My mother could never shut up. I thought to myself.

"We didn't realize you had an ex-husband."

I wasn't surprised that my mother had ratted me out. Good thing I didn't go to her house to dry out. She probably would have gift-wrapped me for the cops to take. And to think I was just about to surprise her on Mother's Day. There went that plan.

"Well, you found me." I shut up after that.

"Do we need to handcuff you?" the male cop asked me when we arrived at the airport.

"No, I'll be good. I promise." I was feeling deflated. The cops were one thing. It was inconvenient to be dragged back to prison, but I knew I didn't murder anyone. What worried me was the crack. Six weeks wasn't long enough to get clean. I had hoped for six months. Just to be safe. To be sure I wouldn't use again.

"All right."

None of us had any bags to check. We moved straight to the airport security. A simple metal detector separated the airport from the gates. The male cop removed his wallet, watch, and pen. He walked through no problem. I passed next, no problem.

BEEEEEEEEEP! The metal detector sounded when the female cop went through.

Oh my God, look at all those bracelets! Her arms were covered. She slid them over her hands one by one, putting them in the bin. *BEEEEEEEEEP!* Off came her necklace and earrings. *BEEEEEEEEEEEP!* She rolled up her pant legs and took off her shoes to remove her ankle bracelets. She put her shoes back on. *BEEEEEEEEEEEEEEP!* The woman took off her shoes and finally went through with no sound. The security guard waved her through. It made me think of Donald's prison social and Miss Jingle Jangle. I laughed to myself.

The female cop dusted herself off and guided me to some seats near our gate. Our flight wasn't going to leave for a while.

The more immediate threat of what might happen to me when I arrived at the Montreal headquarters started to compete with my worries about crack. I didn't have a lawyer or any witnesses to observe my condition going into jail. If nobody knew where I was, who knew how long they might keep me?

"Can I call my sons to say goodbye? This is going to be hard for them. We were just starting to settle back into being a family." I looked at the male cop. I didn't bother with the female.

"Fine." He brought me to a payphone and put in some change.

"Hello," Danny answered the phone.

I looked at the cop. "A little privacy?" He moved back a little. "Danny, it's me. I don't have a lot of time to talk. The Montreal police are here and they're taking me back to Montreal. Tell the boys goodbye from me. Also, can you call Wayne and tell him what's going on?"

"Give me the number," Danny said.

"Thanks, Danny. I'll talk to you soon." I hung up the phone and looked at the cop. "Thank you," I said. I walked back to my seat.

It had been decided that 1:00 a.m. was too early to go to the headquarters. Instead, when we arrived at that ungodly hour, we would take an airport hotel room.

As I walked into the hotel room, the female detective said, "Once we get to headquarters, we're going to give you a lie detector test. If you pass, you're free to go."

"Oh, is that all?" I was surprised.

"Yeah, get some rest." The cop took off her shoes and waited for me to lie down. I sat on the bed closest to the wall. *What a waste of a trip. I didn't murder anyone.* I wasn't going to sleep after that. I wanted this to be over and done with as soon as possible.

At 7:02 a.m. I woke up the female cop. "Come on, it's after seven. Let's get this show on the road."

The cop rolled over and looked at me. "Are you serious?"

"Yeah." I got up to gather up my purse. "I want to get this done." I started moving towards the door.

"Hold your horses." She grabbed the phone and called the other cop in the next room. He sounded equally pleased at being woken up.

We drove back to the station in silence. I was not offered coffee or breakfast. They handed me off to other officers who put me in an interrogation room. Once again, I found myself in the basement of the Montreal headquarters. The place hadn't changed. The two cops from the airport reappeared in fresh clothes. The lie detector guy followed.

"Now, Victoria. I'm going to ask you some questions. It's important that you only answer yes or no. Do you understand?"

"Yes," I responded.

For about an hour, they grilled me over and over again. I understood, based on the questions they were asking me, that there was a witness who had placed me at the scene of the murder. I hadn't been anywhere near there. I had been high, alone in my home. I left out the part about the crack and repeated over and over again:

"No."

"No

"No

My only 'yes' came when they asked me if my name was Victoria.

"All right, I think we're all done here." The lie detector guy got up to leave; the two cops followed him and closed the door behind me.

I rapped my fingers on the table. Now that the test was done I was starting to get hungry and looking forward to getting a real night's sleep.

The door opened. "Victoria, stand up. You're being charged with accessory to murder."

"Excuse me, I told you I didn't do it. I wasn't there. You gave me a lie detector test. I'm not lying."

"You failed." The male cop read me my rights and stuck me into another holding cell.

Well, this is fucking stupid, I thought to myself. *Now what? They'll have me pass court and I'll try to get bail.*

Did I want bail? Jail was as good a place as any to dry out. I would be sent to Tanguay, which wouldn't be that bad for a few weeks. I would be safe from crack. I could hire a lawyer, and wait for this mess to clear up.

I was brought to the holding cells to await a court hearing. The air hit you walking in; it sucked the air out of your lungs. The room was badly lit. It was nothing but bars in front of bars. No doors. No windows. Nothing but cages. I was put in a room with thirty other women. Most of them were smoking cigarettes, adding to the smell and smoke.

I looked around. The only thing in the room besides the benches we were sitting on was a toilet in the corner of the room. It was completely visible from every angle. I saw a woman move towards it, and we all averted our eyes as she pulled down her pants. The walls were the same horrible beige as they were at Tanguay; I began to have serious second thoughts about going back there.

They called my name and I was brought into court. My lawyer, Pierre Morneau, stood there.

"Bail?" the judge asked the Crown prosecutor

"Remand, Your Honour," he replied.

"Let's call it $50,000 cash or property."

I was ushered out. I was finally able to use a phone.

"Linda!"

"Victoria, is that you? Wayne called. He said the police came for you in Edmonton."

"Yeah, I'm at the courthouse. I need bail. It's fifty thousand cash or property."

"No problem, Victoria. I'll be down soon. Let me make a few phone calls."

"Thank you, Linda. Thank you so much."

"What did they charge you with?" she asked before I hung up.

"Accessory to murder."

Linda laughed. "I'll be right down. I know you didn't murder anyone."

I hung up the phone and waited in line to be taken back to that hell hole.

I stood in the sunshine taking deep breaths after Larry and Linda bailed me out. Linda had brought a Rolex and Larry had left the title to one of his cars.

"You had better not run," Larry warned me.

"She won't run," Linda assured him.

I had called Kenny and Moira since they were supposed to have my stuff. They told me I could stay at their place. Linda dropped me off and I went inside.

CHAPTER 104

"Surprise!" Kenny stuck a pipe in my mouth and lit it. I hadn't even put down my purse. I took a massive toke and all the magic came back.

"Welcome home." Moira hugged me. I went into their bright kitchen. They had been smoking all day already by the look of the stove.

"Thanks."

"How did the Albertans treat you?" Kenny asked in his British accent.

"Great, but unfortunately it all ended." My mind turned to the happy parts of my trip. I didn't think about the murder charge and the high kept me from thinking about my sobriety.

"Good morning champ," Kenny greeted me the next morning.

"I hate you, Kenny. How are you so okay? You were up as late as us. You smoked more than I did. How do you do that? I heard you snoring the moment your door closed. You never go through this anguish."

Kenny shrugged his shoulders.

I grabbed a coffee and sat down. "In all seriousness, just so you know, I had six weeks dry."

"Wow." Kenny put his fork down. "Victoria, if I had known I wouldn't have stuck that pipe in your mouth."

"I know, Kenny."

"We can talk about this later. I have to get to work." Kenny put his plate in the sink.

"Is that a good idea when you've been smoking all night?" I asked.

"Oh, it's just fixing airplanes. What's the worst that could happen?" He laughed as he closed the door behind him.

I settled into Moira and Kenny's house and their drug habit. It felt like home and it felt like cold ice. I couldn't handle the thought that my escape hadn't worked. I had to keep that from my mind. I could get sober later. When I beat the murder charge.

Once I'd hired the lawyer, there wasn't much else to think about; the lawyer was handling it. I also didn't want to think about the fact that I gave him the seven grand Jimmy had given me out west. However, Pierre was one of the best lawyers in Montreal, so I trusted that he would get me acquitted.

My mind had become a minefield of things I had to suppress. I needed something safe to think about. I wanted to think about love. I thought a lot about John. Donald was not on my radar. If he had been out, I doubt I would have been in this pickle of a mess. It definitely would not have gone this far. But Donald chose to stay inside, and John was the closest thing I had to someone who understood me the way Donald had. A lot of things had been left unsaid when John went to jail. Now, all charges against him and his Outlaw brothers had been dropped and he was back in Montreal. He was trying to get his life back together. I knew as soon as he saw me, everything would be fine. Kenny wasn't so sure. He had gotten John a job at the airport working for him. I begged and begged Kenny to take me to see John. He said no to me so many times and slammed his bedroom door in my face. That did not stop me. After a week, Moira commanded Kenny to take me to John so I would shut up.

Kenny didn't tell John I was coming. That suited me just fine. I waited for him outside the airport. I had on a sexy dress and boots. I positioned myself so I was leaning against the piece of shit car I had scavenged.

I saw John walk out of the airport and in my direction. I knew the second he saw me. A big smile broke out on his face. I couldn't help but grin back. He came up and put his arms around me, encircling me in his warmth. Then he bent down and kissed me.

CHAPTER 105

"So, I've looked at the evidence. The Crown doesn't have a good case. There seems to be only one witness putting you at the scene. From what I read in between the lines, they don't look like a reliable witness."

"Who the hell would have put me there? Because I wasn't."

"They're keeping that information confidential for now. I asked them to just drop the charges, but they declined. I guess they want more time to try to build a better case."

I rolled my eyes.

"I know. As soon as we get to the preliminary next week, I'll ask the judge to throw out the charges. Then it will be done."

"I can't wait."

He was right. As soon as we got to court he and The Crown had a conference. When it was over, my lawyer said, "They're dropping the charges. Their star witness is a junkie. No one else came forward and they don't have any other evidence." As it turned out Darlene, Wayne's then-girlfriend, who was probably more of a junkie than I had ever been, must have been having strong hallucinations when she signed a statement in an interrogation saying I was there!

As I stood before the judge, he threw out the charges. *I know I should have been happy. It was done. The charge was gone, and I was free of the police. But it had cost me. Paying the lawyer $7000 for a few conversations with The Crown and a visit with me was bad enough. The worst part was I was back in Montreal and smoking again. But I had my freedom…*

"How did it go?" John was waiting for me at my new apartment on Dorval Avenue.

"It was thrown out, as I knew it would be." I smiled at him.

"Well, I knew that, too." John put his arm around me. "Now what?"

The apartment I was living in on Dorval Avenue was getting too cramped. The building's main purpose was to help women in need get back on their feet. That wasn't me; I had my life back. What I needed was more space. It didn't take me long to find the house in Dollard Des Ormeaux. John and I weren't a couple, but he was always around and we were sleeping together.

"You're funny." John patted my leg one day when we were sitting on the couch. I sighed and cuddled up to him.

"This is nice." He adjusted his arm so he could hold me better.

"I know." *Well, this seems as good a time as any to ask*, I thought. "So, when are you going to leave your wife and move in with me?"

John stopped for a moment and looked down at me. "I didn't think I'd leave one drug addict for another."

"Is that the only reason?" My eyes went wide. *Why hadn't he told me sooner?*

"Yeah." I could see John was wondering what my next move was going to be.

"Well, then, I'll quit," I replied. "It's simple. If it's a choice between you and crack, I'm going to pick you. Honestly, John, if you had told me sooner I would have quit sooner." It was true. My addictions were always based on my emotional problems. Donald had made the same demand of me about my drinking, and I even quit smoking cigarettes as an added bonus. I left my last pack on top of the fridge to always remind me and I had never touched them.

I was true to my word: I quit crack cold turkey.

I had my radio on in my car coming home from the gym. It was coming up to the half an hour when the news would be read out. Then I heard it. "There was a shooting today in the east end of Montreal. A man known as Fuzzy, a member of the Outlaws Motorcycle Club, was gunned down in the street."

"Oh my God, Fuzzy!" I said out loud in shock. Fuzzy was a long-time member of the Outlaws. He and John had known each other for years. Not just as members but as friends. They were brothers.

The next afternoon John showed up, swinging his keys as he entered the house, like always. He looked at me and said, "You're in luck. I need a place to hide."

"Great, John." I waited for him to go on.

"I'm not sure why, but the cops think I was involved with Fuzzy's murder." John joined me on the living room couch.

"That's ridiculous! Fuzzy was one of your best friends."

"I know." John shook his head.

John stayed with me over the next few days. We had a good time enjoying the simple things in life. I knew he was watching and waiting to see if I would go back to crack. I didn't. I kept dealing, but I never touched a pipe, I never did a line.

After a week John went home and gathered his stuff. On his way out the door, Lucinda asked him, "Do you love her?"

John told her yes. She asked if he would still be visiting his daughter, Alysha. To that he replied, "I'm leaving you, not her. I'll see her every weekend."

Lucinda didn't say much after that. She pawned all of his first edition books on the occult that John left behind. John was truly upset about this and talked about it for days.

John was a collector. He collected books, art, animals. He came to my house with a lot of baggage, and a dog. I didn't love the dog; he was old and really didn't do much. But John loved him unconditionally, the way he loved me.

A few weeks later, we found out Fuzzy left his life insurance policy to Lucinda. John was actually relieved to know that Lucinda would be taken care of now. Sadly, the extra money also meant Lucinda stopped doing coke and graduated to heroin.

"I'm glad you quit drugs. It's good to see you so healthy and happy."

"That's because you make me happy, John." I smiled at him. "But what about you? What do you want to do?"

"What do you mean?" John looked at me.

"Well, do you want to split my business with me or do you want to try to do something else?"

John was silent for a moment. "No, I don't want to try something else. I'll split the business with you."

"Wonderful." I kissed John.

"Come here." He rolled me over and spooned me from behind. I fell asleep almost instantly.

I was in love with a man who loved me back. He accepted me and welcomed my intimacy. Our days were simple because I was happy. John reminded me of a giant teddy bear. On the outside, John was over six feet, covered in tattoos and looked the part of a biker. Inside, he was as gentle as a newborn kitten.

When I quit smoking crack, I went back to making the respectable amount of money I had before. It was easy to make between $500 and $800 a day. For each gram of coke I sold, I made seventy dollars, and it was easy to sell seven to ten grams of cocaine a day. We would buy an ounce of coke and keep it at our stash house. The house was in Pierrefonds. I had a friend who lived there. I paid her rent as compensation. As the amount of dealing John and I were doing went up, it made sense to start buying coke in kilos. I would work the noon to 6:00 p.m. shift and then it was John's turn. He would work 6:00 p.m. to 11:00 p.m. Most of the time, though, we ended up working the whole day together.

Soon I was able to buy myself another Corvette; John used some of his share to buy a Harley off of our friend Blake. John's bike and my Corvette made a cute couple parked in our driveway.

Since I had quit smoking crack, I had suggested to John that he quit drinking. I had been too skinny smoking crack and John had some extra pounds to lose because of the booze. I also wanted to curb John's tendencies to get new tattoos when he got black-out drunk. His most talked-about tattoo was a naked women with her legs splayed around his belly button. I told him I didn't want him to end up with another belly button vagina tattoo. John agreed. He got up with me to go the gym. He headed to the YMCA and I went to a smaller gym. I've always preferred smaller gyms. I don't remember how it started, but we began having one day a week where we only ate vegetarian. After a month of this, John had lost most of the forty pounds he needed to. Clearly, drinking creates a beer belly. I gained the twenty pounds I needed. We were truly good for one another.

Blake was out of prison and came around almost every day. I had met him back in the late 60's when Heather met John. He too had been a member of the Satan's Choice. I had always thought Blake was unique. I had never met anyone like him. He was a very straightforward guy, smart, creative. He was always up to something. There wasn't a business Blake hadn't tried. Around this time, he bought himself a crematorium. He wanted to go into the pet cremation business.

The house that Blake owned was forty-five minutes away from Montreal. He put the crematorium on his land. Blake and John went into business together. John handled the sales calls and drove halfway to meet Blake to give him the deceased pet. Blake did his thing and then drove halfway to John, so John could deliver the urn to the pet's owner.

One day, Blake drove all the way to the house to give John the urn. While he and Blake were talking, I decided to go and check the mail. We had a long driveway that ended at our gate where the mailbox was.

I heard the front door open and close. Then I heard Blake's car start up and he drove towards me. We reached the gate at the same time.

He rolled down the window. "Oh, by the way, I've been meaning to tell you I have some news on Donald."

I stopped and looked at Blake, taken aback. "Oh?" I didn't know if I should expect good or bad news.

"Yeah, I heard he got married," Blake said.

"Really?" I said.

"Yeah, to some young thing." Blake looked at me, waiting.

"Good for him," I replied.

Blake said a few more things but I didn't really hear them; my mind was busy processing what he had just said to me. I walked back in the house. As I was saying goodbye to John, I remembered the last letter Donald had ever written me.

When John left and I was alone, I went to the garage where I kept my box of letters. The letter stuck out in my mind because I recalled him asking me if I knew any gold-hearted whores.

I found the three paged letter and read the part I recalled. Here it is, unedited:

I hope you send me lots of nice photos of yourself in your jean shorts and swim suits so that I can look at them and say to myself she does not hate me and if I could of changed my ways that is the girl I would of made my wife. As no man could of asked for more from a girl I only hope that you say to yourself I do care for Donald, but I must make my life as Donald could never be more to me then a friend. But I want him as a friend. But do you? Could you? I am happy that your two jobs are going good. I wish you the very best.

P.S no one will ever replace you ever. I can never love like that again also I can never trust like that again. I will love again as a person needs love but I will never get that close again to another person. I will just give what love I can. I love women do you know any why don't you find me a whore with a heart of gold? Or maybe it would hurt you to do that but if I knew a guy who I thought would be Mr. Right for you I would send him to meet you but all the people I know are in jail and I would not do that to you as I know it's a bad trip. I love you and care for you and I wish you the best in your work and I hope you meet a good guy who will do good by you.

Take care love you always and will care for you always. Your best
friend in your life I hope. I love you friend. I will never fuck up your
head again love always Donald. xoxoxo

So, it wasn't a golden-hearted whore; it was a whore with a heart of gold.
Is there really any difference? I guess he found one.

CHAPTER 106

I had stopped seeing Heather a few years after John left her. Donald had come into my life and my circle of friends changed. After John came into my life, I met Angel, Heather's daughter, now grown. She wasn't living with Heather at the time, but we had reconnected and now she was friends with my son, Emmett.

On a whim, I decided I wanted to look Heather up. I thought it would be nice to get together again.

"I got Heather's number from Angel." I handed John a piece of paper.

"This is Heather's number?" John looked at the paper.

"Yeah, I'm going to give her a call. See if she wants to get together."

"Okay." John handed me the paper back.

I picked up the phone. "Hello, is Heather there?" I said.

"This is she," she replied.

"Heather! It's Victoria. I haven't seen you in years and I wanted to look you up, see how you're doing."

"Oh my God, Victoria! It's been so long! Angel mentioned she was cleaning your house for you for a while."

After chatting with her for a bit, I said, "How would you feel about John and me dropping by?" I didn't really think she would still have feelings for him. I would've been happy for my ex-husband if he found love again.

"Okay." I heard Heather pause and the sound of pages turning. "I'm free on Saturday, if you guys want to stop by." She gave me her address and hung up.

"She sounded very happy to hear from me."

John didn't say anything for a while. "Next Saturday?" he finally asked.

"Yup, she's living in Verdun," I answered.

John drove the Corvette to Heather's house.

"Oh my God, John! I haven't seen you in forever." Heather opened the door and threw her arms around John. John hugged her back.

"Victoria." She hugged me, too.

I smiled at her. "It's nice to see you, Heather."

"Yes, come in please. This is Marcel."

I shook the man's hand. It was clear that he and Heather were living together.

"I really am so happy to see you both. Victoria, we were together at the Bus Stop when we met John, remember?" Heather was beaming at me.

"Remember the Bus Stop, John? The underground café where I met you?"

"Yeah, I do." John was not saying a lot.

"You used to dress in suits and have your Choice colours on underneath." Heather reached out to John. "It was such a surprise when you finally took your coat off."

John nodded his head.

"We were living on Pierce Street. Right, Victoria?" Heather looked at me.

Marcel sat quietly, watching everything. Heather was so focused on John, she didn't see Marcel's dirty looks.

"You were driving a Harley at the time. Do you still have the bike? What do you drive now? Besides the Corvette."

"The Corvette is mine." I caught Heather's eye.

"Oh." She looked back to John.

"I sold that bike years ago. I have another Harley now."

I could tell that Heather was overwhelming John with all of her questions, and his answers were getting shorter and shorter.

Heather talked about their previous relationship. She talked a little about Angel, and what they had been up to the last few years.

John and I were ready to go after an hour. Heather wanted us to stay, but we had friends to meet.

"Heather is still in love with you, John." I waited until he started the car to tell him.

"No, she's not," John said absent-mindedly.

I answered the phone a few nights later. Heather interrupted me before I could finish saying hello. "You're my best friend, Victoria!" Heather was drunk, very drunk. "You're my best friend. He is the love of my life, Victoria. The love of my life."

I looked over at John, eating his supper. "Who is it?" he mouthed.

"Okay, Heather." I gave John a look. He shook his head.

"You don't understand. He's the love of my life and you're my best friend. My best friend is with the love of my life." Heather sobbed a little.

"Heather…" I didn't really know what else to say. There is no reasoning with a drunk. The sooner this conversation ended, the better. "You're drunk. We can talk about this later." I hung up the phone.

"Not in love with you, my ass," I said as I sat down next to John.

"What did she want?" John put down his fork.

"To tell me you're the love of her life. She's devastated that her best friend is with the love of her life."

John rocked in his chair. "Okay?"

My thoughts exactly.

CHAPTER 107

John and I enjoyed the contentment we brought one another. Living with him was a lot like living with Donald. John accepted me as I was. That gave me the space to be happy, and that made being sober easy.

Working together, John and I were making enough money to be comfortable. When we weren't working, we would go for drives in the country, brunches on Sundays and spend our summers at a cottage on the lake. We were always looking for new adventures. When Emmett came to visit with us in summer, we went river rafting, a tradition Emmett and I had started when he was fourteen years of age.

John had stayed committed to going to the gym and being sober. His body became hard and muscular. He looked like a much younger man, full of vigour and passion. John complimented me often, telling me I wasn't looking too shabby, either. Sex with him was like something out of a romance novel. The tall, strong martial artist sweeping me off my feet and into bed.

John never stopped studying. One day, he was out at a martial arts weekend seminar. I had the house to myself. I was sitting in my kitchen, contemplating life, as I often did. *What the heck was it all about?* was the question I mused most about.

I let my head rest gently on my hand, one elbow on the table. The next minute, I was out of my body in a box, if I can call it that. My brother was there on a motorcycle, driving in a circle around me. My brother had died in a motorcycle accident many years back at the age of fifteen. I had been seventeen at the time. I was so shocked, I bounced violently back into my body. This took place in under five seconds. The way I would describe the landing is this: you go to sleep for about five minutes and suddenly you are jolted awake harshly. Most people I have spoken to have experienced this. I was absolutely, totally wide awake.

I blinked, staring at nothing for a while, processing what I had just experienced. It was not so much a "visual" experience as more of a telepathic moment. I knew with complete certainty, life existed after death.

A few days went by. I was spending time with my friend, Ginette. Ginette owned a casting company; she hired extras for movies that were shot in Montreal. I explained to her the immense, powerful, energy journey I had experienced in those five seconds.

Ginette looked at me. "You know, Victoria," she said, "every Sunday I go to this cabin in the woods. There is a group of us and we meet there to meditate. The teacher is amazing. I've experienced all kinds of miraculous things there."

"Really?" I was starting to get excited. *Ginette had never touched drugs or alcohol in her life. Her only vice was smoking.* I wasn't even sure you could call her smoking a vice.

"One day, our teacher told me to lie on the floor and close my eyes. Close them very tight, he instructed. I did, but it was so hard. My mind wouldn't stop. I couldn't seem to close it down."

I waited for her to continue, captivated.

"The teacher came, and he sat with me. He coaxed and coached me until it happened. All of a sudden, I left my body." Ginette looked deep into my eyes. "It was like nothing I had ever experienced before. I was in a box exactly as you described. Except my grandmother was there."

"I know," I said. *How many other people have had these amazing things happen, and kept them to themselves out of the fear of being judged as crazy?*

To this day, I know my brother is one of my spirit guides, angels, whatever you want to call him. He is with me every day, and he guides me. I also wonder if he was the voice I heard from the staircase.

CHAPTER 108

Lucinda had run through all the life insurance money. With less money and more time on her hands, she began to intrude into our lives. It started to get out of hand when she called our house phone.

"John, how does she know our phone number?" I asked him point-blank while he sat on the couch.

"I don't know," John stammered.

"Well, think, because we've been very careful with this number." I raised my eyebrows at him.

"I'll ask Alysha the next time I see her, okay?" John offered.

Friday came, and John had his weekend visit with Alysha.

"Alysha said Lucinda was at the welfare office. She looked inside the file and it had our phone number."

"Right, 'cause you would have gone in and updated your forms." I rolled my eyes and walked away. Apparently, his welfare file also had our address. I suspect Lucinda had gotten her information a lot closer to home, considering neither John nor I were on welfare.

This was getting out of hand. John worried about Lucinda's unpredictability. I took a more proactive approach. You can't trust a heroin junkie to begin with; I certainly wasn't going to trust Lucinda. I did what any reasonable woman would do. I sent people to talk to her. I wasn't going to let her maim my new Corvette, or abduct John's Harley.

I got what I wanted, but John intervened. It triggered something deep inside me. He was still the first person she called. And John ran to her right away, putting her on the first bus to Manitoba.

"Why did you get involved, John? I was handling this."

"I thought this would make you happy." He looked at me incredulously. "She's gone now."

"You were wrong." I was pacing our bedroom; a part of me was tempted to throw him out. My method for dealing with relationship problems had always been to hurt the person before they hurt me.

"I made it clear to Lucinda she can't come back. I won't help her a second time."

"And I'm just supposed to believe that." I could feel my emotions swirling. "If you don't have any feelings for her, then why did you get in the way?"

"I don't have feelings for her. How can you say that? I'm glad she's out of my life." John was looking straight at me with his blue eyes.

"Bullshit." I decided it didn't make sense to kick him out. So, I walked out of the bedroom and out of the house, slamming the door on my way out.

John and I fought the way Donald and I fought. Except about different things. We were mad for a few hours, maybe a day, and then we made up. I would calm down and let it go. We would get on with our lives. We didn't talk about it. It was just something that happened.

I loved John and he loved me. I tried hard to make things work between us, but every time I felt like we were making headway, something would happen. My emotions would flare back up and things between John and I would get worse.

Before John left Heather twenty years ago, he had fooled around on her. Shortly before John's break up with Heather, Louise and I had come out of a dépanneur on Saint Catherine Street, bumping into John. John had his arms around a woman who was definitely not Heather. It was Carol, a stunning long legged beauty, a girl we both knew.

While John was married to Lucinda, he had two affairs that he admitted to. One had been with Alysha's babysitter, Carly. The other was with a woman named Jody. Jody and I had a history together, going all the way back to 1972, when she slept with my then-husband. I hadn't been with John when he cheated with Jody or Carly, but still, it made it worse. Technically, I guess I was also an affair for a while. I hurt the way I had hurt when I knew Donald was going back to jail. Rather than pulling away as I had done in the interrogation room, after the country house raid, I was pushing John away. It's hard to trust a man who you know cheats.

I never encouraged or discouraged a relationship with John's mother. When Lucinda left, I knew she was no longer dropping in on his mother. I assumed that John's mom was no longer relaying messages between them. Since it had been two years, I decided it was time for her to come for Christmas dinner.

I went up to the attic in early December to pull out our Christmas decorations. While I was looking around up there, I found a box which contained some letters between John and his daughter, Alysha. Curious I sat down to read one. The letter was actually from Alysha, but forwarded to John by his mother. All this time, John and Alysha had been communicating secretly through his mother, instead of writing to our house directly. *What else could his mom be telling her son behind my back*? Here I was making plans to get to know her and possibly become her new daughter-in-law.

When he came home, I confronted him. There wasn't much that he could say. He called his mother and told her what happened. Her only response was, "I guess I'm not coming to dinner anymore…"

John and I got back on track after Christmas, but now I was on high alert. I became suspicious of all other women. Contact with his mother to me meant contact with Lucinda. I didn't want John to be gone from my life, but I felt powerless to stop it.

John's business with Blake began to pick up in the spring. They had done a second round of handing out business cards at veterinarian offices and dog groomers. Dealing blow together, John and I had made a good amount of money. But having a straight job and a way of paying taxes is just common sense for a dealer.

It was the last week of April, and we had just sat down to lunch. It had been a nice morning so far. We were both enjoying the spring sunshine when John's business phone rang. "John A. Pet cremation… Yep… Yep that's me… This is what I'm doing now… Thanks for calling. It was nice to hear from you, too," John said quickly before getting off the phone.

"Who was that?" I asked.

"Carly," John replied, getting back to his salad.

"Repeat her name."

John did.

"Isn't that the babysitter you had an affair with?" I narrowed my eyes a little.

"Yes." John kept his eyes on his plate.

"Why the fuck is she calling you?" I could feel blood rushing to my head.

"She's a vet receptionist now. She saw one of my business cards and wanted to know if I was the same John from the Outlaws, the one she babysat for." John shrugged his shoulders.

I just started at him blankly.

John sighed. "What do you want me to say, Victoria? I got off the phone quickly."

"You could have told her not to call you again." I stood from the table and said, "I'm not hungry anymore."

That woman calling, the way John's voice changed when he talked to her bothered me.

How do you trust men when they've screwed around on every other relationship? You don't. My intuition knew the relationship was over; I just wasn't ready to admit it to myself yet.

CHAPTER 109

"Happy Mother's Day, Victoria." John walked out of the shower.

I had just woken up. "Thanks."

He leaned down and gave me a kiss on the way to the closet to get dressed. "Do you want me to leave now, and see my mom for an hour? Or do you want me to see her later tonight?" John turned his head to me.

"Go now. The sooner you go, the sooner you can be back. Then we can really celebrate." I smiled at him.

"Okay," he replied and finished getting ready.

My kids weren't in Montreal to celebrate with, so I went down to the kitchen to make myself breakfast. I called Linda and wished her a Happy Mother's Day. I read the paper, enjoying the peace and quiet, and my freshly perked coffee.

Two hours went by. The first hour, I didn't wonder. The second hour, I expected him to walk through the door at any minute. At least call me. The phone did ring, but it was my kids calling.

When hour number three came around, I began to get upset. *What the hell is he up to?* My mind went to all kinds of places. *He's with his mother, and his mom likes Lucinda. Did Lucinda plot something?* I paged him; he ignored me. I paged a second time, still no phone call. The third page worked. The phone rang, and I said, "Where the hell are you?"

"I'm with my mother. I decided to take her to lunch."

"That wasn't what you told me. You told me you would be back right away. Couldn't you have phoned?" I was beside myself now.

"That was my plan, but my mother started crying so I took her for lunch." I couldn't see John, but I could tell from his voice his shoulders were probably starting to sag.

"What? So you can discuss Lucinda again? Come get your fucking stuff. I'm done," I said, hanging up in his ear.

I hung up the phone, then I went upstairs and started pacing. My insides felt raw. My throat hurt, my muscles were tense. John didn't rush home. I heard him come in around 9:00 p.m. He knew I was serious this time. John didn't fight with me or for me. He started looking for a new place to live right away.

The timing worked out well. John moved into a room for a couple of months, and then my friend Sue moved to Two Mountains. I had been paying Sue's rent to use her apartment as my stash house, but now the drive was too long and inconvenient. I offered John the same deal. I would pay his rent in exchange for stashing my blow. We were no longer business partners. I kept my blow in a blue trunk with a padlock only I had the key to. I moved it to John's new apartment.

Soon after John was settled into his new place, my lease came up. The house felt different now that I was alone. It was cold, and old. The landlord wasn't motivated to make repairs quickly. It was time for a fresh start in a new house.

My intuition was right about Carly. Within weeks of our break up, John told me they were dating. There is no way you jump into a relationship that fast. They must have been talking for a while. Fury swept over me when I found out. *How could he fucking... That conniving little bitch*! I felt well within my rights to call the girl, and explain how things actually went down. I knew where to find her; after all, that is how she found John—when he dropped off his business cards at the veterinarian's office where she worked.

She answered the phone at the vet's.

"Carly?" I asked.

"Speaking."

"Not a wise move, Carly. Dating John like that, it's not wise." I didn't threaten her. I just described the situation for her.

"Wha—"

"Listen," I cut her off, "The reason I threw him out of the house was because I knew you had something up your sleeve, bitch!" I hung up the phone.

The girl dumped him right away. Honestly, I didn't think what I said was that scary. I guess she really didn't like him that much after all.

"Victoria, what did you say to Carly?" John demanded after stopping by my new house.

"The truth, John."

"Which is?" he asked.

"That you and that bitch must have had something going long before you and I broke up."

John didn't say anything.

"So, it's true."

John still didn't say anything. Finally, he asked, "Do you want me back, Victoria?"

"No, but I'm just not ready for you to be with somebody else," I responded. *Why don't I want him back? And why don't I want him to be with somebody else?* I didn't understand my feelings, I just felt them. Strongly.

"Okay."

What else could he say? I had scared away one girlfriend. I had encouraged his ex-wife to leave town. Arguing with me wasn't worth the hassle to him, and that's how we carried on for at least a year.

It was starting to get rainy and cold in Montreal, and I needed to do an inventory of my stash. *I should really take everything to my house and take my time.* When I got to John's apartment, I decided it didn't make sense to take the risk driving the blow all the way back to my house and then back to the apartment. I undid the padlock, grabbed my little black scale from my purse, and began to take stock of what I had.

It took me a couple of hours. But when it was done, I was happy. I had more than enough to keep going and I already had almost as much money as I would need for the next deal.

"Hello?"

"Something's happened. I'm coming over."

I didn't need for John to say his name; I knew it was him. "Okay…"

John rushed over. He looked grim when I answered the door. "I've been raided."

"Fuck," I swore.

"I came home to find one of my kittens in the hall," John said. "I went in and my place had been torn apart. They left a business card on my table and your trunk is gone."

"There was a decent amount of blow in that trunk. Why do think you were raided?" I shook my head.

"I don't know. I'm going to turn myself in with my lawyer, and see how this plays out." John looked at me. "I'm going to make sure this is handled fairly and try to get bail. But I'll be lucky if I do."

With that, John got up and left to see his lawyer, Dave Linetsky.

CHAPTER 110

"Hello, Victoria." Dave, John's lawyer called me. We had been in touch constantly since John had turned himself in.

"Hi, Dave. How are things with John's case?"

"I have good news." He sounded excited. "I was able to get John bail."

"That's wonderful…" My voice trailed off as my cell phone rang. "Hold on, Dave. I have a call on my other line. I think it might be John." I switched lines. "Hello?"

"Hi, Victoria."

"Hi, John. Good timing—I'm on the other line with Dave."

"Really?"

"Yeah. He says he's gotten bail for you." I waited for John to say something.

"Seriously? I couldn't get bail in Ontario. Are you sure?" John asked.

"Yes! Dave wants you to call him," I replied.

John hung up.

I went back on the line with Dave. "I was right, Dave. It was John. I told him the good news about you getting him bail."

Dave made a noise. "Why did you tell him? I wanted to be the one to tell him."

Lawyers never like to have their thunder stolen.

John called me back later that day. Before the bust, John told me, he had started seeing a girl in Châteauguay whom Blake had introduced him to. He asked me if I was okay with it and I was. I realized at that moment I didn't love John anymore. I was ready for him to move on. I was starting to understand the cause of my addictions were my emotions. I was ready to be single for a while and work on myself.

Beth, John's new girl, was able to come up with $4000 of John's $5000 bail. I reluctantly paid the rest. John was out by the end of the day. He went to stay with Beth. I went home to the east side of Île-Bizard, to the house I had rented after I moved. My two cats, Kali and Chocolate, greeted me. "Good news, guys! John got bail."

I could see Kali knew who I was talking about. She stopped mid-chew and looked up at me. "I know. I feel the same way, Kali."

We waited for John's court date. There was never any doubt John was going to take the charge from the apartment bust. Like I said, I could trust John because I knew he wouldn't rat. It was a miracle the cops hadn't come an hour earlier. I would have been caught red-handed, my scale and blow everywhere. However, if I had listened to my intuition that was nagging at me to take the trunk home to do the inventory, nothing would have been there. I made a point of saying to myself, "Stop ignoring these feelings and listen."

John's lawyer tried to get John to plead guilty and take a sentence of two years. John declined the offer and Dave wanted more money. At that time, rumours were starting to spread that Dave was involved in jail-time trading. Selling out clients by convincing them to plead guilty in exchange for the cops dropping charges against other clients. Whether this was true or not, I have no clue. I only know it was the rumour on the street. John continued to wait for his day in court.

CHAPTER 111

"Vic, have you seen the paper?" John called me very early on the morning of June 16.

"No, I've been sleeping." I was unimpressed.

"Well, it's a good thing I didn't take that deal. The Montreal police who were investigating my case were just charged with evidence tampering. All their cases, including mine, are going to be thrown out. It was the Matticks bust that finally did them in." Everyone knew the Montreal police coloured outside the lines. But Operation Thor had been especially bad. Operation Thor started in 1993 and ended on June 15, 1995. It can be googled on the web, but better still, there is a great description on pages 191–193 in the book *Montreal's Irish Mafia* by D'Arcy O'Connor, where you can read all the details in full.

I hung up the phone, feeling happy for him.

CHAPTER 112

The house I rented at the beginning of 1995, now on the west side of Île-Bizard, was lovely. The house I had been renting on the east side had sold. This was a small, cosy house that backed onto the Parc-nature du Bois. It felt as if I had a forest with all its creatures in my backyard. Kali and Chocolate loved the house, as well. The cats explored outside, and I began to explore myself. I had no man to anchor my life to. That meant there wasn't a man to set it adrift, either. I focused on myself and getting my business back on track.

When John was busted, the coke I lost was easy to replace. Finding a new stash house was more difficult. Thankfully, Sunshine came into my life. I don't remember how I met her, but she worked at the Dorval Airport as a car rental agent. I offered her the same deal I had offered Sue and then John. I paid her rent and she kept my stash.

Life continued to be two steps forward, three steps back. After John left, I continued to make progress in my life, and then suddenly life would send me a new curveball.

"Chocolate!" I called, walking through my backyard into the forest. "Chocolate!" I called again. Kali rubbed against my legs, helping me look for Chocolate.

It was starting to get dark. Chocolate hadn't come home the night before. All night, I heard coyotes calling. I tried to tell myself he would be fine, that I would find him waiting for me in the morning. But as soon as I heard that first coyote howl, I felt sick. Chocolate had been doing so well. The runt of the litter, he was born with a weak heart. John and I had taken him to the vet right away. The vet prescribed some medication. He also told us Chocolate wouldn't live past three years of age. However, the medication worked and Chocolate grew stronger.

Another night went by. "Kali, don't you know where Chocolate is?" I asked her as I brushed her fur. She just purred. *Maybe Chocolate is okay...*

It had been a week since Chocolate disappeared. Kali still didn't seem upset, and I held on to the hope he might come back.

"Chocolate won't leave you guys. Is it okay if we take him?" a voice woke me up three days later.

Half asleep still, I mumbled, "Okay." I felt a rush of air and then nothing. I fully awoke. This voice was similar to the voice I'd heard in my house in Dorval, yet it was different. It was like an energy vibration with an accent. Somehow, I knew this voice looked after animals. I wish I had fully awakened and asked what happened to Chocolate, but just like the voice in Dorval, it came quickly, said what needed to be said and was gone. I wish I had said, "Wait, let me say goodbye," but at least I could stop looking now.

I must have drifted back to sleep.

When I woke up, Kali was beside herself. She wouldn't get up. She wouldn't eat. She looked distraught.

"I think your cat is depressed," Joey a friend who had dropped by to visit commented, looking at Kali.

"I know. She's been like that for days. I don't know what to do." I stroked her head and she ignored me. "I think I'm going to get her a new friend, maybe that will help." I put Kali's food in front of her. She turned her back to it. This was the eighth day she hadn't eaten.

Two days later, I came home with Lucas. He was small and spunky. When I brought him home in my Corvette, Lucas sat on my lap and purred. He seemed excited to be on a new adventure.

"Kali, I'm home!" I walked through the door, holding Lucas.

Kali looked up from where she lay on the carpet. I put Lucas down. He started to move towards Kali. Kali got up. *This is working!* I thought. Then she let out a hiss and ran. She hissed and growled from the spare bedroom. She wouldn't let Lucas or me anywhere near her. I had to sleep with Lucas that night.

"Kali, no!" I swerved my car to the side of the road. "No, no, NO!" I jumped out. Kali's lifeless body was by the side of the road. Devastated, I said to her, "You never cross this street!" I picked her up and brought her back up to the house.

She's committed suicide...

I called John, and he came over right away.

We sat on the couch and he comforted me. Kali had been the one to open my heart and allow me to accept her unconditional love. I learned to give that back to her, Chocolate and now Lucas. John had taught me how to love animals, but now they were causing me to feel all of the same emotions. Unconditional love, followed by devastation.

"You shouldn't blame yourself." John wiped away one of the tears that escaped my eyes.

"I should have never let Chocolate outside. I knew he was sick."

"Victoria, we both let him out at the other house all the time. There was no way you could have known. Kali and Chocolate were inseparable. She couldn't survive without him."

That brought me back to the voice I had heard at the beginning of Kali's depression. Before that, she had been fine. The voice had asked me if they could take Chocolate and I had felt his spirit leave the house. I didn't even say goodbye. I hadn't realized then what was happening.

"I think I should give Lucas back. I don't want anything to happen to him." I stroked his ears. He was on my lap, purring.

"I don't think so, Victoria. Lucas loves you already, but I think you should get him checked. He seems listless."

I looked down at him, and noticed his blue eyes had become rather dull. Lucas took my finger between his tiny paws and chewed on it weakly. John was right.

I rushed Lucas to the vet. It was evening, so only the emergency vet was open. When they saw Lucas, they rushed him in right away.

"Your kitten is very sick," the vet said gently.

"What do you mean?" I asked, alarmed.

"He needs IV fluids. You'll have to leave him overnight. We'll call you when we have more information." The vet wasn't looking at me; he was totally focused on Lucas.

"All right." I dragged myself back to my car and drove home. The house was horribly empty with no cats. I sat on the couch, waiting.

After an hour, the phone rang. It was the vet.

"Your kitten is ill because he has a very bad parasite infection. He has worms."

"Is he going to be all right, though?" I was clutching the phone to my ear, my hands shaking.

"It's touch-and-go right now." The vet paused. "If he lives through the night, you can you pick him up in the morning."

I was stunned. I thanked the vet and hung up the phone. I paced back and forth in my bedroom. I missed Kali terribly; everywhere I looked around my house, I had memories of things she and Chocolate had done here.

Lucas hadn't been in my life very long, but he was such a loving personality that he had already taken over my heart.

I called the vet a few hours later. They told me Lucas was still resting and on an IV.

I waited some more. There was no way I could sleep. I couldn't distract myself. TV didn't hold my attention. I couldn't focus enough to read. So I sat by the phone, waiting.

I called the vet twice more. Each time, they told me Lucas was holding his own.

At 7:15 a.m., I called the vet. They had told me to expect their call by 8:00 a.m., but I couldn't wait.

"Lucas is ready to come home. He's still weak but you can come and get him now," the vet tech who answered the phone told me.

I rushed over and brought Lucas home. He was still groggy but very happy to see me. I laid him on my bed. He snuggled up beside me, and I finally fell asleep.

Still, I felt like Lucas was lonely. I walked by a pet store a few days later and stopped for food. Walking by the cat cages, I spied the most amazing-looking Siamese kitten. The cage for the kitten was terribly small. The kitten came up to me the second I looked at him.

I flagged over the owner. "How much is this kitten?"

"That's a Lilac Point Siamese. He's $900."

"Nine hundred dollars for a cat? That's outrageous. Sorry, kitty." I turned around and walked out of the door. All week, that cat was in my head. When Lucas ran around my house, I remembered how tiny the cage was. When I fed Lucas the food he liked, I wondered what the pet store was feeding the kitten.

"I'll take him!" I handed my $900 to the pet store owner. I had managed to last a week before I went back. "Come here." I picked up the kitten. He was a little more timid then Lucas was, but he nuzzled into my neck and purred.

"Wise choice. I think you'll be very happy with this kitten."

"I know I will," I said as I left the pet store.

Sammy hid on the drive home.

Lucas ran up to the door. I lowered Sammy down to the floor and let him go. Lucas moved towards him and, with a sound of joy that I had never heard before, wrapped his paws around Sammy's head, and then they took off down the hall together. They were like two lost souls who had finally found each other.

CHAPTER 113

In Montreal, dealing makes you part of a clique. Everybody knows what you carry, when stock is in town and if you have it. I needed to send some pot out west because there was a drought. I knew that Sam could get me the pot I needed. So I set it up and waited for him to page me.

It didn't take him long to find the twenty pounds I wanted and page me back.

I backed my rented Jeep into Sam's driveway. He was already outside with his garage door open. "Hey!" I got out of my Jeep.

Sam nodded at me. "Come on in." He ushered me into his garage. Sam seemed a little nervous. "My family is in the house, so let's do the deal here."

"Okay." Something felt a little bit off. He showed me the pot. I opened the bag and inspected a few of the buds. Everything looked good.

I handed him his money. It was more expensive than what he quoted me. "Take this for now and I'll get you the rest later," I said. I knew that the $2000 owing would be Sam's profit.

"Sure." He helped me to load the pot into the back of the Jeep. We covered it with a blanket. Then I got into the Jeep and started to drive away. Sam had seemed off some how. I could see my friend Harold's place coming up the block. *I should really drive there and ask him to hold this in his locker,* something told me. But I ignored the feeling and made the right onto Saint-Jean Boulevard. I drove a block farther, and then, to my utter horror, I saw flashing lights in my rear-view mirror. I pulled over, got out my license and registration, and then started to get out of my Jeep to talk to the cop.

"Stay in the vehicle." The cop was already beside my door. He poked his head through the window and sniffed. "I smell pot." The cop pulled his head back out of the window. "Now I need you to get out of the vehicle."

The cop handcuffed me, and put me in the back of his car. He walked to the Jeep and shut the engine off. *What had just happened?* I asked myself. *Had I been ratted on? Did Sam set me up? Or were the cops already watching the place Sam picked up the pot from?* My mind swirled with a thousand different possibilities.

The cop looked in the back. He turned around, locked all the doors, and came back to his car with my purse in tow. "You're coming with me," he said.

Back at the station, I was put in a holding cell. I knew that the cops would be watching me with their two way mirror, so I put my head down on the table to rest my eyes. I continued to think about what was coming. The cops had my scale, some blow and a lot of pot. *This is not going to be pretty,* I thought to myself.

The door opened an hour later. The cop that entered looked very pleasant. "We're releasing you," he said. He had the keys to the Jeep in his hand.

I blinked to make sure I had heard the cop right. The word "stunned" didn't do justice to what I felt in that moment. I shook my head and chuckled. "Can I have my stuff back, too?"

The cop laughed. "No, we're going to keep that." He handed me my keys.

I didn't want to push my luck any farther. "Where is my Jeep?"

"In the parking lot. We had someone drive it here and now it's waiting for you." The cop kept smiling at me.

"Okay." I walked out of the police station and got into the Jeep.

I started driving in the direction of home, not because I planned to go there, but because I didn't know where else to go. My thoughts felt slow and fuzzy. *I'd better talk to Victor.* I stopped to use a payphone, then headed over to Vic's place.

Victor answered the door and let me in.

"Seriously, Victor, I picked up the pot, drove a block, and then a cop pulled me over. There is no way he smelled that pot," I said.

Victor nodded his head. "And then?"

"And then the cop put me in the back seat of his car and searched my Jeep. I had an ounce of blow, a scale, baggies and twenty pounds of pot. When they took me to the station, I waited an hour. Then some cop comes in, as happy as can be, and hands me my keys. He says I'm free to go." It still didn't seem real.

"You're right, Victoria. That is crazy. I've never heard of that happening before." Victor sat back in his chair. "Maybe it's the Matticks case—the cops are watching each other now. They have to make clean arrests." Victor paused. "Or you are just incredibly lucky."

"True," I agreed. "But I don't have to pay Sam the balance, right? I've been busted, so the deal is void."

"Yes, the law of drug dealing says when there is a bust, everyone takes the loss and calls it even."

Victor and I sat for a moment longer, thinking about why the cops had done what they did. "I should probably go and talk to Sam now." I stood up.

"Yeah," Victor agreed and walked me to the door.

I called Sam from a payphone to let him know I was coming. He didn't look happy to see me when I pulled up. He didn't say anything; he just raised his eyebrows at me.

"I was busted less than two blocks from your house, Sam." I emphasized the words "your house."

Sam waited for me to continue.

"The pot's gone, so I can't pay the $2000."

Sam didn't accept that. "Yes, you are. You still have to," he informed me.

"No, I don't Sam. That's not how it works," I said and left him there, sitting on his sofa.

Later that evening, when I was home and it had gotten dark, I heard *a thump, thump, thump,* on my deck outside. I wasn't expecting company. I had a .22 rifle that was legal. I grabbed it and headed for the door.

Sam was standing on the other side. "I just want to talk," he said.

Who in the hell told him where I live? "Get off my property," I said sternly.

Sam didn't move.

I raised my rifle and pointed it at him. Then Sam ran. He ran as fast as he could to the car waiting farther off.

I opened my door and went out the front, rifle still raised, trying to see who was stupid enough to drive Sam to my house. But it was too dark, and the car drove away too quickly.

I wasn't afraid of Sam; I'm not the kind of person to worry. But this had to stop. I went to see Victor again the next morning. When I told him what Sam had done, he shook his head and asked me if I wanted him to talk to Sam.

I said yes and put them in touch. It was a calm conversation. Sam and Victor agreed to go for breakfast. When Victor got back, he told me that it didn't take long for Sam to see I was in the right. Again, there was no malice in this conversation.

It was just two people having a breakfast meeting. After that, I never heard from Sam again.

CHAPTER 114

When summer turned into fall, my life settled into a better rhythm. I had my two boys in my life, Lucas, and Sammy. I didn't need John, and I certainly didn't need Donald. However, on occasion, I wondered how Donald was doing. But then I remembered he got married and I put an end to my thoughts. I was taking care of myself and I was doing well for myself again and that was all that counted right now.

I found something I liked way more than I had ever liked booze: blackjack! There is only one casino in Montreal. It looks like a floating palace on Île Notre-Dame that never sleeps. Five storeys tall, the casino has several restaurants, bars, and entertainment stages. When you arrived, valets parked your car and you walked into to a bright, expansive casino.

I would drive up in my Corvette and be noticed before I even left my car. Gamblers are a breed of their own. It would be the same people day in and day out. I made the rounds, greeting all the regulars before I settled in at the blackjack table of my choice.

Blackjack is a fast game not too many women play. The other players were almost always surprised by my skill. My love of numbers and the lightning-fast pace my brain craves allowed me to be the anchor of the table on most days. That way, I would get to decide the outcome of a pull on sixteen, with the dealer showing a seven or higher. I always hit.

My life was speeding along, and I kept my eyes on the road ahead. I didn't look left, I didn't look right, and I certainly didn't look back. I wasn't on drugs, so I wasn't paranoid. Life was good, and I was enjoying it.

February 13th 1996 began like every other day.

I drew open my bedroom curtains in the morning and there was a man walking quickly to the end of my driveway and then heading back from the way which he had come. *Strange,* I thought and then I stupidly forgot about it.

In the winter I always rented a vehicle. The Corvette was not a winter car. I hopped into my rental and ripped out of my driveway; I was heading to Pierrefonds Boulevard to see a client. Traffic was light, so I drove fast. A beige car had pulled in behind me. For some reason, my radar told me to keep an eye on him, and just as I was getting a wee bit suspicious, he turned left. I breathed a sigh of relief and kept going to my clients.

Ava and Calvin lived in a basement apartment. When I parked, I walked around to the back door, passing another beige parked car. When the driver saw me, he ducked.

That's strange. I buzzed the doorbell, and Calvin let me in. He answered the door right away when I knocked.

"Come in." Calvin waved me inside.

"Hi, Ava," I said as I moved to the couch. I noticed her hands were shaking. "What's wrong, Ava?" I asked. "Why are you shaking? Are you coming down or something?" I put my scale on the coffee table to weigh out their half gram.

They watched me in silence. I handed the baggie to Calvin, took the money and left.

The cops appeared out of nowhere. I had only been driving for a few seconds before they surrounded me. In an instant, all the signs I had missed throughout the day flooded my brain. The man at the end of the driveway. The bloody car that followed me. The man in his car who ducked when I walked by. Ava, nervous out of her mind.

That bitch! Those bastards set me up!

"Can I see some ID?" I mouthed through my window. The cop laughed and said, "Come on, you know who we are."

The cop opened the door and hustled me out. By this time, another car had driven up and they put me in the back and took me to the nearest station.

If I had just ditched the scale somewhere in the hall, or at least washed it off... I could have flushed the coke. It was a tiny amount in the grand scheme of things. If only I had listened to my intuition. When was I going to learn to listen to this now very obvious feeling?

I was a small-time dealer. Normally, the cops didn't bother with dealers on my level. I guess my name had come up too many times. *Maybe they will just take my stuff and let me go again?* I grinned to myself at the thought. *Well, why not, this is a heck of a lot less than the amount I had last time.*

I was fingerprinted and processed. The silver lining on this disastrous day was that I knew my prints wouldn't pop. I had applied for a pardon six months ago. Nothing had come up when the lawyer looked for my record. I can only assume that the burns from the crack pipe changed my prints. Or it was the angels; I'm grateful either way.

Back at the station, I told the cops where to find the pot I had in my kitchen drawer. It was seven grams and I didn't want them to tear my house apart looking for it.

The cops booked me for trafficking. I was taken to the courthouse. I counted the minutes until I could escape the smoke-filled, underground, hell hole of a holding cell. I passed court the next day and was given a signature bond.

Linda picked me up. "Seriously, Victoria. We have to stop doing this." She laughed as I got into her car.

"Just take me home, Linda. I have a massive headache."

"Okay, Miss Daisy," she said.

CHAPTER 115

I was in a deep sleep, in the middle of the night. The cats cuddled beside me.

"You would be better off in English Canada." The now somewhat familiar voice woke me again. I was instantly filled with the same warmth and love I felt the first time it spoke to me. I sat up quickly in bed.

"Wait!" I called out to it. "What do you mean, English Canada?" I asked. But the voice didn't respond. I lay back down, basking in the glow the incident left me with. *English Canada? Ontario is a forty-five-minute drive away. Technically, it's English Canada,* I thought. I wished the voice had been more specific. I wish words could accurately convey the emotional effect the voice had on me. But only when I tell the story in person do people really understand how profound it was. I fell back into a deep sleep.

Dave, my lawyer, the same one John had used, was confident I would get off easy. Kali's breeder had called me a week later and I was overjoyed. When Kali passed, I had asked her if she had any more female kittens from Kali's parents. She didn't, but she told me she would call me if she did. It had taken a year and I had never stopped thinking about Kali. Kali's mother had finally given birth to a new litter, by a different father. All the kittens were boys but one. Before I drove over to pick the little girl up, I called my lawyer. I wanted to make sure I would be free to take care of my new kitten. My lawyer told me to go ahead and get the kitten; I would for sure not be going back to jail. When I arrived at the breeder's, there was the daintiest kitten I had ever seen. She was the spitting image of Kali. I named her Princess.

Dave was right to be so confident. The Crown offered me a deal: 100 hours of community service in exchange for a guilty plea. Dave strongly suggested I take the deal. I would have a year to finish my 100 hours.

My first community service job was at a second-hand clothing store. When you do community service, everyone you work with knows why you're there. The women who worked in that store enjoyed trying to make me feel bad. They had me do the most demeaning jobs in the store. The last straw came when they told me to take out the garbage. I had never taken the garbage out in my life, and it was the dead of winter. I quit on the spot and applied for a new place to do my community service. I would do anything but work at another clothing store. Prison time felt like it went by faster than working at that thrift store.

I was still dealing to make money, but now I was being very careful. I only dealt to people I knew. People who I knew weren't rats!

CHAPTER 116

It was now May 1996. My lease was coming up and I had decided to move. I had found a brand-new condo off the island, but still on the water. Third-floor with a balcony, carpeted and clean. I had signed a lease and would take the month of May to move in. The lease sat on my desk in my front room. My pager went off with Celine's number with the code for half a gram.

I went into the front room to make sure my sliding patio doors were locked. The week before, two boys had wandered into the house, apparently very impressed by my big-screen TV. I heard them from my bedroom. The boys did what Debbie and I had done. They asked if so-and-so was home. I told them no, that I had never heard of so-and-so, and then the boys took off running through the back woods. My neighbour hadn't been as lucky. She had her garage robbed a few weeks prior. The robbers had gotten in because she forgot to close the garage on her way to work. I wasn't going to make that mistake. Now, I made sure all my doors were secure. As I looked at the lease, the same feeling I had about bringing the pot over to my friend's that I had ignored came over me. Which was the same feeling I had before that; I should have taken my inventory home from John's to calculate. That same feeling overtook me. I guess you call that intuition. I wasn't going to ignore it a third time. This time I took the lease, put it in my purse and left.

I grabbed half a gram from my fake Ajax can. I was being more cautious with my inventory, so I only brought what I needed. Before heading over to Celine's, I first stopped at my new condo and dropped the lease off there.

Celine lived on Pierrefonds Boulevard. She had been my client for some time. I always had a routine with my clients. There was a specific place and a specific way we would meet. When I pulled up, Celine was waiting outside of her building, looking cold. Our arrangement had always been to meet in her apartment.

What the hell? I pulled up beside her and opened my window. "Don't get in. Why are you outside?"

Celine shook a little. "My boyfriend is home. He doesn't know I do drugs. He can't know! I'm going out later tonight and I really want this."

"I gave you very clear instructions."

"But my boyfriend… He would leave me if he found out."

"Tell him to go to the store or something and I'll come up."

Celine's eyes went a little wide. "That won't work."

"Why not?" I asked

"Because I said I'm going to the store. That's why I'm out here. If I ask him to go now, he'll be suspicious."

"Fine." I traded the half gram for Celine's fifty dollars and I left.

A dark car started driving beside me on the way home. I looked over and saw an older man behind the wheel. A younger woman was in the passenger seat. They weren't talking; they just stared straight ahead.

Then the feeling came over me again; I knew they were cops. *Argh! I'm busted again!*

On cue, when I turned the corner, I was surrounded by cops.

At least I don't have any blow on me. I waited for the cops to come. I got out of the car quietly. "I have nothing on me," I said to the young female cop who began searching me.

"Well, it doesn't matter," the male cop said. "We're taking in the person you sold to." *That junkie bitch!*

The cops took me down to the station. I looked, but I didn't see Celine anywhere. I was put into another interrogation room. While I waited, I made sure to keep my face calm. Inside, though, I was freaking out about Lucas and Sammy and Princess. *This is my second arrest and I'm on probation now… What if they don't let me out?* Either way I was concerned because today was Friday. I wouldn't see a judge until Monday.

The male detective from the car sat down in front of me.

I didn't say anything. I kept my expression blank.

"We're going to go and search your place now," he informed me.

"Are you going to be the one doing the search?" I asked.

The cop looked at me a little funny. "Yes."

"My three kittens are there. Can you please put out some extra food and water for them?" That was the most I had said up to that point.

The detective nodded. "Sure, I'll make sure your cats are fed."

When the detective left, a uniformed cop came in and put me in a holding cell to wait. All my coke was in one fake Ajax can. The can was right where it should be, under my kitchen sink, with my actual cleaning supplies. I really hoped the cops wouldn't find it. I really didn't have anything else in the house.

I was brought into an interrogation room again. The male and female detective were already sitting down.

"We found six grams of pot in the pocket of one of your fur coats," the female detective started.

Six grams of pot? I didn't smoke… What was it doing there?

Both detectives looked at me, expecting an answer. I continued to stare at them. *So, they didn't find the blow,* I thought to myself.

"With that pot, plus the scale we found in your home, we are going to charge you with trafficking," the female detective continued.

I shrugged my shoulders. *Oh my God. What about the cats?*

Dave came to see me later that evening. I had spent the last few hours imagining what my poor cats would go through if I didn't get out. The cops had fed them today, but what about tomorrow?

"Why are you crying?" Dave asked me when he entered the room.

"It's not for me. It's for my cats. I'm worried about them." I tried to stop crying.

"Oh." Dave paused. "Well, did you tell the cops anything?"

"No. Can you make sure they let me call someone to get my house keys?"

Dave nodded his head slowly. "Cheer up, they're going to take you to Tanguay now. Stick out the weekend there and I'll have you out on bail Monday morning."

"Really?" I brightened up a little.

"Yes." Dave nodded his head and then slowly left the room.

The cops let me call my friend Jack. He came and got my house keys. I knew he would take care of Lucas, Sammy and Princess.

Dave was right; I was able to pass court on Monday and get bail, no problem.

When I got home, Sammy, Lucas and Princess came running to greet me at the door. I knelt down and petted them all. I felt so relieved to have them in my arms again.

CHAPTER 117

Celine was not a strong person. Nor was she particularly smart. That is why I had always insisted on doing deals in her apartment. I knew she couldn't be counted on to make sure she wasn't seen.

I went to see my lawyer. He already had the evidence from the cops. They had coke residue on my scale, as well as the pot. The only evidence they had linking me to an actual deal was Celine.

Dave was very happy to hear that Celine would be saying I hadn't sold her any coke, that she already had it when I stopped by. The judge had set the date for my preliminary hearing when I got bail.

When my court date arrived, I didn't take any chances. I picked Celine up from her house and brought her with me to the courtroom.

At the courthouse, I introduced her to my lawyer and then went to use the washroom.

When I came back, Dave looked like he was going to have a stroke. He grabbed me by the arm and pulled me into a corner. "What kind of a stupid fucking friend do you have over there?"

The question was rhetorical. I raised my eyebrows at him and shrugged my shoulders.

Dave leaned in and whispered in my ear, "She just told me that you actually sold it to her. I don't need to hear this."

I marched over to Celine and said, "Are you a fucking idiot?" and then sat elsewhere.

Dave walked back to his table. He gave Celine a dirty look. "Sit here and don't move. Don't say anything."

"All rise." The judge walked into the room. The bailiff rattled off the case number.

"All be seated." The judge looked down at his papers. He was older, with pink skin and a soft body type. His wig sat a little too forward on his head. "This is a preliminary hearing?"

"Yes, Your Honour," Dave replied. "I would like to make a motion to have the case thrown out. The Crown doesn't have sufficient evidence."

"Your Honour," The Crown counsel's voice went a little squeaky. "As you can see, we have the marijuana found in the defendant's home, along with a scale containing cocaine residue."

"Your Honour"—David pointed at Celine–"the person is here in court today who my client is accused of trafficking to."

"Very well, swear the witness in." The judge was staring at Celine.

Celine made her way to the witness stand. The judge looked down at her and asked her one question: "Did the accused sell you cocaine that day?"

Celine looked up and said, "No, Your Honour, she did not."

The judge said, "I don't believe you. Court will resume in three weeks."

I shook Dave's hand. Celine and I got into my car and drove to the casino. That night I won $600 while Celine sat beside me.

CHAPTER 118

The voice may have been right that I would be better off in English Canada, but I still wasn't ready to leave Quebec. What would I do out there? I knew I had to do something with my life. Dealing drugs was no longer working for me. I sold my Corvette to buy myself some time to figure out what my next step should be.

Back when I was married, I had been an electrolysis technician. To me, becoming an aesthetician seemed like a nice fit. I could open my own business in my neighbourhood.

When I researched becoming an aesthetician, it appeared I needed my high school diploma. I made some more calls and learned where I could take my GED. On August 13, 1997, I went down to the school, prepared to take the test. I sat down and looked at the different sections for different subjects. I left the French language test for last and got to work on English and math. I flew through those and started on science and social studies. Then there was nothing left but French.

"Time's up," the teacher at the front of the classroom said.

I looked up. I had just finished my French test; I wasn't confident about what I had put on the paper, but at least I had finished. I walked to the front of the class and handed in my papers. The tests scores would be available soon. I sat down to wait. I kept going over the French test in my mind. I didn't really read French. I had never learned because I hated the way French is shoved down people's throats in Quebec.

"Hi, Victoria. Can you come into the office now, please?" a pleasant woman said.

I followed her to the office and, again, waited for someone to speak to.

Finally, an older woman ushered me into her office. "Have a seat, please." The woman smiled at me. "I have good news and bad news," she said.

I looked at her.

"On your math, social science, English, science and comprehension tests, you scored between 95 and 100%, which is really quite impressive…" The woman's voice trailed off.

I knew what was coming next.

"On your French test, you scored thirty-five per cent." The woman shuffled some papers on her desk.

"Seriously?" *French shouldn't even be on that bloody test!* I thought angrily. *It's not on any other test in any other province.*

"We can arrange for you to retake the French test"—she checked her calendar—"at the end of the month, if you like."

"No, there's no point." I got up and walked out of the office.

So much for becoming an aesthetician.

Sometimes you feel defeated. Each and every person reacts differently to this. At first, I was okay. Then I realized that I was spending more and more time alone. This led me back to drugs. I didn't go back to smoking crack. I just started doing lines. I didn't go out when I was high. I answered the phone with a different name, so my friends would know I was high. Most of them knew I was extremely paranoid when I used that name, and that there would be no hope in trying to see me or get me to sell them anything. The more time I spent alone, the more blow I started to do.

Gradually, the paranoia returned with a vengeance. However, I noted that if I stayed awake more than thirty hours in a row, my paranoia would disappear. I often stayed up thirty hours and beyond. I would do a run of a few days on coke. Then I would sleep. After I woke, I would stay straight for a week or so. Life was a series of being high, dealing to make some money and trying to complete my 200 hours of community service. After Celine testified, Dave told the judge I wanted to go out west and clean up my life. The Crown offered me another deal in exchange for additional community service. David told me I should take it. On his advice, I pleaded guilty and took the additional 100 hours.

I had Cat or Linda to do lunch with. I had other friends as well—Michel, Joe, Mike—but nothing else. Time passed without much personal growth.

It wasn't for lack of trying, though. After my dreams of being an aesthetician were crushed by Quebec's language law, I began to consider putting my psychic skills to work. I had always said that I would not become my parents. I think a lot of people say that. It had been difficult to process the changes in my parents after

Dad's first spiritual experience. Before that, my parents had been typical Brits. They believed children should be seen and not heard. After that, my parents became sort of hippies. Dad grew his hair and called his sandals "Jesus boots." All of a sudden, when I would go to visit my parents, there was a good chance some weirdo would be rolling on the floor, speaking in tongues.

I had a shelf of spiritual books however, and had always been fascinated by tarot cards. Psychics aren't common in Quebec because they aren't exactly legal. A province of Catholics who look upon psychics as the devil. It was a huge part of why my parents moved out west. Whenever I found a new psychic in Montreal, or when I was out of town and saw a psychic, I would have a reading done. My father always gave amazing readings; only one of the psychics I went to came close to doing as good a job. It told me that most people who claim to be psychic really were not.

I could read tarot cards, but I judged myself according to my father's standards. I never felt my readings were as good as his. I had done readings for some of my friends. John, who had a love of all things supernatural and occult, was fascinated by my readings. I had gotten some cards that were specifically designed for doing past-life readings. John was the first person to get a reading from them. When I did the reading, it said that he had once lived in ancient Pakistan, where he spoke Sanskrit and practised Zen Buddhism. John looked as if he could be from that part of the world, and he loved spicy foods; the hotter the food, the better. He had embraced my suggestion of only eating vegetarian one day a week.

I had seen ads in the paper and commercials on TV advertising psychic readings. The psychic, Jo Jo Savard, was on every night after the news in commercials asking for phone psychics. I called and was hired right away. When the phone line for psychic readings was installed in my house and I started doing them, I wanted to take things a step further. I made myself business cards. I called myself "V." I felt that was appropriate as the V in numerology represents the number four. Four means "foundation" and that was what I was looking for. A foundation in a business I could build. A singles' group booked me to do couples' readings at their Saturday "Singles Ready to Mingle" events.

Psychic readings, community service, dealing, my friends—all of these things— couldn't fit into the schedule coke was keeping me on. Life was propelling me forward, but drugs kept holding me back. Even when I tried, Quebec was telling me to move, not just the voice. I had been arrested, community service was terrible, relationships didn't work out, I couldn't learn French, I couldn't find work because of this. Quebec and the voice were telling me to leave. Still, I stayed. I do not know why.

CHAPTER 119

It was one of those days. I was still not smoking crack, just snorting lines. When coke is pure, you get a truly strong high. Most dealers on the street cut their coke, sometimes so badly that most people can't even imagine the experience of uncut coke. If you know the importers, and get the coke fresh off the boat, you can experience uncut coke.

The day started out like any other: one line, then two, and so on and so on. I don't know exactly how many hours I had been high, but it was past thirty. My paranoia was gone and I was in the sweet spot. All of my senses were amplified, and I was able to go deep into my subconscious. Visions overtook me, and I settled in to watch. I saw all kinds of things.

For instance, I was able to channel almost a whole science fiction novel about nine worlds, and duplicates of all of us in each world. It was intricate when I think about the concept today, and read the pages I have. I often wonder if I should turn it into a book at some point.

My subconscious would take me to other places, including my past lives. One time, a Scottish fellow was on the other side of my couch; somehow, I knew I had been him in that past life. At other times, the visions would be more intense, and I would actually relive scenes from my past lives. Once, I was in a gunfight with a hit man. It was during a war between two mobs. When I came out of the blackness, I was behind my couch, pointing my fingers like they were a gun. I just knew what had happened. I also knew this was a lifetime I had lived with Donald.

That cold November day seemed no different than any other. Until I smelled smoke. I've always been sensitive to the smell of smoke. My heightened sense of smell alerted me to it right away. I looked and saw smoke coming from my office.

The cats! Oh my God, the condo is catching fire! I went to get my cats, but they were curled up under the middle of the bed. No matter how I tried, I couldn't reach them. They wouldn't come when I called to them.

I began to really freak out. I decided the best course of action was to jump from my third floor balcony. I don't know why I didn't think of using the front door to escape, or to pull the fire alarm in the hallway as I left. Coke highs can be strange.

I had just showered; my hair was freshly washed. I had on clean jeans, a burgundy woollen sweater and black cowboy boots tucked over my jeans. I swung myself over the edge of the balcony, and then I jumped.

I could feel myself leave my body. My body fell faster than I did. I don't remember landing; my spirit continued forward. I could see all kinds of spirit people around me, but what caught my attention the most was a cat. I began to follow it.

"What is she doing?" one of the spirit people asked another.

"She's following that cat," the person answered.

Something else caught my attention and I looked down at the waterfront. A spirit lady was sitting on a rock, looking out at the water. Everything shimmered, including the spirits. To me, it was a completely different dimension of energy.

Suddenly, I was back in my body. All of me felt fine; nothing was broken. I had not one scratch or bruise on me. I walked around for a bit, settling back into my body, then I headed back to my condo.

When I got back, I saw what a disaster it was. When I did lines and waited for the sweet spot, my paranoia took over. I had checked all the wires in the house. I started thinking that the TV had been watching me, so I had unplugged it and started taking it apart. I did the same thing to switches, looking for listening devices. And I had done nothing to clean up the mess.

KNOCK, KNOCK, KNOCK.

I startled at the knock on my door.

"Montreal Police! Open up!"

Cops!

I did a quick inventory. I had just done the last of my coke and, for some reason, flushed the baggies. Someone had looked after me there. I opened the door and the cops barged in. I was told to sit on the couch.

"What happened here?" one of the cops asked me.

"I have no idea. Someone must have broken in," I replied, proud of my own cleverness.

"What do you mean someone broke in?" the same cop asked.

I wasn't going to repeat myself. I stayed quiet while the cops bombarded me with questions. I didn't notice when they called an ambulance. But, all of a sudden, a paramedic was walking through my door, stretcher in tow. They put me on the stretcher and I was on my way.

In the ambulance, the paramedic asked me what day it was.

I don't remember if I answered, but if I did, what I said was definitely wrong. Luckily, I was ready to sleep.

At the hospital, I was put in a bed. The two cops from my condo showed up. They stayed beside me. I could see them fidget and look at their watches. It was taking forever for anyone in the hospital to see me.

Finally, one of the cops asked me, "Will you stay here until a doctor sees you?"

"Sure," I agreed. "I'm tired and I just want to sleep."

That was enough assurance for the cops to leave. I lay still for another five minutes. Then I simply got up, walked down the hall and out of the hospital. I realized I was on Hymus Boulevard in Pointe-Claire, at the Lakeshore General Hospital. I walked to the corner and hailed a taxi. A cab stopped right away, and I hopped in. I gave the cabbie my address. On his dashboard was a large picture of Jesus. As I looked at the picture, I realized Jesus was staring back at me. I was filled with a feeling of calm so strong I will never forget it. I looked at Jesus the whole way home.

When we arrived, I got out of the cab and told the cabbie, "Just a minute, I have your money upstairs." In my hurry, I forgot about the one-foot-high chain-link fence that surrounds the grass in front of our building. I tripped over it and fell hard.

The cabbie jumped out and helped me up. We went to my apartment together. I found my jar of change and paid him. Then I crawled into bed.

I slept for the next two days. Nobody came back to get me.

When I woke up, I called Kenny and Moira. I filled them in and told them about my three-storey jump.

Kenny looked at me like I had two heads.

"You know, Kenny, not all of us can be high for days and then go fix airplanes," I said.

He nodded his head and looked at Moira. Moira was like me when she did coke: paranoid. We both never stopped until the coke was gone and then had strong withdrawals, or we stayed up until we dropped from exhaustion. Kenny looked back at me and said, "I'm just glad you're okay." He didn't understand, but he was worried about me.

Kenny took a walk around my condo to make sure it was safe. "Hey, girls! Come here," he called from my office. Moira and I joined him. "Look at this." He pointed to my baseboard heater. On it was a candle. "Maybe this is what you smelled when you thought your place was on fire?" Kenny suggested.

Sure enough, a candle had fallen off my office desk and onto my heater. The candle hadn't burned, but it had melted into a pool of wax.

"That must be it," I said. *Your senses are so much more profound when you're high.*

Both Kenny and Moira nodded their heads in agreement.

My only unanswered question was why had the cops come? Little did I know, the janitor for my condo building and the one across the grass, had been watching me all night with his binoculars. When the janitor finally told me he had called the cops, he said, "I had to stay up all night because of you."

I decided to stay off coke for the rest of the month. That episode had truly made me think. My thoughts constantly flashed back to the spirit people I had seen when I left my body. It had been an amazing trip. It reminded me of the only other time I astral-travelled. That time I was able to spend those five seconds with my brother, Jeremy.

I guess I inconvenienced the janitor enough that he reported me to the rental office. The rental office waited until I had paid my rent on December 1st. By December 3rd, I had been served an eviction notice. The eviction notice was entirely in French, which for once, was actually illegal. In Quebec, at that time, if you signed a lease in English, which I had, then all communication that followed had to be English. I was able to understand the gist of what the notice said. I took it to Cat, one of my French-speaking friends, to be sure.

The rental company had set a court date. I could go to court and fight my eviction. I thought about it and decided it wasn't worth it. Part of me was too worn out to care, and it was easy to find places to rent, so I just left.

The ground-level duplex I moved into had a whirlpool tub in my room, a fireplace in the front room with a mantle that I put all my faux Fabergé eggs on, and a sunken living room. It also had a small back yard; it was tiny, but big enough to sit two chairs in it.

Money was tight for me now. When I had to pay the movers, I was $100 short. My son put it in the bank for me, I paid the movers and then I paid my son back later that night. After I moved, I leased a little black Honda. Predictably, my business picked up as soon as I stopped using. I always made good money when I was sober.

In 1998, computers and the Internet weren't that big of a thing. What I had learned about the Internet made it sound like a fancier version of the *Yellow Pages*. I didn't really understand how computers worked, but I was fascinated by them. When I had some money saved up, I went to the store and bought a top-of-the-line computer. I paid $2000 and had to have my friend Drew put it together for me. When I looked at my newly assembled computer, all I saw was a hunk of metal that needed to be plugged in. In my heart, though, I knew having a computer and learning to use it was important. I kept the computer, even though I did nothing with it.

Drew lived in the country. As he and I began to hang out more, we spent a decent amount of time on the road driving and talking about different things. One day, I was telling him that I wanted to build a psychic business like my dad's. I explained to Drew that I had been working for Jo Jo's psychic hotline and had recently starting working for a few others, as well.

"I'm just stuck on a name," I said to Drew as we drove. "I can't have a company that doesn't have a neat name. Everything should have a name: people, places, cats and businesses. They all need names!"

Drew was quiet for a moment. "You are the Alternative Universe!" he said.

"Drew, that's perfect! I love that name. Can I use it?" I had a big grin plastered on my face. *I had never felt like I truly belonged. To me it felt like I was from an alternative universe.*

"Sure, you can use it. Use away," he said as we pulled into his driveway.

I didn't waste any time after that; I designed my business that very afternoon.

CHAPTER 120

The road to hell is paved with good intentions. I had every intention of staying off coke. But it started to tempt me. Good intentions on their own don't stand up to addictions. You have to find the reason they exist within yourself, then the strength to change what you find.

Nothing inside of me felt happy. I wasn't kidding when I said I felt like I was from an alternative universe. I would ask myself all the time, *Am I on Mars? What the heck am I doing here?* I still didn't see the point of waking up and doing the same mundane things day in and day out. I knew that one day I would die and that, most likely, this may all make perfect sense then, but right now I could not find that sense. That feeling made it worth getting high and suffering through my paranoia until I reached the blissful state I felt after. There, deep in my subconscious, I found the answers I was looking for. When I was sober, I couldn't figure out how to make changes. I couldn't figure out where to start. I couldn't figure out where to start when it came to the process of seeding, germinating, growing, maturing, and enjoying life.

After my stint at the second-hand clothing store, my community service was changed to a restaurant. I was given the position of cook, but I asked the owner if I could work as a waitress, instead. I hoped it was a job I would find tolerable enough to leave dealing for.

The owner told me she wouldn't even consider it because I didn't speak French. *Goddamn French language laws.* I fumed after she told me. *How can I stay in such a backwards province that won't let me do any job I enjoy?*

I resigned myself to working in the kitchen. On the days I would work, I made breakfast and lunch. I have always liked to cook, and I enjoyed the fast pace of the kitchen. But at every turn, the owners and staff went out of their way to remind me I was a criminal.

"You're not a true volunteer," the owner sneered at me one day. "You're only here because the court forced you to be."

I rolled my eyes and walked away. *Sure, some people are lucky enough to be supported and have nothing else to do with their time. That, my dear, is not me. I take care of myself... and pretty soon I'm going to turn things around, and really take good care of myself!*

That's how I spent the winter between 1997 and 1998.

Then came the spring of 1998.

I was drowning. Cat and Michel were still my friends. A few of my clients were still willing to buy from me, but money was tight. In March, I was twenty dollars short on my rent and the landlord was pissed. What kept me going was my cats. Princess, Lucas, and Sammy were the loves of my life. Not everyone can understand, but my love for them was stronger than anything else; stronger than any love I had experienced before. Without them, I would have told the restaurant owner to screw off and take the year of jail time the court kept hanging over my head. I would have had a chance to dry out and get my life together. But I could never have deserted them...

To me, my cats were little beings in fur coats who purred when you petted them. They ran to you when you came home and when you fed them. My cat's dependence on and love for me was unconditional. My love for them had to be equally unconditional. No matter how depressed I was, I had to be there for them. Watching them play with one another amused me for hours. I *loved* these cats. Their love had taught me to swim. But I could only swim when I was with them. I had to learn to expand that into the rest of my life.

In April 1998, I went on my last binge. I got high and stayed high all night. When daylight came, I didn't care; I kept snorting. Around noon, I did one of the largest lines I had ever done. Normally my lines were small. I didn't think of myself as a glutton. Why I did this, I do not know. Was it the universe taking me to where I would go?

Typically, I would have laid back to enjoy the bliss I felt when I entered the spiritual realm. This time it was different. My head spun. The world around me changed. My duplex became dark and sinister-feeling. I knew in my heart I was in a dangerous place. I had to escape as fast as I could. I noticed my cat's empty food bowls as I fled out the front door.

I jumped in my Honda and drove. As I headed down the highway, my car began to sputter. I pulled off to the side of the road before my car died. In my paranoia-fuelled panic, I started to go through my glove compartment, looking for wires and things that might allow others to be watching me. It's called severe paranoia.

In that moment, I believed that the aliens were finally coming to rescue me. They were going to take me home. The aliens had started to come and talk to me when I was high. They told me that I was from Planet 8511. They were the ones who gave me the inspiration for my science fiction novel.

I didn't find anything in my glove compartment. Except now, I had pulled about every wire possible from under the dash that I could find. And there were a lot of wires under there. Defeated, I sat on the side of the road in my car calling out, "Eight-five-one-one, I'm here!" I waited and kept watching for the spaceship that was coming to take me.

I don't know how long I sat there. At some point, a tow truck driver pulled over and knocked on my window. I turned to him, excited my saviours had finally come. Alas, it was not to be; the aliens had not yet arrived.

"Can I help you?" he mouthed, standing close to my window.

"I'm fine." I waved him away.

They must not have figured out I need them, I decided. I began to search for anything in my car that would let me contact their planet. Now, I really pulled the car apart. I pulled out all the wiring from my steering wheel column. When I didn't find anything there, I looked under my seats. Then I desperately tried to start my car.

Planet 8511 and it inhabitants never came for me. But the cops did, and they brought an ambulance with them.

I later learned the tow truck driver had driven by me four more times. Hours had passed. Each time he had driven by, he slowed down to peek inside my car. The cops didn't ask me anything. They took one look at my car and motioned for me to get out, then they hustled me into an ambulance.

"You can't start a car that's out of gas," the paramedic riding in the back with me muttered.

"What did you say?" I asked him.

The man narrowed his eyes at me and I think he repeated himself. I don't know. The more I looked at the paramedic, the scarier he seemed. This guy was not sympathetic like the last paramedic. In my panic, I felt myself go into another life. The paramedic stared at me. That pushed me deeper into the vision. I saw tunnels littered with gurneys. All of the gurneys had patients strapped to them. When I looked at the walls, I saw locked cell doors. Each of the doors had small ports. I could see faces screaming looking out of these tiny windows. I knew this paramedic had been one of the keepers of that place. I knew that he had tortured many people in that life.

I don't know what I did to trigger the paramedic, but when we arrived at the hospital, I saw the flash of a long needle. I watched it come towards me and stick into my arm. The last part of the past life came to me. I was in a mental institution and I was being tortured. Mercifully, I passed into a deep, dark much-needed sleep.

Later on, I awoke, tied down to a bed in four-point restraints. It was just like what I had seen in the vision. As I stirred, my body was starting to feel that feeling I always have whenever I have been held down. A feeling of sheer panic. It's hard to explain this feeling. Of all the feelings I have ever had, being tied down is the worst form of torture I have ever felt. Luckily, there was an attendant nearby. The woman who was sitting at the desk got up, came over and looked at me. I smiled at her and she undid all four restraints. Even with all of that medication, while I was unconscious my muscles and bones continued to be tense. They didn't relax until I was finally free of the restraints. I lay there thinking: *I'm exhausted.*

I was moved into a different room. A psychiatrist came to see me. I asked him if I could make a phone call. He said yes and had a nurse take me to a payphone.

"Wendy," I said after she answered the phone. "I'm in the hospital. Could you please come get my house key so you can feed the cats?"

There was silence on the other end of the line for a moment. I explained some more and then she said, "Of course, Victoria. I'm on my way."

Wendy came right away. She assured me that she would feed the cats and take care of them. Once she left, my worries were over. I only worry about things that are important in the moment. I crawled back to bed. *My feet! Oh, my feet.* I realized how badly my feet hurt. I could barely stand. I felt everything in my body ache before I fell into a deep, deep sleep.

Every so often I would wake up. I checked and noticed my door wasn't locked. I was able to go and get water. That would be enough exertion for me and I would go back to bed. After two or three days, the psychiatrist came to see me again. I told him the same thing I had told the psychiatrist in Dorval.

"Honestly, Doctor, I don't know what I was thinking. I was a fool. I did way too much cocaine," I said to the psychiatrist.

I don't know why, but doctors like it when you tell the truth about your drug use. Just like the psychiatrist in Dorval, he discharged me.

Wendy came and picked me up. On the ride home, she assured me over and over again that the cats were okay. She tucked me into bed and made me eat something before I went back to sleep. I was ravenous.

I slept for four more days, only getting up in-between to drink water and order pizza.

About a week later, when I was feeling better, my friend Lawrence, who had been a long-time client of mine whom I met when I moved to the West Island, came over and together we tried to track down my Honda. When we found it, I had it towed to the dealership. The dealership promptly told me that not only could they not fix my car, they were keeping it. No doubt because the monthly lease payment hadn't been paid. I really do not recall whether that was true or not. Lawrence drove me home. When he dropped me off, I was alone. I was alone again and only had time to think.

What a mess I had made of my life. What a mess of our lives we had made. Why, Donald? Why did you choose life in prison instead of coming home to me?

I had no money and now my computer was at the pawn shop, my two fur coats at another. Not all pawn shops took furs. Lastly, all my gold jewellery had been hawked. I had no car, and barely any friends. Victor had put me on a "cash only" payment plan. I had none of that left. I could no longer accommodate any of my clients.

CHAPTER 121

Around that time I looked at a calendar and saw that Easter had passed. *I had missed my community service!* When I called them later that day, the owner of the restaurant told me I was no longer welcome. She had also notified the courts. *Great!*

My next call was to Dave.

"You've really done it this time," Dave told me.

"What do you mean?" I asked. "They won't give me another chance?"

"Not a hope in hell. The judge is done giving you chances. You're going to be sent by the court to jail to finish your time."

When I got off the phone, I looked at the three innocent faces staring up at me. My greatest loves, who trusted me and loved me back unconditionally. I knew I could not leave them.

We would all be going.

It was time to stop sinking and to swim!

Dave had told me it would take a few weeks for my warrant to be processed by the system. I had some time. I looked around at what I owned. It seemed obvious. I could sell everything and have enough money to head out west. *I'll trust the voice*, I said to myself. I made a sign: Everything Must Go. I put my address at the bottom and placed it outside.

The doorbell rang within minutes. I was so busy, you would have thought I hired a skywriter and hung up a neon sign. All day people came and went. They paid me money and came back with vehicles to take their purchases home. In those few hours, I sold my waterbed, bureaus, desk, large-screen TV, designer couch, loveseat, fridge, stove, dishwasher, and all the other household items I had. I made $3000. It was incredible!

Once I had finished selling everything, I rushed back to the pawn shops. First up was the one I had consigned my furs to.

"Oh, good, you came back," the pawn broker said to me. "I think I paid you too much for those furs."

"Okay." I handed him my money. It turned out to be true.

At the next pawn shop, the owner greeted me, saying, "I was so hoping you wouldn't come back. This is an excellent computer."

"I know. That's why I want it back." I handed him my money, took my jewellery as well, and left.

The next day, Cat and Michel came over. They would help me pack and then stay at my place for a while. At least until it was time for them to send me the rest of my clothes and whatnot, when I was settled in a few weeks.

I knew I was still going to need a van. I was taking the cat's eight-foot-tall scratching post, litter box, toys, and food. I also had some of my own stuff I wanted to bring. The one credit card I had left worked at one specific car rental company. I called their Dorval airport location.

"Hello. Do you have a van for rent?" I asked the clerk.

"No, I'm sorry they're all…" the clerk's voice trailed off. "Oh, wait a minute. I can see one coming in. It's early."

"Hold it. I'm on my way!" I hung up the phone to tell Michel. He drove me to pick up the van while Cat started packing for me. I came back with a lovely van.

When Michel saw what Cat had finished, he exclaimed, "Let me handle this. I can pack a van like nobody else!" He was telling the truth. I have yet to meet someone who could pack the amount of stuff he was able to.

"This box has all of your psychic stuff in it," Cat said. She carefully placed it in the van.

I remember her saying that because when the rest of my stuff came a few weeks later, she had neglected to pack my skis, important papers and the majority of my clothes. *Damn that woman for being the same size as me!*

I had always planned to leave mid-evening. The van was packed and ready on schedule. I went to grab the cats. Sammy and Princess were lying on the mattress I had left for Cat and Michel to sleep on. It was one of the few things that hadn't sold.

"Lucas!" I called.

I searched high and low for Lucas. He was not in my duplex. My house cat had somehow gotten outside! I started to fan out from my building, calling for him. I searched until midnight and returned devastated, sobbing.

Michel looked at me. "Tabernacle! It's just a cat."

That made me cry harder. "I'm not leaving without him!"

Michel shook his head. He and Cat went to bed. I left my front door open a little, and settled on the couch I had sold to Cat. I tried to sleep but I couldn't. I dozed in and out but that was it. Around 5:00 a.m., I heard the tiniest *meow*. I bolted upright. There was Lucas, looking at me. I grabbed him and burst into tears. This time I cried tears of joy.

"Tabernacle! What is it?" Michel flew out of the bedroom, ready to defend me in his underwear.

"Lucas is back." I sniffled.

Michel stopped and looked at me. Then he looked at the door and back at me. "Tabernacle! That's it? The cat?"

"Yes." I stood up. "I'm ready to go now."

"Thank God." He turned around and went to get Cat. We loaded the last of my stuff and Lucas, Sammy, and Princess. Cat and Michel followed me to the Ontario border for breakfast. I knew it would be the last time I saw them. They knew it, too. We took our time eating. I hugged them goodbye and we both went our separate ways. I went west; they went east.

I'm never coming back, I thought to myself. In my heart I knew I would never return to Quebec. I replayed the events of the last few weeks. I had a lot to think about. My mind kept coming back to the voice and its insistence I leave for English Canada. Like I said, Ontario was technically English Canada, but at the border in the restaurant I still heard French. *I wonder how long it will take for me to hear only English? That way I'll know I'm truly in English Canada.*

It turned out I had to drive all the way to Thunder Bay, Ontario, a 1500 km, seventeen-hour drive. That truly surprised me.

Long before I reached Thunder Bay, I stopped to eat. I left the window open a crack for the cats and headed into a busy diner. Almost all of the tables were full of truckers and families. I ate leisurely and paid.

"Excuse me." A lady stopped me as I opened the door.

"Yes?" I replied.

"Do you have Siamese cats travelling with you?" she asked.

She had my attention now. "Yes." I looked over at my van.

"I think one of your cats got out." She pointed over to some grass.

I looked to where she pointed and, to my horror, Sammy was wandering around. "Oh my God! Thank you so much," I called over my shoulder as I rushed to retrieve Sammy. I scooped him up. When I was back in my van driving, I wondered, *How did she know Sammy was mine? Why did she assume, out of everyone in that restaurant, that I was the owner?* I was starting to see the miracles that were lining up for me. I smiled to myself. *Everything is going to be okay.*

Most of my trip was uneventful. I stopped when dusk came and, to my surprise, all the motels I chose allowed cats. In Saskatchewan, the province before Alberta where I was heading, I was pulled over for speeding. Really, I was just driving like a typical Montrealer.

"Get out of the van, please," the RCMP officer said and then ushered me to the back of his police car.

I stayed quiet while he took his time doing whatever it was he was doing. Inside, I was freaking out. *Had the warrant for me already been processed by the system? Had he pulled it up? Was he calling Quebec right now?* A million scenarios played out in my mind.

"Okay, Miss, you can get out now." He opened the door for me.

"You can't be travelling with cats loose in the car. They were distracting you. That's why you were speeding. You need to have these cats in cages while you drive," he told me.

"Sure…" I nodded my head. "Okay, Officer." I started walking back towards my van.

"Cage those cats up. I've radioed to the next town. If they see you driving with those cats loose, you'll be arrested."

"I'll put them in their cages for the remainder of the trip," I lied and hopped back in my van.

I was not stopped at the next town and I let the cats out for the rest of my trip.

Lucas, Sammy, Princess, and I arrived in Edmonton on April 22nd, 1998. It was Earth Day. At that time, I didn't know what Earth Day was about. Now I celebrate it every year. My son and a lot of my family was living in Edmonton. I was in English Canada and I decided I was going to stay a while.

CHAPTER 122

Miracle #1

The cats and I spent the next few days staying with my son. I was able to spend time with him and my three young granddaughters. It was a change after living alone for so long. My son married a woman who is a lot like me, which is common enough. People often don't like themselves, and my daughter-in-law didn't like me. She helped me find a place to live quickly after I arrived.

Finding a place wasn't easy. The rental board in Alberta gave landlords near-absolute power. They decided if you could smoke, have pets, if someone else could live with you based on your lease, and charged an outrageous amount for things like keys and security deposits. None of that was allowed back home. I still thought of Quebec as home. My daughter-in-law did find a place for us to live, eventually, at Stony Plain Road and 162nd Street. My apartment was a three-storey walk up. I found my furniture at a garage sale. The couple who had the sale even delivered.

I settled in and began to consider my options for work. My father had lived and worked as a psychic in Edmonton. He was well known and well liked. Heck, this won't be hard. I'll just say that I'm his daughter and people will line up for readings. It was not to be so.

I did, however, meet one of my neighbours while I was doing laundry in my building. Another John, he told me about a teahouse that psychics worked out of.

"They work in a restaurant, out in the open?" I asked him.

"Yes," he confirmed. "It's right downtown."

"They can't be very good psychics if they work out in the open." No decent psychic in Quebec would work like that.

Miracle number one, and I ignored it.

It didn't take me long after I paid for rent and furniture to get down to my last few dollars. I contacted my ex-sister-in-law. Her husband took me to a good credit/

bad credit/ didn't matter car dealership and bought me a car. He put it in his name, and insured it. I paid him. I returned my rental van and began to look for a job.

John had a different suggestion. He told me to go to Rosie's, a restaurant on 124th Street, and ask for Rosie. I was hired on the spot as a waitress. A restaurant waitress, not a bar waitress. The two jobs are completely different. I was terrible, but I stuck at it.

A few weeks after I started working at Rosie's, I heard the door open and I saw a man walk in. He was about my height, and there was something about him. Again, I had that feeling of instant attraction. My co-worker told me his name was Al and that "he was here all the time." She introduced us. I impressed him enough to take him home for supper. Just supper.

I had my second job to go to. I left Al in my apartment and when I came home hours later at 11:00 p.m., Al was still there. Al was a Scorpio, just like Donald, and just like John. He never really left after that, just like my other two Scorpios. In bed, Al was like Donald in size, but not technique.

Al was different than my other two Scorpios: he did drugs. Crack, specifically. Al was a crackhead. But, Al was a crackhead like Kenny back in Montreal. He was never paranoid and actually pleasant to be around when he was high. Still, Al was a crackhead nonetheless. I refrained from using. After all, I had not come all the way across Canada to become an addict again. Al stayed with me, smoking crack, making me tea and sharing my bed. *Was this the voice testing me to make sure I was ready to get on with my new life?*

Miracle #2

When my second miracle arrived, I didn't ignore it. When I moved into my new apartment, I started having the *Edmonton Journal* delivered. I read it every morning, as I had always done. I particularly enjoyed reading the business section.

"Oh my God, look at this," I said to Al one day.

"What?" Al looked over my shoulder.

I pointed to the column I was looking at. "This guy, Andy, answers questions about computers."

"That's interesting," Al said and went back to what he was doing.

This was perfect! I had my computer set up and Telus had been in to install my phone and the line to the computer. I went into my office and turned on my computer. I connected to the Internet, waiting for the dial-up beep. Then I opened my email and began to type.

After forty-five minutes, I was done. Well, I had something on the screen. I didn't know how to type. My email was all one paragraph. I explained to Andy that I wanted to start a tarot card reading business. I needed a website and I needed help to figure out how to get one.

I read over what I had written and hit the send button. Something flashed back right away. I didn't understand what it meant. It took me the whole day to realize the email had been returned unsent. I looked at the *Edmonton Journal* again and saw Andy's email address had been printed with a hyphen.

If this comes back, I'll leave it be. I took out the hyphen and spent the next forty-five minutes retyping my email. I had no idea about copy and paste. I read over the email again and hit send. This time nothing happened. The email didn't come back. Nothing happened for two days. At the end of the second day, I found a reply from Andy in my inbox.

> I don't know why I'm answering this email as I get tons of emails, but here goes. If I am to understand your email correctly, this is what you are trying to do: make business cards/ set up a website/ work from home on this? And learn how to use all the other options on the computer. If I am correct, I have an offer for you. Each night, I will send you an email with directions on how to use something that you want to know. You will practise this and keep a journal. Once you feel that you are somewhat computer literate, we will take your journal notes and make a story for my readers. I think they would enjoy this. Are you interested?

Was I interested? I was ecstatic. I wasn't going to pass up this new opportunity, this new miracle. I sent back a reply right away, agreeing and thanking him profusely.

Each night after that, Andy would send me a new email with instructions for the next thing I was to learn. I printed out the email and spent hours methodically deciphering what it meant. I emailed back and forth with Andy slowly, painstakingly absorbing the concepts of floppy discs and Lotus.

I worked at Rosie's and, in my free time, learned to use the Internet, and still found time to read the *Edmonton Journal*. This time, I saw an advertisement for a psychic show that would be happening downtown that weekend. I wanted to go but what if my dad was there? Drugs separate you from your family and it was no different for me. You speak to your family less and less, trying to hide your addiction. Eventually, enough time goes by that it feels too late to reconnect. I hadn't been in touch with my family in a while. Thankfully, Al agreed to go with me and make sure my father wasn't working.

"No, he's not there," Al came back downstairs and told me. We went back up together and started to look around at all the booths. "Hey, I know her." Al pointed to a booth in the next row. "That's Mavis."

"Hey, Al," Mavis greeted us.

"Hi, Mavis." Al looked over at me. "This is my friend, Victoria."

"Nice to meet you, Victoria." Mavis handed me her business card. "Have a seat. I'll give you two a free couples' mini reading." She asked us our birthdates and then did some quick calculations. "Look at this," she said. "You two are soul mates."

I beamed at Al and he smiled. Secretly, I only thought of Donald as my soul mate but I said nothing. Why hurt Al's feelings?

A few months after I had been in town, I got a photo radar ticket. In Alberta, the police set up cameras and wait for you to speed by. When I looked at the date, I was certain the car had been in the shop. My brother-in-law didn't care; he was livid. In the middle of the night, he picked up the car. Now, I was livid. *Seriously. Shoot my car or steal it from me; it doesn't matter, both are completely unforgivable.* That was the end of my friendship with my ex-brother-in-law and sister-in-law.

Miracle #3

I don't remember how I met Larry, but he was my third miracle. Larry was at least six-foot-six, red-headed and extremely helpful. Larry attended different auctions around the province, buying cars and then selling them for a profit. He supplied all the local "dial-a-dope" dealers. He sold me a car and told me to pay him the $500 when I could. It was a cheap car, obviously, but when it broke down, Larry simply switched it for a working one.

Even better, Larry asked me to do his numerology chart. I had told him I was trying to build my business as a psychic. After I did it for him, he introduced me to someone else who wanted their chart done.

The angels—or the voice, as I like to think of them—told me I would be better off in English Canada, and I was. I truly was; things were just falling into place. I met the right people and they helped me. Even when someone tried to do me wrong, everything turned out right.

I was fired from Rosie's after two months. The owner told me it was because I couldn't carry two plates of food on one arm. I think it's much more likely her daughter encouraged her to can me. As a fellow crackhead, she had spent a lot of time with Al before me. They had been crack buddies. Now Al was at my house, and she never saw him. I found a job at a golf course right away and carried on.

The girl didn't have to get me fired to get Al back. He'd always been highly functional when he smoked crack and I enjoyed all of the time we spent together. But when his mother started giving him prescription pills, he changed. His mom worked at a walk-in clinic. I don't know what kind of pills she was stealing and giving to Al, but they turned him into a sullen and nasty man. When I first moved to Edmonton, Al had kept me company; I wasn't ready to be on my own yet. He kept me from being lonely and missing people back in Quebec. I had to break things off with Al early November. Al had been what I needed in the moment, but now I had outgrown him. I wished him well but I didn't want him back.

When I changed jobs, I thought it would be a good time to change locations. I still liked to move around, and I was a little sick of the hookers who worked along my street. I moved to a condo in Surrey Gardens. The landlord was happy to write an exception into my lease, allowing me to have three cats instead of two.

Miracle #4

My miracles continued to pile up. Number four came when I received an email from Andy. I had learned everything I needed to know from him; now it was time to put it to use. Andy emailed me to tell me he had set up an interview at Canadiana, a web design company that also hosted websites. They were going to make my website. I had no money, but I expected my income tax refund from Quebec any day.

It hadn't come when the day of my appointment arrived. Out of respect for Andy and everything he had done for me, I didn't call to cancel my appointment. I went to Canadiana to tell them in person I didn't have the money right now.

When I walked into the boardroom, Canadiana's owner and head web designer sat me down. Before I could get a word out they told me, "Andy has done a lot for us over the years and we are very grateful. As a favour to him, we are going to design your website free of charge. We will also host your website for free for the next two years."

I didn't realize until later how much the offer was worth. It was October of 1998 and websites were expensive. What Canadiana gave me would have likely cost around ten thousand dollars. It took three months to design and it launched live in January 1999. I was one of the first psychics to have one. Canadiana also let me use their merchant numbers, as my credit prevented me from getting my own. Canadiana kept half of my web sales, but I still made fifty per cent more than I would have without them. I hadn't tried as hard as I should have with my journaling, but Andy was still able to write his article. It was a full-page article in the business section of the *Edmonton Journal*. It ran the same day my website launched. *This is it*, I thought. *People will be lining up to get their numerology charts done tomorrow. I'll be rich.*

It was not to be so.

Miracle #5

Summer had passed, and the golf course closed for the season. I filed for unemployment. Then I waited and waited for it to come in. I was getting desperate. Mavis's business card jumped out at me. It fell off my fridge one day. When I found it on the ground, I dialled her number.

"Hello," Mavis answered the phone.

"Hi, Mavis. I don't know if you remember me, but I met you at a psychic fair in town with my friend Al a while ago."

"Oh yes, I remember you."

I was surprised to hear that. "Okay, well, I'm having a really hard time here in Edmonton. I was wondering if you could help me? I'm looking for work as a psychic."

"I had a really hard time when I moved here, too," she replied. "There's a psychic show in Calgary the first week of January. I'm registered. Do you want me to see if I can get you in?"

"I have no money, Mavis," I said hesitantly.

"Well"—she paused for a moment—"let me talk to Don and see what he says."

"Thank you so much!" I gave her my phone number and hung up

Mavis called me back almost immediately. "Hello," I answered.

"Hi, Victoria. Don says he'll pay for your hotel and you can arrange a commission with him for the booth."

I rolled my eyes. *Sure, and I would be paying him back for my hotel room, how?* "Thanks, Mavis," I said. "I need to think about it."

"Okay," she responded and hung up.

My phone rang almost as soon as I hung up with Mavis.

"Hello," a man's voice said on the other end. "This is Don calling. Mavis told me you want to take part in the show. I had this feeling that you won't come unless I talk to you, personally."

Wow, he couldn't have been more right. Don told me he was married—to a lovely woman named Irene. It turned out they had worked together with my dad, doing psychic fairs in the '80s. They both knew my parents very well; I actually have the pictures to prove it. "I'd love to come, Don. I'll see you in Calgary."

"Great," he said and we both hung up.

I then called Mavis back. "Hi, Mavis. I talked to Don and I'm going to do the show. Are you driving to Calgary?"

"I am," she replied.

"Can I drive down with you and give you gas money after the show?" I asked.
"Sure."

Mavis didn't end up driving down. It snowed hard the week between Christmas and New Year's. I had to plug my car in every night. I knew how cold Alberta could get, but I didn't understand it until I lived through it. Mavis called and told me she was going to take the bus. I didn't have the money for the bus, I told her. I looked up how much a ticket would cost and then I checked my bank account. A paycheque had been deposited from a one-off server job I had worked six weeks ago. The people that ran the banquet had said my money would be deposited in six weeks. It was exactly six weeks later, and it was exactly the amount I needed for a bus ticket. I called Mavis back and told her I was coming. I would drive to her house and we would head to the bus depot together.

The day I drove to Mavis's, it was brutally cold. I asked her if I could plug in my car at her place and she said no. I didn't argue with her. Her daughter drove us to the bus depot.

The Calgary show went well. When it was all said and done, I came home with $400 cash. Don and I agreed that I would do the rest of the shows that season. Mavis and I drove home with Don and his wife in their RV. When I arrived at

Mavis's house, my poor "dial-a-dope" had been outside in the cold all weekend, not plugged in. I opened my car door and sat down. I could see my breath. I put my key in the ignition and turned. The car faltered once, twice, and then turned over. Soon after, my unemployment cheques started to come in. I could see that all these people, places and things were connected. It was creating a journey for me. Now, I started to see life as a "seeding."

Mavis worked at the same teahouse my old neighbour John had told me about nine months ago. Mavis took me down there and personally introduced me to the owner. The owner agreed she would call me when she had work for me.

She ended up calling me the next day. There was a party coming in and she needed an extra psychic. *I'll go down there and see what it's about,* I decided. I didn't really expect to see any clients. I was wrong again. The owner sent me clients throughout the night and when I left I had $100. I was delighted. The owner asked me to come back the following Thursday and every Thursday after that, so I could cover Mavis's shifts when she had a show the next day. Mavis and I were doing the same shows. She insisted on leaving Thursday and driving down during the day. The shows started on Friday and you were able to set up your booth the day before in order to be all rested for the opening. Plus, driving in the day is much easier. I worked her Thursday shift at the café and drove through the night to the show, then set up the same day of the show. Although it was exhausting, I was not in Alberta to be lazy. I was here to grow my business and find the life I kept looking for.

I was starting to feel content.

The show season was coming to an end. The second-to-last show was in April of 1999, in the town of Jasper. Jasper is a quiet mountain town that at the time was extremely religious. We were picketed that Saturday. I guess it took them a day to find out we were in town.Don refunded everyone's money and closed down the show. I had my cats with me and my hotel room was already paid for. I asked Don if I could stay. "Sure, if you want to," he told me. Once the psychics left, the protestors had no reason to protest. They went back to church, I assume. Slowly, the more open-minded people started to trickle in. I was the only psychic left in town. I was busy the rest of the day and made $265 in cash.

Driving home on April 12, 1999, my birthday, I thought to myself, *I wonder what will happen to me now? The shows are stopping for the summer and I only have one more left...*

I walked into my condo. The phone rang even before I had time to unpack the car. It was the owner of the teahouse. "Can you start work the following Monday?" she asked. A direct woman, she continued, "I have a four-day shift for you, working 11:00 a.m. to 5:00 p.m., if you want it." *Happy Birthday to me*, I thought with a huge sigh of relief.

"Yes, I would, thank you," I said, being equally direct. We hung up and I started to dance. I was filled with the joy that one only feels when life comes to you. My life was now "germinating."

I was evicted from my condo because of my three cats. As it turned out, in Alberta, the only people more powerful than the landlords were the condo boards. Someone ratted to the condo board about the three-cat exception I had written into my lease.

One of the members of the condo board showed up at my house. She had a lit cigarette in one hand and she pointed at me with the other. "You have three cats in here," she told me. "You can't have three cats in here."

"It's in my lease. I can have three cats. The owner said I could."

"It doesn't matter. I'm with the condo board. You'd better pick one of your cats and get rid of it."

"That's never going to happen." I slammed the door in her face.

A month went by. I tried to keep the peace and keep Lucas inside, at least harness him to the balcony. But Lucas was a regular Houdini. There was no caging him.

After her initial visit, Connie, the annoying woman from the condo board, picked up a cat trap and tried to sneak it under my balcony. I watched her do it. I waited until she was out of sight, then I put a teddy bear in the cat trap. I waited and continued to watch. This woman got on her stomach and crawled under my balcony. She kept trying to look in the cat trap. She crept closer and closer to it. When she was right under me, I leaned over my balcony and said, "Can I help you?"

The woman lost it. "No, but you're going to regret this!"

"Really? What are you going to do?"

"I'm going to"—she pulled herself up to her full height—"have a motion passed before the condo board. We can kick you out in three days."

"You're blowing smoke out of your ass. There is no way you can kick me out in three days."

"You just wait and see!" The woman stormed off.

Yeah right. That's ridiculous. It was ridiculous, but it was also true. I called two different lawyers because I didn't believe the first one. They both told me the condo board could evict me, but they would probably give me thirty days to move.

The condo board gave me the minimum three days. I had no choice but to rent a house sight unseen. When I called the landlady, she told me I could live there with my three cats. Nothing else mattered, and I took it. In June 1999, I moved to 109th Street and 69th Avenue for the next four years. Unfortunately, Sammy was hit by a motorcycle in a hit-and-run in the year 2000. He was so badly injured that I had to put him down. I now only had Princess and Lucas.

Miracle # 6:

Out of the blue, my son phoned me one day. "Do you want the van that's sitting in our driveway?" he asked. "It was my mother-in-law's. Her transmission blew. She put a new one in, but now her engine is shot, too."

"Yes, I want it," I told my son. I hung up and called Larry. He knew exactly where to take the van. Larry had the van towed to a local scrap yard. There, they replaced my engine with one from an old Valiant. They put in a new battery and replaced four tires. It only cost me $1200. I had the money, plus, I had already paid off Larry for all of his "dial-a-dope" cars. I drove that van for three years and still sold it for $1000.

During the summer, I worked at the tea house and began to take on extra shifts. A reader was sick and took time off. Working her shifts and my own added up to my working seven days a week. I did that the entire six months the reader was off. When she came back, I continued to work my four-day shifts, Monday to Thursday, and doubles on Friday and Saturday. I saved what I could. I took my reiki course and was able to earn my teacher's certificate by April 2001.

In 2001, I took some time off from the teahouse and headed to Vancouver to take a colour therapy course. I had met two people at the tearoom who helped me out in this regard. One set me up to teach my first reiki class in Dawson Creek, British Columbia while the other invited me to do readings in Yellowknife in the Northwest Territories. I would start off in Vancouver, do my course, and then head north.

Before I went to Vancouver, I found the courage to track down my parents. They were now living in Christina Lake, BC. It was on my way to Vancouver. I had not seen them since the mid-'80s when my drug addiction started to be a problem. I was also so pissed when my mother turned me in while I was in Edmonton that

I had all but cut ties with them. They came out into the driveway as I drove up. It's funny because when you see someone every day you don't see the aging. When you see someone after years and years, the aging is much more noticeable. That was the first thing that came to mind. *Wow, how they have aged.* It happens to us all, I now realize. Lucas had been stung by a bee while we were at a rest stop. He reacted horribly to it and the top of his head was swollen beyond belief. Funnily enough, my dad had a vet appointment booked for their cat that day. I joined my dad and we both went off to the vet's. Lucas was shaved and the swelling drained.

When we got back, Mum asked if I had taken Princess with me. I told her "No, I left her in the house with you." We searched high and low, in the back in the fields, and I even drove around for a bit. No Princess. I was sad and feeling depressed. My mum said that if we couldn't find her, they'd keep looking and ship her back to me when she was found. I was sitting beside my dad in deck chairs in front of the earth house they lived in when suddenly that feeling came over me. I knew where Princess was. I turned and said to Dad, "I know where she is." I got up. I felt like I was a robot and had been programmed to walk where I walked. I got to my van, opened the door and pulled the engine hood lever. I opened it in a trance and there was Princess, sitting beside the battery, all curled up and looking scared. I couldn't believe it.

That night, I slept in my mother's room and she took the couch. Princess, Lucas and I curled up together and I fell asleep. I was vividly dreaming and, all of a sudden, I started to leave my body. I awoke from my sleep in the middle of this. On top of our heads is a weak spot. It is the reason we wear helmets—to protect this soft part. It never hardens. Well, here I was with what felt like a worm spinning out of the centre. As I awoke, it stopped in place. I said out loud, "So this is how it's done" and immediately fell back to sleep, and the energy or worm kept going and I flew away. It has never happened to me again. I will never forget it; I know that the soul leaves that way. It was an amazing experience and one that I attribute to my parents living in an earth house.

One last interesting thing happened before I arrived in Vancouver. I could not afford the pricey hotels and had booked a motel about 30 minutes away. As I was unpacking and taking the cats to my room I had this sudden urge to put my hand down the edge of the back seat. Why? I will never know. Something was there. I pulled it out and in my hand was a magnet about three inches square. On the front was a picture of an Angel and the words beside said " if an Angel gives you a message, pay attention." I stood silently taking this in. Why would this be there and why would I suddenly put my hand down the back of a seat and find it. To this day the magnet sits on my fridge and I read it every time I look at my fridge.

I taught my first ever reiki class in Dawson Creek. As I say to people, there is a first for everything. Let me just say it was very obvious this was my first class and leave it at that… I taught Reiki Level I and II. I was not invited back to teach Level III. Undeterred, I continued north to Yellowknife in the Northwest Territories. As promised, the woman I had met at the teahouse had clients waiting for me.

Six weeks later, I returned to Edmonton and my tiny house on 69th Avenue.

By then, I had enough money to open a small metaphysical store. I don't know why I thought it was a good idea. My store was open from late 2001 to April 2003. I am a big enough person to admit I am not a good boss. I went through nineteen employees in eighteen months. After that, I closed my store and went back to the teahouse.

Miracle #7:

It was early summer 2003. Lucas had been trapped while outside playing. He had been taken to the animal control centre. He was always home by 7:00 a.m. without fail, and when I awoke at 9:00 a.m., I knew something was wrong. I took my bike and rode all around the neighborhood calling him.

Next, I called the animal control centre. They assured me that they did not have him. *Liars.* At eleven o'clock that day he was put up in the Found photos online. I was furious that they made me worry for so long. I raced to get Lucas.

I decided that it was time to move. The city was changing. A lot of the neighbours I liked moved away and were replaced with bitches and drug dealers. My favourite neighbours were elderly. They kept a nice garden and thought Lucas was the most adorable thing. He would come to play in their lilac bush early in the morning. Old people–early: 5:00 a.m. They would play with him and give him little treats. When the couple left, Lucas didn't understand that the new neighbours didn't like him.

At that time, the animal control website showed the area of Edmonton that the animal was trapped in. I studied the map online; every part of Edmonton showed an animal that had been trapped and sent to the pound. The only answer seemed to be to move out of the city. That meant moving to an acreage. Then and there, I decided, *That's what I want to do. That is what I will do.*

While I was looking at the animal control website, a five-month-old Siamese kitten caught my eye. He was the spitting image of Sammy. I called and was told he would be kept for ten days because the kitten was a purebred. As long as he was in good health, after those ten days he would be put up for adoption. I checked every day, and he was still there. On the eleventh day, I stood outside waiting for the ESPCA to open. I adopted him and named him Solomon on the spot. He was such a cute, happy kitten. All he wanted to do was play. All Lucas and Princess did was hiss and hit him. I felt sorry for Solomon. He was all by himself. I looked back at the ESPCA website and saw another Siamese kitten, a tiny three-month-old female. I read on her profile that she had been surrendered to the ESPCA for being disobedient. How a kitten could be disobedient was beyond me.

I once again rushed over to the ESPCA. In the cage, I found a terrified ball of fur. The sign said her name was Cook; it also said, "I am shy and very timid. I will likely never be a very affectionate cat." My heart went out to her. I adopted her, and they put her in the adoption box. I went to my van, closed the door, and did what I always did. I let the kitten out, expecting her to be grateful and sit on my knee. I had done it with Kali, Chocolate, Lucas, Sammy, Princess, Solomon, all of them. This was the first abused cat I had ever adopted.

The kitten climbed up under the dash amid the wires and stayed there. Once home, I spent thirty minutes carefully going into the wires and retrieving her. Putting her back in the box, I stepped out of the van. I put the box down to lock my doors, and the kitten promptly shot out of the top of the box and ran under the neighbour from hell's cement steps.

Miracle #8

It was getting close to midnight and I hadn't seen Lucas all night. I was getting worried, so I went out and called him.

Nothing.

I walked down my steps, calling his name. I went out in the street. A man was walking quickly towards me. He had a bundle tucked under his arms. I felt sick.

"Is this your cat?" he asked.

"Oh my God, Lucas! What happened?" I took him from the man.

"I found him crawling around in traffic. I think he's been drugged. He can't seem to walk." The man looked at me. "Come on." He took my arm. "My car is over here. I'll drive you to emergency."

"Thank you," I said, not really knowing what I was saying.

We rushed to the emergency vet. When the vet looked at Lucas, he found a puncture mark where Lucas had been injected with some kind of drug. The vet gave me the option of doing drug tests. But each drug test was $1000. Each type of drug would need its own test. The vet put him on an IV. Even if we knew what drug Lucas had been injected with, the treatment would be the same.

"You can go now. He's going to be here all night." The vet went to take Lucas to the back.

"I can't leave him." *This is just like the night in Montreal when he was a kitten.* I couldn't bear the thought of being at home, waiting by the phone.

The vet stopped and looked at me. "Are you sure?"

"Yes." I grabbed a chair and sat next to the cage he was in. I moved him to my lap, stroking Lucas's fur, trying to keep him calm. A few times his breathing got ragged and I prepared myself for the worst.

"I think it would be good to draw another round of blood." The vet looked at his watch. "It's 4:00 a.m. We should be able to get a good idea if he's getting stronger."

"Okay."

At 7:00 a.m., the vet came to tell me I could take him home. The blood test showed improvement. "I'm glad you stayed up with him," the vet told me. "It was touch-and-go tonight, but I think you saved his life."

The power of love!

When I brought Lucas home that day he still could not walk.

Cook, who I had decided to name Venus—since it is the planet of love and love was what she needed right now—was still under the steps. She would need to be trapped if I was ever going to get her out. I headed down to the animal control centre and rented a cat trap and set it up in my yard. I made sure to explain to them what happened and that I was not some horrible person who trapped animals.

Then I had to call my parents to come and look after Lucas while I worked. They had sold their house in Christina Lake and moved back to Edmonton.

I had been allowed to work on the street during the Edmonton Fringe Festival, with permission from a wonderful store owner, doing psychic readings. In Edmonton you could get a ten-day licence and be allowed to work festivals if you could not get directly into them. You just needed permission from a store owner to sit outside their business. I told my parents about Venus. My mother raised her eyebrows. I had four cats now. She suggested that perhaps I should put Lucas down since he couldn't walk.

There was no way in hell I was doing that. I told her the vet said Lucas should be back to normal in ten days. Until then, he needed to be carried to the litter box and his food. I promised I would be home at nine.

Much to my mother's disappointment, Venus had not come out. My mother had checked the trap every hour, on the hour. All we could do was wait.

At 4:00 a.m., I woke up with that intuitive feeling. I jumped out of bed and headed to the yard. There, curled in the trap, was my tiny new bundle of joy. I took her in and put her in the bathroom. She stayed there with the door open, an open cage with a blanket, food, and water. When I left the house, I made sure to close the bathroom door.

Miracle # 9

Lucas recuperated and was back to his normal self within ten days.

While I was still living on Stony Plain Road, one of my more aggressive creditors tracked me down. Darling Cat from Montreal had given them my address soon after she had shipped my stuff over. Most of my stuff, that is, minus my skis and a heck of a lot of clothes. Moira had spotted Cat taking my shoes and putting them in her van. Moira gallantly retrieved my shoes and sent them to me herself. The creditor had badgered me to the point that I felt I had no other option but to file for bankruptcy. It turned out to be the best thing I could have done. I then began the rehabilitation of my credit.

In Alberta, people look down on renters. It's like they are some kind of second-class citizen who can be abused by their landlord. What Alberta had that Quebec didn't was an assumable mortgage. That meant a mortgage could be transferred from one owner to the next without changing the original terms of the mortgage. It was perfect for someone like me who was fixing their credit. It really levelled the playing field; you could be out of work, on welfare, in debt, under bankruptcy, and it didn't matter. You could still own a house. Clearly, the voice had directed me to the right province in English Canada.

My mother was very much on board with the idea of me buying an acreage. She and my father had decided they were done with their acreage. They wanted a property with less work. My mother told me that when her acreage sold, she would give me $10,000 for my down payment.

After that terrible night at the vet, I sat down and leafed through the *Edmonton Journal*. In the "Houses for Sale" section was this ad:

Acreage for sale. Owner willing to hold second mortgage. Assumable mortgage.

I called him and arranged to see it. My mother and I had been through all the real estate magazines. In the magazines, all of the houses with assumable mortgages were dumps in terrible neighbourhoods. Once again the *Edmonton Journal* had what I needed!

Since I had a tarot party booked, I told him I would come by the next day. I called my mother to tell her and she said, "Go now. Just be late for the party."

"No, Mum," I said. "I'll see it tomorrow."

Sunday came and I drove out with a friend of mine. The house was lovely. I fell in love when I turned into the driveway that was long and straight and private. Oh, so very private. It had four acres of land. I asked the owner if $3000, which I had managed to save since going back to work at the café, would hold the place until my parents' acreage sold. He wanted $15,000 to assume the mortgage. "No," he said. "I'm sorry, but this is my business. I bought this house a few days ago. I'm trying to flip it as soon as possible." I left very disappointed.

My parents use real estate agents, which meant there was a big sign in their front yard. But did the potential buyers call the agent? No! At 8:00 a.m. the very next morning, these people rang my parents' doorbell. My mother answered. She showed them the acreage. This random couple bought the acreage on the spot. They paid cash. It was to be a ten-day transfer. My mother was good enough to wait until ten o' clock to call me. She told me very excitedly what had happened. I called the fellow who was flipping the acreage I wanted. "My parents' house just sold. Would three thousand dollars be enough now for you to hold the place until the sale of their house goes through?"

The guy was over that night to sign papers. The acreage was already vacant, so on August 28th, 2003, Lucas, Princess, Solomon Venus, and I moved in. We would stay there for ten years.

In 1983, when I moved to Lac-Brome with Armand, it had felt like a prison sentence. I didn't know what to do with myself in the country. I hated it and I wasn't even living by myself.

Now I was content. I didn't need to have someone there and I didn't need to keep busy. I would enjoy my own company.

I had been in Alberta for five years. The more time went by, the more I felt myself heal and evolve.

Life on the acreage amplified and accelerated the process. The work and concentration required of owning that much land forced my brain to grow and repair.

I became organized and disciplined out of necessity. When you own an acreage, you have to keep on top of your well, septic tank, and gutters. Also, the town of Tofield was so small you had to shop in the city. When you went into work each day, it was important that you remembered if you needed to pick something up. I loved living there. I loved the transformation I was going through. I was starting to love me. I was starting to realize that once you loved yourself, you could experience contentment.

I quit the teahouse again in 2006. A nasty client pissed me off and I walked out in the middle of a shift. I sat in front of my computer the next morning. The client had sent me an email gloating about how much she enjoyed making me so mad I quit. Disgusted, I turned the computer off. I looked out the window thinking about what I should do next. My acreage was in Tofield. It was far enough east of the city that most folks thought I'd moved to the moon. I opened the *Edmonton Journal once again*. It didn't let me down. In the classifieds was an ad for offices for rent on the south side of the city. The rent was $250 a month. I went to see them and rented one.

For the next eight years I taught tarot classes, reiki, numerology and palmistry at my office. I started to do more local festivals: The Fringe, K-Days, BVJ, and expanded to shows outside of town. Everything was balanced. I had meditated, and found myself and my calling while living at my acreage. I had dropped my ego. I had discovered I did love myself. I had become vegan after eating only raw food for two years and changing my entire DNA! I was blissfully happy. My life was growing.

In 2013, I started to lose my love of driving. *Holy,* I thought. I had loved driving all my life. Now, though, with a forty-five-minute drive each way to my office each day, and then having to drive around for chores, it was becoming like work not pleasure. I had already figured out by now that if you don't like something, you need to change it. Something better always comes along if you put the effort into it. So, I called a real estate agent and put my acreage on the market, planning to move to the city. That way I would not have to drive as much. It was the only action to take.

In January 2014, it sold, making me a $100,000 profit. I paid off my debts. Within a few weeks, I found my dream house in Edmonton. I moved in on March 28, 2014. Just in time to be settled in for the beginning of April.

All the work I had put into my business paid off. The phone was always ringing. I had a fireplace to sit by while I watched TV and snuggled with my four cats. Lucas had passed in 2005 from a leaking heart. In 2006, I adopted a poor, crying, tiny eight-month-old kitten that I found wandering around a Canadian Tire parking lot late at night when I went to pick up my van after a night shift at the café. I named her China.

A month into living in the city, I realized this is what the voice had promised me all those years ago. The voice had undersold itself. I was doing so much more than "better" in English Canada. I had been taught the process of seeding, germinating, growing, maturing, and enjoying life; I flourished.

CHAPTER 123

My business was booming. My home was awesome. I had, and still have, the most amazing neighbours. I had no reason to feel restless, but something was missing. I knew what it was: Donald had come back into my thoughts. Over the past two years, I had dreamt of him periodically.

My intuition tugged at me, nagging me. I put his astrological information in my computer and I looked up our compatibility. I hadn't known how to do that in the '70s when we were together. Our charts were so compatible it was crazy. *Did I want to go backwards? Did trying to find him mean I was going backwards?* I decided I would leave that up to the voice. Every good thing that had happened to me in the last twenty years had come from the voice. Life had come to me, and I had not had to do much but put some effort into it as it arrived at my doorstep. My life had now matured. And so had I. Crime did not exist as a thought in my mind at all. In fact, I felt almost as if that life had never existed, yet I knew it had. I felt like two different people. A new soul.

Soon after I moved, Emmett and I went to dinner. We talked about the old days in Montreal.

"Did you know that John got married?" he asked.

"Really?" I said, surprised. "To who?"

"I don't know. The pictures are up on Angel's Facebook page."

Hmm... I'll look at that later, I thought. "I wonder what Donald is up to," I said to further our conversation.

Emmett looked up at me and said without missing a beat, "Probably enjoying married life."

Damn, what a memory he has, I thought to myself a little proud.

"Yup, probably," I said and went back to eating.

I peeked at Angel's Facebook page the next day. There was John, all married. I looked closely; his wife looked a lot like Heather... wait, it was Heather! *So much for her not being in love with him...* I was happy for John. He was long gone from my life. My intuition had been so right, even back then.

Still, on and off, I thought about Donald.

Finally, in 2015, I gave in. I asked my granddaughter to contact her cousin. I wanted to find out Donald's sister's number. *It couldn't hurt to at least find out what he's up to.*

No reply. *How rude!*

My granddaughter texted her cousin twice more after that. Each time her cousin failed to answer for no reason.

The year 2016 arrived and I asked Kirsten to give it one last try. This time I asked her to write "How is Donald?"

Kirsten's cousin texted back:

He's in Montreal now and that's a good thing.

Kirsten again asked for Donald's sister's number. Once again, her cousin failed to respond.

Strange. It had crossed my mind that maybe she was the "some young thing" Blake had told me Donald married.

I went online and entered his name into the computer. His murder conviction came up. The fact that he had been turned down for parole in 2012 came up, but nothing else. Then the strangest of all things happened. To this day, I am stunned by this. An online memorial for Debbie opened up on the computer. I couldn't believe my eyes. "Debbie? Are you speaking to me from the grave?" I went into the online memorial and noted that some girl named Maureen who appeared to be related to her had created it. I left a note and some cyber flowers. I sat back and thought. Then I took it as a sign. After all, who had introduced us? None other than Debbie.

I called a lawyer.

When she answered, I told her, "I'm trying to track down an inmate who is in Montreal in a penitentiary. Do you need my credit card to bill for the time?" My experience with criminal lawyers had been that they always wanted the money upfront.

"No, I don't need your credit card," she said. "That is a weird question, though." I could almost hear her smiling.

"All I know is that he is in jail, but I don't know which one."

The lawyer told me where to call in Ottawa. The office would tell me the next steps. I thanked her and made a note to use her if I ever needed a lawyer again.

I called the office in Ottawa. A lovely man answered the phone. I explained to him about Donald and gave him his full name and birth date.. All I wanted was to know if Donald was still inside.

"I would really like to help you, but due to privacy concerns I can't tell you. Let me put you on hold a second and check."

The man pretended he forgot to put me on hold and loudly said, "Oh, he is still with us." He came back on the line. "As I said I can't confirm or deny if the man you're looking for is in custody. However, this is the address you can send a letter to. If he is still incarcerated, they will see that he gets it."

Getting off the phone, my mind spun. I could not process the fact that he was still inside. That would make it forty years, more than forty. *Is that possible? Maybe he got out and then went back in?* I had to find out.

What fun it would be if we found each other again. I could tell him all about my last forty years in detail and then hear about his last forty years. I wondered if he still had my letters from forty years ago. I still had his. It was how this book got written.

I sat down and wrote:

Hi, Donald,

I know you may be surprised to read this, but here I am. It's me, Vikki, now known as Victoria. If you write back, please call me that.

I will make this short, as I do not know if you care to stay friends at this late date. I had heard you were released and had married some young girl inside and assumed that you were playing house and all was well. Recently, I found out that you are still not out. Hard to believe it's been forty-one years.

If you care to correspond, it would be lovely to hear about how you have survived and what you have done. It's hard to write, sorry. I have tons to say but don't know if you'll even get this letter. No one in Montreal seems to want to share information with me so I am assuming you're married to someone I know. If so, I am happy for you; you do deserve to love again.

If you do get this, please write back to me even if it's just to tell me you do not wish to hear from me again, then I will not wonder about things. I have no clue what prison you were transferred to, so I am sending this letter through the regional headquarters with the hope that they will get it to you. I also do not have your prison number anymore. Seems it was changed from 8012. Make sure you print the address neatly if you write back and want me to reply.

In a nutshell, my life is fabulous. Moved to Alberta eighteen years ago and life just seemed to take off in the direction of success. Not before that, though.

Take care, Victoria

I walked across the street on August 23, 2016, and dropped the letter in the mailbox.

Now I would let the voice decide.